THE
EVERYTHING®
GUIDE TO
STRESS MANAGEMENT

Dear Reader,

May this stress-management book grant you peace as you mastermind the many pressures on your time, energy, and resources.

I am no stranger to stress. I have struggled with anxiety, irritable bowel syndrome, emotional eating, low self-esteem, and the helplessness that comes with letting stress hold the reins in my life. While writing this book, my computer died, I worked a temporary full-time job, and my cat got sick. Just a regular life accompanied by stress!

As a professional chaplain, I have had the privilege to share the experiences of people undergoing heart-breaking emotional stress—illness, fear, pain, and death—and have seen the resilience of the human will to survive and thrive. If they can do it, so can you.

As you read this book, remember who is in control. No matter how bad your life is or may become, you still have choices over what you put into your body, what you think, and what you believe. You are your choices.

Many blessings as you bust stress to survive and thrive!

Melissa Roberts

Welcome to the EVERYTHING® Series!

These handy, accessible books give you all you need to tackle a difficult project, gain a new hobby, comprehend a fascinating topic, prepare for an exam, or even brush up on something you learned back in school but have since forgotten.

You can choose to read an *Everything*® book from cover to cover or just pick out the information you want from our four useful boxes: e-questions, e-facts, e-alerts, and e-ssentials.

We give you everything you need to know on the subject, but throw in a lot of fun stuff along the way, too.

We now have more than 400 *Everything*® books in print, spanning such wide-ranging categories as weddings, pregnancy, cooking, music instruction, foreign language, crafts, pets, New Age, and so much more. When you're done reading them all, you can finally say you know *Everything*®!

QUESTION
Answers to
common questions

FACT
Important snippets
of information

ALERT
Urgent
warnings

ESSENTIAL
Quick
handy tips

PUBLISHER Karen Cooper

DIRECTOR OF ACQUISITIONS AND INNOVATION Paula Munier

MANAGING EDITOR, EVERYTHING® SERIES Lisa Laing

COPY CHIEF Casey Ebert

ASSISTANT PRODUCTION EDITOR Jacob Erickson

ACQUISITIONS EDITOR Katrina Schroeder

SENIOR DEVELOPMENT EDITOR Brett Palana-Shanahan

EDITORIAL ASSISTANT Ross Weisman

EVERYTHING® SERIES COVER DESIGNER Erin Alexander

LAYOUT DESIGNERS Colleen Cunningham, Elisabeth Lariviere, Ashley Vierra, Denise Wallace

Visit the entire Everything® series at *www.everything.com*

THE
EVERYTHING®
GUIDE TO STRESS MANAGEMENT

Step-by-step advice for eliminating stress
and living a happy, healthy life

Melissa Roberts

Avon, Massachusetts

*To Steve, Mari, and Renita, who taught me
how to mastermind stress, and to everyone
who reads this book—you are the expert on
you, and you can bust your stress.*

An Everything® Series Book.
Everything® and everything.com® are registered trademarks of F+W Media, Inc.

Published by Adams Media, a division of F+W Media, Inc.
57 Littlefield Street, Avon, MA 02322 U.S.A.
www.adamsmedia.com

ISBN 10: 1-4405-1087-3
ISBN 13: 978-1-4405-1087-8
eISBN 10: 1-4405-1153-5
eISBN 13: 978-1-4405-1153-0

Printed in the United States of America.

10 9 8 7 6 5 4 3 2 1

Library of Congress Cataloging-in-Publication Data
is available from the publisher.

This publication is designed to provide accurate and authoritative information with regard to the subject matter covered. It is sold with the understanding that the publisher is not engaged in rendering legal, accounting, or other professional advice. If legal advice or other expert assistance is required, the services of a competent professional person should be sought.

—From a *Declaration of Principles* jointly adopted by a Committee of the American Bar Association and a Committee of Publishers and Associations

Many of the designations used by manufacturers and sellers to distinguish their products are claimed as trademarks. Where those designations appear in this book and Adams Media was aware of a trademark claim, the designations have been printed with initial capital letters.

*This book is available at quantity discounts for bulk purchases.
For information, please call 1-800-289-0963.*

Contents

PART I: THE ENEMY EXPOSED: STRESS AND YOU / 1

Acknowledgments

Thank you to my family, my friends, and my beloved Mark for your support during the writing of this project. I know I was a stressor to all of you, and I appreciate you using your stress-management tools in the face of my deadline.

Thank you also to the students of my stress reduction course at Labette Community College in Parsons, Kansas, as well as the various groups where I have shared my stress reduction and meditation seminars. A special thank you to Lee Ann, Jean, and Brenda at the Labette Assistance Center in Parsons, Kansas, for their volunteer proofreading, quiz-taking, and zeal for seeing this book become a reality, and to Sergeant Neil Springer and the other officers of the Parsons Police Department in Parsons, Kansas, who shared their experiences managing stress on the job.

Top Ten Ways
to Manage Your Stress

1. Mastermind stress before it masterminds you.

2. Accept that stress is a part of life. It will not go away. As long as you are alive, and as long as you care, you will experience stress.

3. Awareness is key to managing stress. If you don't know you are stressed, then you don't know how to stop it, manage it, or thrive in the midst of it.

4. You have the power to change your life, and your stress. Only you let something stress you out. Only you can stop it.

5. There are many tools for busting stress. Know them. Find them. Use them. Have fun, lots of fun, with them.

6. Do not be afraid to say no to anyone—your spouse, your boss, your doctor, your hairdresser, or your kids. No protects your personal boundaries and keeps you safe.

7. Your stresses change depending upon your stage in life. Expect different stressors as you age, and be prepared for them.

8. Constantly seek new ways to manage the new sources of stress in your life.

9. Know when grief is triggering your stress, and honor your loss.

10. A strong person knows when to ask for help, even when it's hard. There's no shame in seeking a therapist, finding a financial counselor, or paying a personal trainer if it helps you manage your stress and live the life you want to live, free from suffering.

Introduction

WELCOME TO *The Everything® Guide to Stress Management.* First, it's important to note that this book does not contain everything essential to managing your stress. You do. You are the expert on you, and only you have the power to choose life over stress every day. You reflect in your stress journal. You choose exercise instead of working overtime. With patience, dedication, and practice, you will master your stress. It's only a matter of time.

Stress has so much power in modern life, but that's only because we let it. Missing meals, ignoring aches and pains, eternal commutes, plugged into computers rather than real conversations—modern life forces people to live unnaturally. This puts pressure on you. No one's designed to work ten hours a day or watch television all the time or eat high-fat foods without health problems. Many people cause much of the stress they experience.

In this book, you'll learn to bust stresses you cause by practicing the Big Five Tools for Stress Resilience: healthy diet, adequate sleep, water, exercise, and fun. Sounds so simple, right? The reality's different. Fast food feeds the family. The gym loses to finishing up that work report. Sleep, well, nighttime is when you clean the house. Wrong! Ignoring your basic human needs sets you up for stress, because you lack the energy to mastermind stress before it masterminds you.

Many people spend their lives riding the stress roller coaster, exhausted and fearful, desperate for an end but with no clue. Whether that's your life story, or just part of last Thursday, you'll nip that in the bud. As you explore who you are, what drives you crazy, and what you need, this awareness will help you grab stress by the horns with your own powerful ally—your own mind.

No stressor is ignored. The many, many stresses outside of you, some constant irritants and others that you've never even noticed but wear you down daily, are here with tips to bust them. The book conveniently divides the subject into themes—family, relationships, finances, and work—as well as stages in the life cycle—child stress, young adult stress, adult stress, and senior stress—so there's something here for the whole family. It's impossible to read this book and not learn at least one new thing about yourself.

With your mind on your side, you can take action against stress. Curious to try meditation? Wondering why your family can really, really drive you crazy? Hungry for ways to beat financial woes? It's all in here, and much more. This book includes many, many tools for busting stress—some new to you, and others that may be old friends. As your toolbox grows, so will your ability to manage any stressful situation. Read on to continue this leg of a lifelong journey to survive stress and thrive as a healthy, happy you.

PART I

The Enemy Exposed:
Stress and You

CHAPTER 1

Stress: Enemy or Friend?

Everyone experiences stress. But for some people, stress can seem like an enemy, hijacking their lives. Even though stress can feel like a war that never ends, believe it or not, stress is actually a sign that you're involved with your life. Learning what causes stress, types of stress, and how to set healthy boundaries are key steps to thriving in the midst of a busy life.

What Is Stress?

Stress is a psychological and physical reaction to pressure placed on an individual by external or internal sources. Pressure can come from the environment outside of you, such as your home life, commute, or work life. Pressure also comes from within you, as your desires, urges, and thoughts struggle within you to meet your needs and achieve your dreams.

External Stress

External pressure comes from people you care about and concerns about your own security. Your job, finances, and family members can all be sources of external stress. External stress can be anything that happens to you; even opening your eyes in the morning and getting out of bed can be stressful sometimes. Anything that happens in your environment: at home, work, or out in the community, can all too easily put varying amounts of pressure upon you, depending on the event and what kind of day you're having.

QUESTION

Is there such a thing as "good" stress?
Eustress is a term for good stress, stress that helps motivate people to thrive. Eustress inspires people to create, produce, and enhance their lives and the lives of those around them. Anyone with awareness and discipline can channel a healthy amount of stress into a creative force.

Internal Stress

All people have hopes and dreams for themselves and for their relationships. Yet everyone alive also knows that there's fantasy, and then there's the reality of the real world. Internal stress is the pressure within you when your fantasies don't measure up to the real world. Your hopes are dashed, and your expectations shattered.

Internal stress can be greater than just lost dreams, however. Internal stress includes your inner life and body. Anything happening in your body and mind becomes a source of stress depending upon how you and your body react to events around you. The drive for physical health and wellness, desire to express your deepest passion, and feelings about a spouse can all be sources of internal pressure, or stress.

Manage Stress: Don't Autodestruct

With so much stress out there, is surviving and thriving completely hopeless? Certainly not! If you've ever played the Sims computer game, you'll be familiar with a great image for seeing stress in your life. Sims are computer-generated people that you feed, walk, dress, and entertain with relationships, jobs, exercise, and comfortable homes as part of the game.

In the computer game, each Sim has a bar above her head. When the bar is green, she is well and happy. If a Sim misses a meal, has a fight, and loses her job, the bar begins to turn yellow. As the Sim loses her home and her spouse leaves, the bar turns orange. When the Sim is starving and bursts into tears, the bar turns red because the Sim's needs continue to be neglected. Eventually, a Sim will throw a tantrum and scream at the player to meet her needs. If the player continues to refuse, the Sim will eventually autodestruct.

Each person is like a Sim, with daily needs that must be met, such as food, exercise, security, intimacy, and fun. If you forget to eat or miss your daily jog, you're more vulnerable to stress, just like that Sim. Perhaps the bar over your head begins to turn yellow. If you experience an unpleasant conversation with your boss and skip your favorite television program to work on a report, the bar may turn orange. Stay up late, miss sleep, and the next day starts out on orange, a disaster waiting to happen.

Everyone has that bar above his head, telling him that stress is creeping in. Learning to notice it before it turns red is a key challenge for anyone seeking to mastermind stress. It can be done. The key is knowing what stresses you out and becoming aware of the trigger before stress masterminds you. This book will be your guide on the journey to keep your stress balanced and the bar above your head green.

Why Do You Get Stressed?

Stress. The word conjures up different images, memories, and perhaps even an audible *ahhh*! There is good news though. You are no different from anyone else. Everyone experiences stress, though what stresses out different people can vary. Everyone experiences expectations, desires, hopes, and their way of seeing the world (internal stress) as well as influences from their families and job (external stress). Enter change and uncertainty, natural parts of life, and suddenly there's stress.

Any relationship, goal, or dream can create stress when expectations aren't met. A boss upset that you missed a deadline is definitely stressful. A friend diagnosed with cancer causes stress because your expectations for the relationship (enjoying time with him) are suddenly shattered by the uncertainty. Unresolved issues in relationships can also be a source of stress.

Some pressure comes from sources outside your realm of control. Work, the economy, family, and relationships can all be land mines of stress, depending upon the type and quantity of events, and your ability to cope with them on a particular day. Juggling all your duties, as many multitaskers know, can become old, fast. The more on your plate, the more likely that any area may become a source of stress. You may have certain expectations for that area, but more obligations than energy to meet them.

Why Is Life So Stressful?

Stress has a stigma, as though being stressed is a bad thing. In reality, stress is a sign of being alive. However, that doesn't mean stress is not important and should be ignored.

Life is busy, and your personal desires and relationships are demanding. If you care about your job, it can stress you out. If you care about your kids or partner, they become sources of stress. That doesn't mean your job or loved ones are bad, just that caring opens you up to pressure because you have expectations for those relationships.

On top of your job and family, modern life is busy, noisy, crowded, and demanding. Take a moment, stop, and congratulate yourself on doing so well for so long. Seriously! Life today is hard and complicated.

Travel, technology, and the breakdown of traditional family structures all take their toll. People today tend to have fewer friends than their parents and grandparents did, though they are also much, much busier. Modern life puts more pressure on you today than your parents or grandparents experienced, making it even more important that you have an arsenal of tools to fight stress ready at your disposal.

Why Do Some People Get Stressed Out More Easily?

Certain people are, unfortunately, more susceptible to stress than others. Dr. Elaine Aron's *The Highly Sensitive Person* describes how certain individuals are more responsive to stimuli from the environment. Bright lights, noises, crowds of people, long meetings, and the drama of relationships can affect these "highly sensitive people" more than others, according to Dr. Aron's research. If you or a loved one experiences heightened stress from events and situations that don't affect others so strongly, taking special care to manage and minimize stress will be especially important to thrive in life.

FACT

Many people who commute spend as much time in a car every year as they would maintaining a friendship. Carpooling saves gas, allows you to use the commuter lane, reduces road rage, broadens your social network, and can even help you make a friend.

How Stressed Out Are You?

Life today is stressful because people are so busy with so many different obligations, yet stopping and listening to the self is becoming a lost art. Could a lunch-hour walk around the park have made the afternoon meeting go better? Might a difficult child respond well to the traditional cup of warm milk and a story before bed?

Remember to pause occassionally as you go through your day. Notice yourself or your loved one, and take time to actually be in the moment. Losing the self is at the heart of much daily stress. Too often, people choose to spend their time listening to another, scanning e-mails, or working through lunch instead of taking personal time to enjoy a massage, sharing a laugh with a child, or hitting the gym. It's no wonder that "stressed out" has become a blanket term for many who are lonely, frustrated, overworked, and just plain exhausted. If you are stressed out right now, is it purely stress, or is there something lurking underneath? What are you hiding from yourself?

Acute Stress

A major change hits your life, and you instantly feel stress. Acute stress, to be precise. Also known as short-term stress, acute stress is current stress, usually caused by a recent event. Think about the most stressful event of the previous week. Did you fight with your teenager over her fashion choice? Did your car break down? Was it necessary to put a pet to sleep? If you're still feeling tired or behind in the midst of it, that event likely left you with some residual acute stress.

A major change, such as a medical diagnosis, job loss, or death in the family, definitely causes acute stress. But even events normally perceived as positive, such as the holidays, a child's graduation, or the addition of a new baby to the family, can create new stress. Any change in the life of you and your loved ones, good or bad, can cause pressure as you struggle to understand it and integrate it into your life.

Though everyone experiences new acute stresses every day, managing acute stress to prevent it from causing episodic stress (a pattern of stress-filled living) or chronic stress (stress that continues over a period of time with no outlet to relieve the pressure) is essential to mastermind stress.

Episodic Stress

Everyone can relate to the stress roller coaster. One event happens, and the stress begins. Then, thanks to the demands of life, the stress builds and builds until you are holding on for dear life, nauseated and screaming. One sick child can lead to a fight with your boss, then your spouse, then you miss dinner, then you forget an important soccer game, and the day just plummets. Stress drives you on a winding, wild ride against your will, and all you want is off at the next stop.

Sound familiar? Episodic stress is a series of difficulties that weaken your ability to live life to its fullest potential. One stressful event usually begins the cycle, and then other events follow, like throwing a stone into a pond.

Ripples spread out from the stone, that first event, until the waters of your life are anything but calm and peaceful.

Too often, it takes time to catch up with an episode of stress. One event leads to another, until stress begins to control you. Catching stress at the first event is key to taking the steering wheel in your life. With time and practice, you can learn to drive your own life again.

Chronic Stress

Chronic stress is the worst type of stress. It is pressure so great over a period of time that you can find no adequate outlet. Sure, you can do something fun or talk with a friend, but after that distraction, you return to find the situation hasn't gotten any better. Pain, grief, and caring for an incapacitated loved one all wear away at your reserves until you're a ball of raw nerves, silently begging for relief from anyone who'll listen.

With acute and episodic stress, the causing events often ease over time. With chronic stress, a stressful situation just doesn't get better. In fact, it gets worse because the longer it lasts, the greater the toll on those involved. The wrong job, a loved one on hospice, or a child with special needs are all examples of chronic stress. All three test a person's limits to the max. There is no relief when you live with the source of your stress every day. You can't just quit a nightmare job, abandon a mother with end-stage uterine cancer, or ignore a child with bipolar disorder.

ESSENTIAL

Catch your breath, literally. Focusing on your breath not only lowers your heart rate and stops your mind mid-worry, but it also feels good. Take a minute or so to focus on your own breath. Close your eyes and breathe as deeply and slowly as you can three times. In. Out. In. Out. In. Out. Doesn't that feel better?

No matter how good you are at managing your own stress, you may not be able to tackle chronic stress by yourself. If you are experiencing long-term chronic stress, explore resources available to you, such as support groups, counseling, or in-home care. The more people on board with you, sharing the burden of your chronic stress, the better chance that you will conquer it, despite the stress constantly snarling at your door.

Can Stress Be Good?

Whether stress is acute, episodic, or chronic, it has the power to quickly make life miserable. How, then, can stress be good? Stress itself is neither good nor bad. Remember, it's a reaction to pressure you put upon yourself or others put on you.

Stress can be good when you learn to wield it in a positive direction. How many college papers were finished thanks to the pressure of a deadline? How many conversations with a loved one or friend about a misunderstanding sprouted a deeper sense of intimacy and connection? Stress can, indeed, be good when you learn to mastermind it. Think of stress not as an enemy, but as a friend who tells you that something's not right and suggests that you take the time to figure out what's going on.

Stress and Boundaries

Here's a revolutionary concept in understanding stress. That gentle or nagging pressure that something isn't quite right is actually an alarm letting you know that your internal protection system is under attack. An event, person, or lifestyle choice has done something to make you uncomfortable, and your body and mind are letting you know by going into stress mode.

Boundaries: Fences Protecting You from Stress

Think of a fence around your yard. The fence keeps unwanted guests or intruders out and your beloved family and pets in. Boundaries are fences around your time, energy, and relationships that keep you healthy, safe, and functioning.

Here's a typical example from the workplace. Ann, an employee, is assigned to a specific project, due the following Monday. It is currently Wednesday. A single mom, Ann arranges for her sister to watch her kids so that she can get the work done over the weekend. Ann tries to keep work separate from her personal life as much as possible, so that she can give her kids the time and attention they deserve. This week is particularly important as Ann's younger son, Jake, has an important baseball game on Thursday night.

Rayna, Ann's boss, suddenly calls Ann into her office and says she needs the project done Friday with no explanation as to the deadline change. Ann feels a lump in her throat. After all her planning, she's going to miss Jake's game. Welcome, stress. The lump in Ann's throat, anger, frustration, or even sadness, is a natural response to a boundary violation.

Even though Ann worked to manage the stress of her deadline by arranging child care and planning to be present with her family, her boss violated a boundary by changing the deadline on Ann. Rayna crashed through the fence Ann created to keep work out of her time with her family when she changed the deadline without consulting or warning Ann. If this theme continues, the stress of working for Rayna may drive Ann to seek another position.

When Boundaries Are Bad, Stress Is Worse

Boundaries are not always healthy. Anyone can let his guard down when exhausted or overwhelmed, but some people have unhealthy boundaries in general due to such things as mental illness, addiction, or poor parenting.

Melanie Beattie's *Codependent No More* explores the theme of codependency, people with unhealthy boundaries due to a lack of self-esteem and self-value. Codependents are unable to have healthy relationships with others because they are looking for other people to meet their needs. Many people exhibits traits of codependency in various relationships, so exploring the subject more may be helpful if the following descriptions of codependent traits ring true for you or a loved one.

People with bad boundaries, either too weak or overly protective, are walking generators of stress, both for themselves and for others. When a person has no boundaries, others may walk into the individual's "yard" and get too close, too fast. Those with no boundaries or very loose boundaries can be clingy, manipulative, and draining. On the other hand, people with super-protective boundaries won't let anyone get too close. Cold, reserved, and withdrawn, people with super boundaries may lash out for no apparent reason at those who try to have normal relationships with them, making them stressful for others to be around.

If an individual in your life fits into either category, don't worry. You can minimize this person's effect on you by reducing contact and setting your own limits on the relationship, which will slowly reduce the stress generated from association with that individual. Even if the individual with bad boundaries is your boss or spouse, exploring what stresses you out will increase awareness and resilience against stress from that individual.

ESSENTIAL

It's impossible to drink a very hot drink quickly. Force yourself to take a break, and reduce your stress, by brewing a cup of hot tea. Many herbal teas, such as chamomile and mint, are particularly relaxing. Spend ten minutes enjoying your cup, and maybe even catch your breath at the same time.

How Do You Get Rid of Stress?

Everyone's dying to get rid of stress, although many people will deny the problem. "I'm not that stressed." "I have my stress under control." "I'm not stressed out enough to need a book or a class about stress management." The reality is, stress is a part of life. Whether it's acute stress or chronic stress, everyone who cares about themselves or others experiences stress.

Instead of fighting to get rid of stress in your life, consider embracing stress. Is this a paradox? No! You are the expert on you. You have lived with yourself and know yourself better than anyone else. Who better, then, to manage your stress than you?

Awareness is key to taking the reins on stress in your life. Notice what stresses you out. Become aware of how you physically, emotionally, and spiritually experience stress. Stop yourself before you step on the stress roller coaster and let stress drive you into the disasters of a very bad day. Now that you've seen the monster, read on to learn how to identify stress in your life.

CHAPTER 2

Signs Stress Is Controlling Your Body

Stress doesn't just feel bad, it is also exhausting. That's because stress puts the body on red alert. The brain, digestive system, cardiovascular system, immune system, the skin—everything's primed for action after the boss's new deadline or the spouse's rant. The problem is, the red alert too often leaves you running on empty. Explore how stress affects the body—and your body in particular—as the journey of masterminding your stress continues.

Stress on Your Body

Each human body is a miraculous collection of cells that work together to create a unique human being. Nothing exemplifies this uniqueness more than stress's effects on the body. Stress can manifest itself in different ways, depending upon the person and the situation. Experience migraines after a hard day at work? Abdominal cramps three days after the car breaks down? Nightmares for months after a divorce? Stress can pop up anywhere, and knowing your body's signals is key to managing stress in your life.

The Red-Alert Stress Response

Why does your body rebel after a stressful event or series of events? Stress literally wipes you out. Your body is pulsing with adrenaline, ready to act. Your senses are heightened, scanning the environment for danger. Like a gazelle quivering on the African savanna, your body's alert and pumping all reserve energy into surviving the upcoming danger, whatever it may be.

Stress's red-alert response is extremely useful to outrun a lion. Though the stress response—turning on red alert—is a natural response to danger, the human body just isn't designed to fight danger all the time. No one can outrun a lion every day, and no one can live in a state of constant stress without costs to the body.

Why Stress Is Exhausting

To understand how stress wipes you out, it helps to have some background on how stress affects the body. Around the beginning of the twentieth century, physiologist Walter B. Cannon coined the phrase "fight or flight" to describe the biochemical changes stress invokes in the body, preparing it to flee or confront danger more safely and effectively. Just like a gazelle, you tense up, scan the scene, and instantly decide whether to fight or flee.

The fight or flight response is a complicated process that affects your mind and body.

Here's what happens inside your body when you feel stress and activate red-alert mode:

1. Your cerebral cortex sends an alarm message to your hypothalamus, the part of your brain that releases the chemicals that create the stress

response. Anything your brain perceives as stress will cause this effect, whether or not you are in any real danger.

2. Your hypothalamus releases chemicals that stimulate your sympathetic nervous system to prepare for danger.
3. Your nervous system reacts by raising your heart rate, respiration rate, and blood pressure. Everything gets turned "up."
4. Your muscles tense, preparing for action. Blood moves away from the extremities and your digestive system, into your muscles and brain. Blood sugars are mobilized to travel to where they will be needed most.
5. Your senses get sharper. You can hear better, see better, smell better, taste better.

Sounds great, right? Heightened senses, increased productivity—suddenly you're a star in the latest Hollywood sci-fi thriller, bounding tall buildings, blasting tentacled aliens, and saving the world.

Side Effects of Stress

You already know you're not a superhero. Stress takes its toll on your body with any of the following unwanted side effects:

- Sweating
- Cold extremities
- Nausea, vomiting
- Diarrhea
- Muscle tension
- Dry mouth
- Confusion
- Nervousness, anxiety
- Irritability, impatience
- Frustration
- Panic
- Hostility, aggression

Even worse, being under stress for extended periods of time has been linked to depression, loss or increase of appetite resulting in undesirable weight changes, frequent minor illnesses, increased aches and pains, sexual problems, fatigue, loss of interest in social activities, increased addictive behavior, chronic headaches, acne, chronic backaches, chronic stomachaches, and worsened symptoms associated with medical conditions such as asthma and arthritis. The costs of red-alert mode are very high. Is it worth it? Definitely not, which is why it's important to find ways to deal with stress.

ESSENTIAL

Make a list of the physical symptoms you experience from excessive stress. Take the time to reflect on each physical symptom, and be attentive to any event that triggers the physical symptom in the following week. Explore ways to minimize the stress causing the physical condition. Do you have headaches as a consequence of fighting with your partner over not spending enough time together? Hire a babysitter for a date night. Your body may just thank you.

Stress and the Brain

The brain is where the stress response begins. All that adrenaline, pumped into every system because the brain fears your life is at stake, can do more than just affect your body. Anxiety, a chronic feeling of stress about everything, forgetfulness, and system overload are also culprits of stress on the brain.

The stress response causes the production of chemicals that make the brain react more quickly and think more sharply. Yet, under prolonged conditions of excessive stress, the response also depletes other chemicals, keeping you from thinking effectively or reacting quickly. So at first, the answers to a test come to you without hesitation. However, three hours into the test and you can barely remember which end of the pencil you are supposed to use to fill in those endless little circles. To keep your brain working at its optimal level on a daily basis, you can't allow stress to overwhelm your circuits.

Brain Brownout

Though most people will never admit it, everyone has experienced burnt-out brain circuits to some degree. Indeed, burnout is becoming an epidemic as people struggle to manage their stress. Many people struggle with anxiety and depression, both signs that the brain's circuits are not firing properly.

Two mental illnesses, generalized anxiety order and depression, exemplify a brain short circuiting. Generalized anxiety disorder is chronic stress for no apparent reason, while depression is a sense of empty hopelessness and a loss of the ability to enjoy life. Both exemplify a brain on burnout that can't tell what's really stressful or even what's pleasurable anymore.

ESSENTIAL

Though medications help many people manage their depression, changing your patterns of thinking can also facilitate healing. Optimism is a key factor in cognitive behavioral therapy, a popular and effective treatment for depression. Hang an upbeat quote above the bathroom mirror, play with a puppy, or volunteer at a preschool to find some daily joy in life and heal a brain short circuiting from stress.

Though understanding mental illnesses' causes and effects is a complicated process, more and more people are being diagnosed with depression and chronic anxiety. If you have experienced either condition, reflect on your life and see if a stressful event, job, or relationship may have been a factor contributing to this condition.

Tummy Trouble

Stress doesn't just affect the brain, but also the digestive system, or "second brain." The gut is the source of hormones and chemicals that regulate mood. Long-term episodic or chronic stress has been linked to a number of digestive maladies. It's no wonder that stress-related conditions such as irritable bowel disease, Crohn's disease, and celiac disease are on the rise as people's guts struggle with stress overload.

How Stress Affects the Digestive System

When the body undergoes the stress response, first the blood is diverted away from the digestive tract to large muscles. Stomach and intestines may empty their contents, preparing the body for quick action. Many people experiencing stress, anxiety, and nervousness also experience stomach cramps, nausea, vomiting, or diarrhea. (Doctors used to call this "a nervous stomach.")

Poor Diet and Stress

Poor diet is also a contributor to digestive distress. Many people forget to drink water and eat well while stressed, which can lead to constipation and even hemorrhoids. Others substitute soda and processed food when life gets tough, and both can cause constipation from lack of fiber and essential nutrients. To maintain a healthy digestive system, be sure to eat well and drink plenty of water, especially when stressed.

Dangers of Emotional Eating

Mood eating can lead to weight gain in addition to digestive problems. Eating to "feel" better is not good, for your feelings or for your waistline. Yet many people grab a soda or eat a tasty, high-fat meal to unwind after a stressful day. To make it worse, many people have a favorite comfort food, sweet or salty, held close like a teddy bear during times of stress. Even people who eat well as a rule break down for a treat in the midst of stress.

An occasional treat is part of a healthy and balanced diet. Eating badly to feel better, however, is neither healthy nor balanced. Explore other activities to unwind besides eating a mixing bowl full of ice cream. Exercise, a healthy snack, or other treat can easily be substituted for a fatty, sugary feel-good friend as a reward for a stressful event or conversation.

Cardiovascular Connection

Heart attacks used to be an epidemic for men, the strong silent types who bore the stress of work and family alone. In recent years, heart attacks have become an epidemic for women, too. In addition to medication and a healthy diet, the cardiologist will advise all heart patients to manage their stress. It's never too soon, however, to manage your stress without the advice of a cardiologist.

Stress and Heart Disease

Some scientists believe stress contributes to hypertension (high blood pressure), and, for decades, people have advised the nervous, anxious, irritable, or pessimistic among them that they'll work themselves into a heart attack. In fact, people who are more likely to see events as stressful do seem to have an increased rate of heart disease. If you are one of these people, your perception of stress is about to change. Remember, you mastermind stress. Stress only masterminds you if you let it.

The high-fat, high-sugar, low-fiber diet (the fast-food, junk-food syndrome) contributes to fat in the blood and, eventually, a clogged, heart-attack-prone heart. Coupled with lack of exercise, the risk factors for heart disease increase. All because you were too stressed out to eat a salad and go for that walk (day after day after day).

ALERT

Polluting your body with too much saturated fat and highly processed, low-fiber food has a direct effect on your health. Just as a polluted river soon cleans itself when the pollution stops, so will your coronary arteries begin to clear out if the body is freed from having to process foods that are damaging to good health.

Stressed-Out Skin

Ever notice how pimples get worse after a stressful presentation, a pallid complexion results in anticipation of a difficult conversation, or the lips get dry after forgetting to drink enough water? The skin, the largest organ of the human body, also shows signs of stress.

Acne, Not Just for Teens

Every teenager is prone to acne, thanks to dramatic hormonal fluctuations. Stressed-out teens may have a much more difficult time getting acne under control, however. Remember getting that big pimple right before your first date? It's no coincidence. That's stress.

Teens aren't the only ones suffering from stress-induced acne, however. Skin problems such as acne are usually related to hormonal fluctuations, which in turn can be exacerbated by stress. Stress can extend the length of time these skin flare-ups occur, and damage can take longer to repair in a compromised, stressed-out immune system.

ESSENTIAL

Stress Buster: Try cucumber slices on your eyes after applying a facial mask or aftershave for an in-home spa experience. Dim the lights, light some candles, lie down flat, and enjoy the cucumber's coolness sinking into your skin. Now, this is refreshing! Try slightly damp used tea bags, a chilled eye mask, or smooth stones as variations.

Chronic Stress on Skin

Long-term stress can lead to chronic acne. Eating badly, forgetting to practice healthy skin care, and chronic dehydration also will affect your skin. Stress contributes to psoriasis, hives, and other forms of dermatitis, too. Stop, breathe, and wash your face. Your skin will thank you.

Chronic Pain

Ever notice how migraines, arthritis, fibromyalgia, multiple sclerosis, degenerative bone and joint diseases, and old injuries all feel worse when you're under stress? That's because, along with stress's other victims, the body's pain tolerance has also succumbed to stress.

Pain is tricky. Pain begins in your head, and how you perceive pain can make it better or worse. For example, a woman hospitalized for back surgery with an angry daughter in her room yelling about the hospital bill is likely to have greater pain than the same woman in an empty room without her obnoxious visitor.

But then again, stress begins in your head, too. If your mind is relaxed, your pain is also reduced. Being aware that stress is exacerbating a preexisting condition is the first step to saying no to stress. A simple note to self—"This is just stress. I can handle this"—may decrease the pain because the mind has stopped the fear and taken control of the situation. No amount of positive thinking should be substituted for medication prescribed by a doctor to alleviate pain, however.

Stress and Your Immune System

Ever notice how a bout with a bug often follows a stressful event? Your immune system is the front-line defense against colds, flu, and any type of infection or illness. But when red-alert mode exhausts the body, stress depletes the immune system's effectiveness.

When the body's equilibrium is disturbed due to the long-term release of stress hormones and its associated imbalances, the immune system can't work efficiently. Imagine trying to finish an important proposal during an earthquake!

FACT

Many studies reveal that patients experience self-healing, symptom relief, and a strengthened immune system when given a placebo such as a sugar pill, suggesting that the brain has amazing healing powers. And other studies suggest that patients can use this power consciously to help themselves heal.

Mind and Body Health Connection

Under optimal conditions, the immune system is much more able to help the body heal itself. However, when conditions are not optimal, some believe guided meditation or focused inner reflection can help the conscious mind perceive what the immune system requires the body to do to facilitate healing.

While some doubt such intra-body experiences, the mind-body interaction is far from understood. Testimonial evidence is widespread that managing stress and listening to the body are essential elements in the promotion of self-healing. Those people who staunchly claim "I don't have time to be sick" and then never catch the bug may just be on to something.

The Stress/Disease Connection

While not every expert agrees on which diseases are linked to stress and which to other factors such as bacteria or genetics, an increasing number of scientists and others believe that the interrelatedness of the body and mind means that stress can contribute to, if not cause, almost any physical problem. Conversely, physical illness and injury can contribute to stress.

The result is a whirlpool of stress—disease—more stress—more disease, which can ultimately cause serious damage to the body, mind, and spirit. The question of which came first may be irrelevant, and quibbling about which conditions are caused by stress and which are not may be irrelevant as well. Managing stress, whether it caused physical problems or resulted from them, will put the body into a more balanced state, and a body that is more balanced is in a better position to heal itself. It will also help the mind to deal with physical injury or illness, reducing suffering. Stress management may not heal you, but it will make your life more enjoyable. Then again, it may help to heal you, too.

That being said, remember that stress-management techniques should never be used in place of competent medical care. Stress management is best used as a complement to the care you are already receiving, or should seek, for your physical illness or injury. Follow the advice of your doctor, and give your body's natural healing mechanisms an extra boost by getting debilitating stress out of the way.

CHAPTER 3

Signs Stress Is Controlling Your Mind

Stress cannot ravage your body unless you let it. Your mind, the command center of your body and spirit, is more than just the brain in your head. How you perceive the world is key to what causes you stress. Is life really too busy? Are you juggling too many things? Control your mind with self-awareness and practice stress busting in daily life, and you are well on your way to masterminding stress.

The Everything Guide to Stress Management

Stress and Your Mind

Your mind is like a computer's central processing unit or CPU. The CPU is the part of the computer that manages all the other programs. If the CPU is beyond repair, it's time for a new machine.

Miracle of the Mind

Your personality, memories, and experiences—what makes you the way you are—are all part of the mind, the CPU of your body and brain. A brain is just a brain without the mind connecting each thought to motion and speech. Stop and pat yourself on the back. You are a walking miracle, fully functioning and enjoying life—at least until stress causes a systems error.

The inner workings of the human mind are as mysterious as computers are to many people. The mind is science's new frontier. Much about how the human brain works is yet to be discovered, but how your own mind works and manages stress is a journey only you can make.

What Stresses You Out of Your Mind?

Everyone has a different mind with different perceptions of reality. When it comes to stress, everyone has different perceptions of what is stressful. Sure, there are certain things everyone finds stressful—being woken up every hour of the night by a screaming infant, experiencing a headache during a boring meeting, or sitting in a traffic jam. Much of what stresses people out, however, is based on perception.

Your mind can be your best friend or your worst enemy, depending upon the situation. Ever hear the phrase, "she did this to herself," or notice a person who's freaking out about something that seems silly to you? This is the power of the mind, specifically, the power of stress controlling your mind.

Running on Autopilot

Everyone knows what it's like to run on autopilot. Those are the days when you don't even have time to sit down for all three meals, let alone take some time out for yourself. Why is there so much to do? First you're bouncing from meeting to meal to meeting, barely there, then someone says something offensive, and then the boss spills hot coffee on you, and suddenly you're descending in the dreaded roller coaster. How did that happen?

Though you may indeed have a busy job, needy family, social obligations, countless errands, and a home to maintain, who doesn't? How do some people avoid the stress roller coaster and others don't? Here's a trick. Turn off the autopilot.

ESSENTIAL

Buddhist monk Thich Nhat Hanh teaches that mindfulness—awareness of what's around you at the present moment—is key to inner peace. Stop and notice a tree outside the window, a picture on your desk, or that beautiful apple on your lunch tray. Take several minutes to just explore the object with one or more of your senses. You have just practiced awareness.

Be Aware to Bust Stress

Awareness is key to stopping stress before it manages you. When you put your life on autopilot, you check your brain at the door. Ever overhear two women in a coffee shop, gossiping about a friend who dates bad men? "She checked her brain at the door," one will sigh. "Yep, she's crazy," the other may reply. As the women try to understand why their smart, successful, and fun friend would stay with a boyfriend who cheats on her, they conclude she's lost her mind. No woman with a brain would stay with a guy like him!

The woman with bad taste in men is not alone. Everyone has moments of checking his brain at the door, especially when it comes to stress. Unfortunately, like a partner who's bad for you, stress is out there waiting to drag you down yet again.

Why Your Perception of Stress Matters

Stop and think of the first three things that come to mind that you hate doing. Does it stress you out having to deal with these things? Perhaps you were even stressing about one of the things on your list as you half-heartedly scanned this book in hope of support. The mind is constantly running various programs, just like a computer, and each program is different depending on the person.

A busy day for one person is a slow day for another. Perception is key to stopping stress before it stops you. The term "perception" simply means how you see the world. A tour at the local art gallery can be inspiring for one person, and torture for another who'd rather be playing paint ball. It's all about perception.

An individual can spend a lifetime in therapy with gifted professionals trying to change her perception of the world. Indeed, the whole discipline of psychology is based on how the human mind perceives the world around it. How you see the world directly affects how you see stress.

Be Aware and Change How You See Stress

If you're afraid of stress or have no clue what stresses you out or why, you're much more likely to become stressed than someone who knows that stress is a part of life and manages stress with meditation, exercise, or positive affirmations.

"But my perception's fine. My life is just crazy, and I don't have time," you might argue, and rightfully so. The modern world is faster than it was even a decade ago. The Internet brings hours of fun online, but also an inbox of work daily, even hourly. Families are smaller and farther apart geographically, meaning less support at home. In addition, the cost of living keeps rising, as it always has, and couples must work two, or sometimes three or four jobs just to pay the bills. Yes, life is indeed busy.

But does that have to make it stressful? A family a hundred years ago had none of the conveniences enjoyed today. Most people lived on small, family farms where everyone struggled to produce food and care for domestic animals. Medical care was limited, and many children died young. Many women, too, died in childbirth.

Imagine living next to the cemetery where you buried several of your children and worrying about having enough food for the winter. Maintaining a farm, family, and food supply is enough to keep anyone busy. Life a hundred years ago, though much slower, certainly sounds equally stressful.

Perhaps the busyness of life is not simply a fact, but a perception of life. Why are some people smiling as they sip a coffee on a park bench, while others are rushing by chattering on their cell phones? It certainly sounds like more fun to enjoy a sunny day than sink into someone else's drama. A beautiful day, no matter what's going on in your life, is still a beautiful day. The question is, did you take the time to enjoy it?

How Do You Make Time?

"That's great, but I just don't have time to sit on a park bench," you may be thinking. There are twenty-four hours in every day. After subtracting eight hours of healthy sleep, you have sixteen hours. That's enough time to fly from New York to Malaysia, yet you don't have time?

"I have no time," is a common perception that welcomes stress. Telling yourself you don't have time to breathe means you don't have time to think, and if you don't have time to think, you certainly don't have time to manage your stress.

How to Make Time

Remember, your mind is the command center of your body and brain. You, and only you, have the power to say, "I'm going to actually take both of my breaks today," or "I'm going to try Zumba. I need to shimmy off some stress," or "I'm going to eat dinner sitting down tonight and actually chew."

ESSENTIAL

Ever notice how hospitals and baby rooms are decorated with pastels? That's because light greens and blues are soothing. Try wearing a light shade of green or blue clothing or jewelry, or, if you have a little time, sit by a lake or ocean of blue water. Isn't that relaxing? Pastels don't just work on babies.

Knowing all the side effects of stress controlling your life—headaches, lost sleep, fights with family, poor diet, and increased risk of disease—how can you afford not to have time for yourself? How can you not spend five minutes a day doing something relaxing and fun, even if it's just machine-gunning enemy soldiers on Xbox or playing fetch with Fido? You spend more than five minutes a day going to the bathroom. Five minutes of something fun and relaxing will do wonders for your stress level, and who knows, five minutes may become ten or twenty as you make the miraculous discovery that you do have time for yourself.

Multitasking: Good or Bad?

If balancing the phone in one arm, a child in the other, and nudging the dog away from the cat with the spare foot sounds like a slow day, you are one of the many people who multitask. Simply put, you are juggling multiple responsibilities at once, working all the time to keep control of family, work, friends, your health, your finances, and every other part of your life. In any given instant, your mind is bouncing back and forth, thinking, planning, and masterminding your life.

Benefits of Multitasking

Multitasking is good when it helps you meet all your responsibilities. Everyone has responsibilities, and if you're not accountable, who will be? Indeed, modern life is so busy that taking much off the plate is just plain ridiculous. Who can stop caring about the kids, or the house payment, or rehab after knee surgery? Is multitasking, then, a way of life? For people who are alive and care, yes.

Dangers of Multitasking

But what about those occasions when multitasking causes problems, when the ball drops—a teenager starts using drugs, the boss is unhappy with a poorly written report, or the phone bill doesn't get paid? Stop; hold it. Why did the ball drop? All too often, the answer is "stress."

Some people thrive on being busy, and others struggle. Some people love doing two or three things at once, while others focus on one task at a time and cross each off the list in their turn. No matter how you multitask, what's important is knowing when you enter the danger zone, an overloaded mind.

The Key to Successful Multitasking

Can you hear your mind yelling "stop" before stress interferes with your valiant attempts to manage your many responsibilities? Take some time to reflect on the last time stress hijacked your ability to get everything done, multitasking gone bad. Can you discover an event or situation that triggered the ball dropping?

Here are possible causes for multitasking gone bad:

- A stressor, illness, family problems, or financial disaster, zaps energy needed to manage life.
- Taking on a new responsibility when you're already stretched too thin.
- A person or event hijacking you in the midst of your responsibilities, preventing you from doing what needs to be done.
- Any area of life exploding into an emergency: a child in the hospital, your job is cut to part-time, your car dies.

Do any of these sound familiar? The above are all signs that multitasking has you on a road to trouble. Your mind, talented though it may be, simply can't handle the extra stress in addition to everything else that's going on. Like a computer stalling, your mind struggles to process everything that's going on.

ALERT

If stress is running high, stop and take a time out to regain control. Learn to prioritize your many responsibilities. Give yourself permission to say no to new demands on your time and yes to whatever keeps you healthy and balanced. Turning down coffee with a friend for time at the gym to blow off steam isn't selfish; it's savvy to bust that stress.

Awareness is key to balancing all your responsibilities. If you are losing the ability to do everything you usually do, your mind may be trying to tell you something. Learn to recognize the warning signs that you're losing control, and respond accordingly. If you can grab the steering wheel to your life before stress does, you are well on your way to stopping the stress roller coaster before it ever hits the tracks.

What Does Burnout Look Like?

Ever notice how your computer slows down when it's overloaded? Whether it's loading a massive file, needs a backup, or has one too many photo albums, an overloaded computer is not the efficient, responsive tool the person with a deadline needs.

Your mind, the body and brain's command center, also slows down under pressure. Like that stalling computer screen, the mind too experiences system errors. With care and attention, a system error can be fixed. With neglect and added stress, a system error can deteriorate into a system failure.

How the Mind Malfuctions under Stress

What happens when your mind goes into system failure? Concentration, response time, access to skills and memories are all compromised, and feelings you've been ignoring because you're just too busy may flood to the surface. In a nutshell, your brain loses the ability to access the power it needs to function normally. Your mind begins to brownout.

Just like a city with a limited power supply, your brain shows signs it's losing power, too. Maybe you're more tired than usual. Stop and reflect—what are the signs of brownout in your life?

Compare your own signs of brownout with the list below. How many apply to you now?

- ❏ Waking up exhausted on a full night's sleep
- ❏ New aches and pains
- ❏ Inability to follow normal conversation
- ❏ Forgetting to eat due to lack of hunger or weight gain due to excessive hunger
- ❏ Nightmares involving stressful situations
- ❏ Lack of emotion or excessive emotion
- ❏ Staring blankly at a computer screen or into space with no idea what you were thinking of
- ❏ No interest in people, events, and activities that used to be fun
- ❏ No desire for sex or impotence once sex is initiated
- ❏ Existing health conditions worsen

If you are experiencing five or more of the above symptoms, your mind is browning out. Take some steps to manage your stress now. Pamper yourself with a massage. Reschedule what you can from next week's obligations. Consider therapy or a consultation with a medical professional. Your mind is screaming for relief, and you are setting yourself up for anxiety and depression, signs that your mind is truly burnt out.

FACT

Screening is the first step in getting help with any major illness, including depression. The National Depression Screening Day is a day in October during Mental Health Awareness Week to encourage everyone to check their risk for depression. Free screenings are available in person, via telephone, or online through the Mental Health America website. Get screened for depression, and take a key step in keeping your mind healthy.

Anxiety Is Not a Way of Life

Anxiety is one sign of a burnt-out mind that has lost the ability to function normally. Anxiety is a state of chronic worry. The mind is always in red-alert mode, anticipating stress even when no stress is in sight. According to the National Institute for Mental Health (NIMH), 13 percent of the adult population suffers from symptoms of anxiety. Many more people may experience anxiety symptoms that do not fit into the NIMH's criteria for an anxiety disorder, such as post-traumatic stress disorder or generalized anxiety disorder.

Anxiety Reveals Stress Is Winning

Stress masterminds those with anxiety. Their minds are so keyed up for stress that they see it everywhere. Worrying consumes them. If you lie in bed at night and cannot get the day to stop running through your head, anxiety is at work. If everything seems stressful, and your relationships, work, and health are at stake, anxiety is at work. If you've totally lost the ability to tell a real threat from a worry—the boss cutting your hours or whether a cake will taste good, for example—and stress about both equally, anxiety is at work.

Anxiety Skews Perception of Life

Anxiety not only skews your perspective on reality, but it's also exhausting. Always looking for stress, like a soldier on patrol, the mind is constantly on red alert. It pumps cortisone and adrenaline from your brain throughout your body and primes the body for a fight, converting energy the body needs elsewhere into a completely imagined need for defense. The body begins to deteriorate behind these defenses, as vital processes such as digestion and the immune system lose the ability to function normally. Anxiety doesn't just affect your mind and how you see the world—it affects the intricate system of cells that is your brain and body.

Healing Anxiety

Although why some people suffer from anxiety is a hotly debated question, preventing and healing anxiety is possible. For those currently suffering from serious anxiety, consulting with a medical professional or trained counselor is the first step to exploring viable treatment options.

For those who suffer bouts of anxiety and hope to prevent future anxiety, awareness of stress is key. Say no to the modern stress cycle of over committing, cutting sleep, exercise, and healthy diet, and avoiding breaks. Instead, listen to your body when it hurts from stress and to your mind when it shows symptoms of burning out. Only you have the power to prevent anxiety and a much more serious sign of a burned-out mind, depression.

The Stress/Depression Connection

Depression is the most serious example of a burnt-out mind. Depression is a general term for a family of mental-health conditions that all include a general low mood. According to Mental Health America, over 19 million Americans may suffer from depression or depression-related illnesses.

Though many factors such as genetics, personality, and history can contribute to depression, there is evidence to link stress and depression. Over time, stress literally overloads the brain's circuits, called neurotransmitters. These neurotransmitters fire the chemicals that begin the red-alert mode, the body's defensive stance against threats. After excessive bouts of red alert, the neurotransmitters begin to malfunction and lose their ability to fire the right chemicals in a healthy amount, and the result is not pretty.

How Depression Affects You

A depressed brain is not getting the power it needs to function healthily. Serotonin, a neurotransmitter in the brain connected with mood and pleasure, is disastrously low. The result is the mind's inability to enjoy life in any capacity. Sure the body's there, but the mind has lost the ability to engage and enjoy it. Symptoms of depression include sad or empty feelings, aches and pains, disturbed sleep cycle, and suicidal thoughts. Depression is an extremely serious mental-health condition and should be treated immediately.

ESSENTIAL

When your mind is overburdened, do something with your hands. Many people find relief in baking bread, painting, gardening, home repairs, or amateur carpentry. Building or creating something helps the mind to focus. When you are hammering a birdhouse together or decorating a birthday cake, you don't have room in your brain to worry.

Depression is also the worst-case scenario for the effects of stress on the human mind. Excessive stress controlling a life may literally gain the power to alter the brain's chemistry. Much can be done to prevent depression if stress is noticed and managed before it alters the brain's chemistry.

Stopping the Cycle

Sometimes depression can be prevented by listening to the body and the mind. Stop running on autopilot and take the steering wheel of your life. Multitask carefully and evaluate what's really important. Make time for yourself. Stop, breathe, and take control of your stress. As you learn to mastermind your stress before it burns you out, your mind will thank you.

CHAPTER 4

Grief: A Major Cause of Stress

No one wants to talk about it, but grief, like stress, is a part of life. For many people, stress is actually a symptom of repressed grief in their lives. Learn to tell the difference between grief and stress, and try to grieve what you've lost in life. That will permit you to better celebrate what you have now, rather than being stressed.

What Is Grief?

Grief is the process of missing something lost in life. Love is the source of grief, because anything loved that is taken away causes pain and tension as the mind struggles to understand what has happened. As the mind recovers from the loss, it works through various feelings and memories to integrate the loss into its perception of reality. The journey the mind makes after a loss is called the grieving process.

Grieving is a lifelong journey, as everyone continues to remember what they have lost at various times in life. A memory, image, smell, or place can trigger a memory of a lover lost, a child grown, or a wonderful night long gone. Nostalgia, the blues, and the good old days are all references to grief, as the person remembering looks back with a mix of fondness and sadness at what used to be.

What Causes Grief

Most people associate grief with death. Bereavement groups are common outreaches of hospices, offering support and comfort to the deceased's loved ones. The reality is, many people need support grieving myriad losses in their lives. The loss of anything or anyone special causes grief as the person struggles to understand life without the beloved spouse, pet, or even personal autonomy. Common sources of grief include:

- Lost relationships—breakup or divorce, or changes in relationships such as a child moving out or a friend moving away
- Decrease in independence due to financial crisis—an adult child moving in with elderly parent after losing a job
- Decrease in independence due to natural aging process—an elderly woman loses the ability to walk and is placed in a skilled nursing facility
- Change in occupation or living situation—new job or moving to a new place
- Illness or other loss of health
- Losing ability to do something you enjoy—a professional piano player diagnosed with carpal tunnel syndrome
- Growing older

Surprised? What other causes of grief are on your personal list? Everyone alive has loved and lost. Despite the cliché, grief is the natural human response when something or someone beloved is taken away.

FACT

The word grief, originating from the Latin term for "burden," came into common English usage during the 1400s, a time when the grieving process fascinated Europe. The Danse Macabre, or Dance of Death, spread throughout popular literature and art in the century after the Black Death killed a third of Europe's population. In the Dance of Death, skeletons spring to life. Surreal as these images were, they reminded people of life's fragility and the need to enjoy loved ones now, before death danced them away.

What Grief Looks Like

Grief pioneer and psychologist Elisabeth Kubler-Ross wrote a definitive book, *On Death and Dying*, where she explains that grief is a process or journey that takes time and patience. Everyone experiences grief differently, even the same person can grieve differently at different stages in his life.

According to Kubler-Ross's research, anger, denial, and depression are few of the ways that grief manifests itself in life. Other signs of grief may include:

- Fatigue
- Retreating socially
- Nightmares or insomnia
- Sentimental behavior toward objects connected with the loss
- Crying
- Repeated memories connected with the loss

Everyone grieves differently, but what is important to remember is that grief, like stress, is a natural part of life.

Change Causes Grief

Life is constantly changing. Children grow up. Retirement hits, and the working life ends. A marriage thought to last forever disintegrates unexpectedly. Any time a change occurs in life, there is loss. With any loss—missing a person, place, or aspect of the self such as financial security and mobility—comes grief.

Society places so much attention on grief and a death that it misses the larger picture: everyone grieves small and large losses in their lives, mini-deaths if you will, as life continues to change around them. The loss of a beloved friend is definitely a death, but losing a pet, a job, a relationship, use of one's legs, or a child to a college across the world are also forms of death. Life has changed forever, and there is loss.

Stop to recall a change in your life, either good or bad. A promotion at work for more money is definitely a good change. Yet moving across the country and leaving friends, family, and a house with beloved memories is a result of the change that may cause pain. You may miss coffee with one friend or holidays with a family member. You may miss aspects of your former home or garden. The food, environment, and feel of your new home are all different. Though it may sound silly, a person in this scenario misses aspects of life before the change. She grieves the loss of her old life, whether she knows it or not.

Why Don't People Grieve?

If grief is a natural part of life, why don't people grieve? One answer is simple: grieving hurts. Anyone who's lost a loved one knows the pain of remembering. The memories flood back, and one is lost in time, thinking about life before it changed.

In today's busy world, people often don't have time, or don't make time, to explore the depths of their feelings, especially when those feelings involve grief. Anyone given the choice would rather be in love than grieve a loss. Grief can feel terrible.

Awareness Is Key to Grieving

Another reason people don't grieve is a simple lack of awareness. Many people don't stop to consider that any loss, not just a death, creates grief.

How many middle-aged parents struggle after the last child leaves for college, but don't recognize their grief over losing a child? Sure, the child is away at college and succeeding at life. "Empty nest syndrome," the neighbors shrug. But a fancy name doesn't lessen the loss of the child leaving home. The couple's lives have changed forever. Some marriages, based around children, actually disintegrate after the children leave because the couple did not maintain a relationship as a couple.

Hiding Grief Causes Stress

Many people don't grieve because they are afraid to show they care, or they have no idea how much they care until they lose what they love. They've been told since childhood to not cry or show emotion. Grief not expressed can join unmanaged stress—a co-pilot on the stress roller coaster—and suddenly the mind loses its ability to balance and cope.

ALERT

In 1991, Japanese researchers discovered that women who experienced a sudden, traumatic breakup and did not openly grieve, suffered the symptoms of a heart attack. Testing concluded that stress hormones literally enlarged their hearts after the stressful event occurred. Termed "broken-heart syndrome," this condition can be prevented by expressing grief openly rather than bottling it up inside.

Signs of Repressed Grief

Whether grief is ignored deliberately or unintentionally, grief will not just go away. You have lost something you love, and your mind is trying to make sense of it. If you fight the tears and try not to reflect on your memories, you won't understand the grief, and it becomes repressed. Repressed grief is simply grief that has not been expressed. Your desire to avoid pain pushes grief down underneath your awareness. You may be able to function for a while, but grief will not give up.

Ignoring grief takes a lot of energy. Stress is only one sign that you are not grieving a loss and the grief keeps recurring. Other signs may include:

- Struggling with bouts of anger or irritability for no apparent reason
- Using food, caffeine, or drugs to control bad moods
- Bouts of uncontrolled hyperactivity and lethargy
- Lashing out at others without knowing why
- Random tears or an all-consuming desire to cry
- Excessive hunger or lack of hunger
- Avoiding anything or anyone connected with the loss

If one or more of these signs apply to you, you may need to devote time to exploring what you've lost in life and honoring it, so that avoiding the grief cannot continue to affect your body, mind, and stress load.

Stress Is a Symptom of Grief

"Real men don't cry" or "big girls don't cry" are two of the most toxic perceptions about grief. In both scenarios, society encourages healthy men and women to repress their grief, to avoid outward signs of missing someone, to keep all the sadness and helplessness inside. Hiding a part of yourself is stressful. Your mind yearns to honor the loss, express feelings around it, and heal. Yet many people manufacture stress for themselves simply by denying themselves permission to grieve.

The Grief/Stress Connection

Keeping grief repressed is extremely stressful, because the mind wants to release tension and make sense of the loss. Imagine a pot of water boiling on the stove. The water is your grief, churning inside and seeking release. The phrase "big girls don't cry" slaps a lid down on the pot. Now, where is the steam going? Eventually, the pot will boil over. This is a person who lets grief take control. What is more stressful than feeling out of control in your own life?

Yet all the ways you avoid grief are also unhealthy, making life even more stressful. You are not in control; your desire to avoid grief is. Not only is stress a result of avoiding grief, stress is also a symptom of grief. Remember, stress is a reaction to pressure put on you by external or internal forces. Grief is definitely an internal pressure, urging you to honor a loss and explore feelings around the loss.

Is grieving stressful? Yes! Tears, memories, breaking down in the midst of daily tasks, feeling out of sync with the present because the past is so real—this grieving takes your mind on a journey of healing. It doesn't always feel good. Often, the grieving process means a loss of control as the grieving individual lets go and releases all the feelings of anger, frustration, and sadness associated with the loss.

ESSENTIAL

A funeral is a fitting tribute when a person is lost. If you are struggling with the loss of something or someone in your life, hold your own funeral. Offer flowers and words to honor the loss, invite friends and family to pay tribute, celebrate with a party, and then frame a picture of the event to remind yourself of how far you've come in your grieving process.

Manage Grief to Manage Stress

It's easy to see why many people avoid grief. It's messy, uncontrollable, and even scary as the mind releases the tension building up after a loss. No one wants to look out of control. Yet, if grief is not addressed, it will soon control you. What choice does a healthy person have but to grieve? Short-term stress while grieving a loss versus long-term stress avoiding a loss that's eating you alive. The choice is easy.

For the person keen to mastermind stress, managing grief is a must. Stop, take time to honor the loss. Put flowers on a grave, and schedule a time to cry, or do whatever you need to do to feel better. When you can smile through tears, you have triumphed over grief. Your mind is healing, and the crippling stress around the loss will soon be a thing of the past.

Self-Evaluation: Are You Grieving?

Accepting a loss takes time and work. For many people who suffer with stress, the grieving process is playing itself out without their knowledge. Can you tell when you are grieving? Do you lash out at others for no reason? Are you tired and irritable? Do you avoid certain places, foods, or people who trigger memories that you don't want to deal with?

If constant stress is a part of your life, maybe it's time for some reflection. Knowing the difference between grief and stress is key to managing your stress. Is stress controlling your life, or is the problem unrepressed grief from a loss you haven't explored? Look at the following list. You may be struggling with a loss if you have experienced any of the following in the last six months to a year:

❏ Lost a loved one due to death.
❏ Experienced a significant change in relationship status: married, divorced, widowed.
❏ Moved more than a commute away from your home.
❏ Been diagnosed, or had a close family member diagnosed, with a serious physical or mental illness.
❏ Unemployment or underemployment.
❏ Lost the ability to do something you love due to illness.
❏ Become a first-time parent or grandparent.
❏ Experienced a significant loss in income that has affected your quality of life.
❏ Struggled with a child who is developmentally disabled or mentally ill to the point where you cannot care for him alone.
❏ Experienced a physical condition that has affected your quality of life.

If any of the above apply to you, stop and reflect on how you have grieved the loss. Did you cry, write in a journal, seek therapy, create a memorial, or channel your energy into something positive? If you can see concrete ways you have grieved, and you feel comfortable with how you have grieved the event, pat yourself on the back. You are doing well keeping stress from grieving at bay.

If you can see yourself going downhill since the event—gaining weight, avoiding social contact, losing the ability to enjoy life—stop and breathe. It's likely you haven't been actively grieving the loss. Awareness is key. Now that you know you've been repressing the grief, you have the power to grieve and not only honor your loss, but also better manage stress around the loss.

If two or more of the previous items in the checklist apply to you, you may be so overwhelmed by the losses in your life that you do not know where to turn. Being stressed out from so much grief is understandable, especially in a busy life where you don't think you have time to grieve. Unfortunately, the grief will keep bubbling to the surface and distracting you from your life. The more grief, the more distractions you will experience.

FACT

Shiva, a Hindu god with arms spiraling out from his body in a circle, symbolizes creation and destruction. For Hindus, life and death are bound in a never ending cycle. Grief, too, is a process of creation and destruction. Loving someone or something, losing it, and rebuilding a new life without it but ever changed by it, are parts of the cycle of grief and loss.

If you have experienced several losses, seeking professional assistance from a counselor, therapist, spiritual director, pastor, or other trustworthy individual is the first step to beginning the grieving process. Don't wait. Take time, commit to honoring your loss, and begin the grieving process.

How to Grieve

Every person grieves a loss differently. Some people need to talk and share memories. Others need time to reflect. Some need to be prodded by a counselor or mentor; others can do it alone. Grieving a loss can be so overwhelming for some that they need counseling for the rest of their lives, and others can manage and honor the loss in their own way.

What's important is not how you grieve, but that you grieve. The key to grieving a loss is listening to yourself. Your mind is struggling to understand what has happened. Tell yourself it is okay to grieve. Silence those voices that tell you that you shouldn't cry or care. You obviously do, so why fight it?

Schedule Grief Into Your Calendar

If you're busy, schedule time to grieve. What is an hour a week if it prevents grief-induced stress from controlling your life? Take a picture of your lost loved one or another symbol of your loss. Reflect on it, and let the feelings flow. Keep a journal or other record of your experience, and continue until you reach a place where the loss is a natural part of life. Find a ritual that works for you, and give your mind permission to make peace with the loss. Indeed, the time you intentionally grieve honors both you and the person or object you have lost. What greater honor is there than taking the time to care?

Grieve to Overcome Stress

Grieving is key to managing stress. Remember, stress is both a symptom of grief as well as a result of avoiding grief. A wise griever makes time to let off steam and to honor the loss so that the grief doesn't control him.

There are many ways to grieve thoughtfully in the midst of a busy life. If it's a deceased spouse's birthday, maybe paring down the daily schedule is a good idea. If you're missing your previous job, take time to contact a former coworker and get the scoop. Give yourself space to grieve and plan that space into your schedule, so that you are not overwhelmed by grief.

If grief is in control, there's a good chance stress will be, too. Become an expert on your grief and how you express it. Be brave and express your feelings of loss in a safe place so that stress can't creep in and mastermind you while you struggle with your grief.

CHAPTER 5

How to Manage Stress

Whether stress is short term or exacerbated by repressed grief, stress wreaks havoc on the body and mind. Everyone knows what it feels like when stress is in control of life. That's why managing stress is so important: to prevent stress from managing you. Learn more about self-awareness, explore what stresses you out, experience daily relaxation as insurance against stress, and practice responding rather than reacting to stress as your journey to master your stress continues.

When Stress Manages You

The stress roller coaster is the classic example of stress managing you. One bad event leads to another, and suddenly you're looking for the Dramamine. Yes, stress can make you sick. It exacerbates pre-existing conditions, messes with your digestion, makes your head hurt, and floods your brain with anxiety as you worry about what's coming next. Being managed by stress is truly no way to live. That's not living at all when you're wound up so tight that you can't live life the way you want.

Say No to Stress

How do you say no to stress in the midst of a screaming child, a blaring cell phone, and a frozen dinner exploding in the microwave? Here's the twist. You choose to say no. Push the phone's mute button and voila! You act, and stress cannot. There, exhale, one less thing to worry about!

Your mind steps in and you think, "This is crazy. I can't do all of this at the same time." You act and manage the situation. Suddenly, stress is halted mid-cycle. Instead of losing your mind to stress, you still have your mind, though your kid may still be hungry and the microwave is messy. You stepped up to the plate and, miraculously, you said no to stress. How did you do it, right there in the midst of chaos? Practice.

Awareness Is Key to Stress Management

To stop stress before it stops you, first you need an idea of what causes you stress. Make a list. Yes, seriously. Check it any time you start to feel signs of stress in your life. Why? This list helps you say no to stress because you are aware of what is stressing you before the stress takes control of you.

Gain and keep control over your mind in the midst of stress. Instead of letting the body blast off into red alert with stress as a guide, stop and think, "Wait a minute. The car's dead, but I'm not. This isn't that bad." It may sound silly to talk yourself out of stress, but if it prevents the stress roller coaster from controlling your life, then isn't it worth it?

Case Study: Say No to Stress

This case study is an example of how awareness can prevent the stress roller coaster. Let's say that Meghan is a woman juggling a hungry baby, blaring cell phone, and exploding microwave dinner. Meghan knows, from her stress list, that dinner is the most stressful time in her household. Her baby is irritable after a day at the babysitter, and her husband is irritable after a day of work. Meghan's irritable, too, after working all day transcribing documents for a law firm.

Trying to get dinner prepared as quickly as possible for the hungry family is always a challenge. Now the phone is ringing, another interruption. Meghan could answer the phone in the midst of the chaos and increase her stress by adding one more thing to her plate. Instead, Meghan knows she's already stressed trying to feed her family. Right now, her family is top priority. The phone can wait.

ESSENTIAL

In the midst of an important meeting, a kid's baseball game, or family pizza night, turn the cell phone/handheld device off. You may experience withdrawal, but it won't kill you. Don't the real people right in front of you deserve your full attention? After all, don't you want to be actually living your life instead of missing it because you're on the phone? Whoever's calling you can wait.

Meghan has prioritized what's going on in her life. She knew when to say no to stress. If Meghan were not aware that having dinner with her family is more important than talking with the caller, she would answer the phone, waste time and energy, and increase her stress. Would answering the phone be the end of the world? Not at all. But it might just push Meghan over the edge and give stress the advantage it needs to control the rest of Meghan's evening or beyond.

In this scenario, Meghan was aware that life had become stressful, and she chose to manage it by eliminating a stressor, something that created stress for her. Meghan said no to anyone interfering with her family dinner.

When Meghan said no, she made a choice to put herself and her needs first. Meghan cleaned up the microwave, fed her family, enjoyed her dinner as she planned, and then she followed up on the phone call.

Self-Evaluation: What Are Your Stressors?

Everyone has different stressors—people or events that cause pressure— at any given moment. Remember that some stressors, like a new job offer, are good while others, like a sick child, are bad. Indeed, even a bad stressor like a sick child can become good when you take a day off work to spend quality time with your child. Much of how you see stress is all about perspective.

Find Your Stressors

How do you find your stressors? If you were a reporter, recording a stress story from your life, how would you begin? Use the following questions to evaluate your own stress in a given situation:

1. What is your name and age?
2. Who are the people—family, friends, coworkers—involved in the stressful situation?
3. What are your eating and exercise habits?
4. What working conditions are difficult for you—sitting at a desk for hours, on the phone all the time, commuting long hours, and so on?
5. What are the specifics of the stressful scenario? Who's involved? What do they say? What happens?

Now write down a case study of a stressful event in your life. Stop the case at the point where you experience the greatest amount of stress. Take a break, and then come back to the case study. Make a list of everything stressing you out in the given scenario. If you have trouble seeing the stressors, give it to another trusted person to evaluate. What does she see that you have missed? Last, rate your stress in that given scenario on a scale between one (very little) to six (extreme and dangerous).

Stress-Proof Your Life

Writing down a stressful situation helps you to see what exactly is stressing you out. The next step, of course, is figuring out what you can change in the future to make life less stressful and maybe even prevent this stress story from happening again.

ESSENTIAL

Stress Buster: Practice sex at least twice a week. If you're too stressed and not in the mood, suck it up and hit the sheets. You may just be glad you did. Sex is proven to lower blood pressure, increase immunity, burn calories, decrease prostate cancer risk later in life, boost self-esteem, manage pain, promote sleep, tone muscles, and bust stress.

Some stressors—such as diet, exercise, and making time for yourself—can be changed with awareness and discipline. Others, like the family and your boss, may take flexibility and creative thinking to manage successfully.

What Are Your Stressors?

Now spend some time with your stress story. Sit down with a favorite but healthy beverage and ten to twenty minutes to spare. Get up a little early, actually take a break at work—whatever you need to do for yourself to find time to focus on you. It's important.

Brainstorm all the stressors in your stress story, and then think of ways to manage each stressor. For example, some ways to manage the stress of marital problems might include therapy, quality time with your spouse, or exploring divorce. See how many different ways to manage each stressor you can find, to offer as many choices as possible.

Make Your Own Stress-Busting List

Next, make a new list with two columns, one for changes you can make daily to fight the stressors in your story, and another for changes you can make in the future. If you want to be especially thorough, break down the stress busters into the next week and the next month. Include as many of the stress busters as you can think of, and you may even find that some solutions will bust multiple stressors.

When you are finished, stop and review your work. This is your plan to manage the stressors in your stress story for the rest of today, this week, and this month. Take a deep breath, and pat yourself on the back. You have taken the first step toward mastering your stress.

Daily Relaxation: Insurance Against Stress

Did you notice, while reflecting on ways to manage the stressors in your stress story, how many stress busters you already use? Taking a walk in the park, spending time with a pet, having coffee with a friend, a weekly massage, or lounging with prime time sports—what things do you do already to manage short-term and long-term stress?

FACT

Stress effects everyone, including the rich and famous. Hollywood stars Johnny Depp, Penelope Cruz, and Nicholas Cage all struggle with anxiety. The late Princess Diana suffered from an eating disorder triggered by stress. Olympic champion Apolo Anton Ohno meditates to relieve racing stress, and even First Lady Michelle Obama admits that she's the one who gets stressed out most in the White House.

You haven't lived this long and made it so well through life thus far without knowing a thing or two about what you need. Remember, you are the expert on you. Though finding new ways to bust stress is great, tried and true methods that have worked for you for years are just as effective, and perhaps even more comforting. The problem is that most people forget to manage stress until they are already stressed out.

Take Time Out and Meet Your Needs

Remember the saying: "An ounce of prevention is worth a pound of cure"? The same applies to stress management. Stress busting before you are actually stressed is insurance against stress.

Remember the image of the Sim, the virtual person, in the computer game, with a bar above her head? The bar turns green when the Sim has all her needs met, but goes yellow and eventually red as she neglects her diet, family, hobbies, and other ways to relax. If the Sim spends adequate time every day eating healthy foods, exercising, spending time with loved ones, and having fun, her bar remains green, and she is content.

You are just like that Sim. If you consistently eat healthily, exercise, have fun doing what you love, and spend time with friends and family every day, your bar is green. Stress is less likely to tear you down because you are already relaxed.

FACT

A 2000 study at the University of Maryland Medical Center found that patients with heart disease were 40 percent less likely to laugh than those without heart disease. Cardiologists found that hearty laughter actually improved the lining of blood vessels as well as lowered blood pressure and heart rate. Lighten up, enjoy life, and laugh at life's stressors rather than fretting about them.

Take some time to explore what you need to do to meet all of your physical, relational, and emotional needs every day. Are you meeting these needs daily and weekly? No one wants to be without health insurance, yet why do so many people live without stress insurance? Don't be uninsured against stress—practice relaxation and meet all your needs daily to keep yourself healthy and stress-free.

Responding versus Reacting to Stress

Now that you've explored the stress-management technique of recording your stress story and getting stress insurance by meeting your daily needs of food, exercise, friends, and fun, here's one more way to manage stress. Ever notice how the silliest things stress some people out? Why, for example, would that driver in front of you freak out and swerve when she sees an ambulance coming? Why doesn't she just pull over and wait like everyone else?

The answer is that many people let stress control them. A stressful event occurs, such as an ambulance screeching down the road, and the woman reacts. She automatically swerves as her body blasts into red-alert mode.

Reacting to Stress

Reacting to stress is a result of cruising through life on autopilot. Something, anything happens, and suddenly it's *red alert, red alert*. The stress cycle begins, and you've literally lost your mind to stress. Your brain pumps chemicals throughout your body to fight the perceived danger, and vital energy is transferred from digestion and immunity to defense. In other words, your body freaks out, and you have lost your mind. Stress is running the show.

Responding to Stress

Responding to stress is an alternative method. When you respond, your mind checks the scenario and decides what to do. You take time to notice what's going on around you, and you choose how to act. In the case of the ambulance, another driver notices the ambulance, but calmly pulls over and waits for it to pass.

Why does the first driver get stressed, and the second driver does not? The first driver reacted. She let her gut instinct—loud flashing lights mean danger—guide her, and her body and brain went into red-alert stress mode. The second driver saw the same situation as the first driver, but he noticed the ambulance. He wasn't driving on autopilot, and he didn't check his brain at the door.

Respond to Stress to Manage It

A key to managing stress is responding, not reacting to life. Are you aware of what's going on around you at home, at work, financially, physically, mentally, and spiritually? Do you take time to notice what's going on in your immediate environment? Are you interested in what your mind and body are telling you everyday about yourself, your relationships, and your world? If so, you have a greater chance of responding to stress rather than reacting, and letting stress control you.

How do you respond, rather than react to life? Turn off the autopilot, start to notice what's going on with you and around you, and you are well on your way to not only responding to life, but responding to stress.

A key difference between reacting and responding to stress is awareness. The mind stops and decides how to act when you respond to stress. The mind's checked out when you react, and the body instantly goes into red alert. Save time and energy, as well as your health and happiness. Choose to respond, rather than react to stress.

Respond to Stress in Healthy Ways

Many ways that people react to stress are unhealthy. Did you consider whether you really wanted to put that 3,000 calorie fast-food meal into your body today? Where was your mind when you made that decision?

Other unhealthy behaviors that stem from reacting to stress include:

- Smoking or using drugs
- Caffeine or sugar consumption
- Overeating or forced anorexia
- Impulse shopping
- Sedentary lifestyle or excessive exercising
- Sexual promiscuity
- Work-a-holism

See what happens when you let stress control you? Stress creates more stressors—smoking to manage stress increases health problems, skipping the gym to crash from a bad day contributes to obesity, and so on. Perhaps you have other unhealthy behaviors as a reaction to stress. It's a good idea to know what they are, so you can look back and see what triggered the behavior. You can track your stressors from your stress story, but also by knowing what you do to try and manage them.

Stop and Think to Bust Stress

Responding to stress takes hard work and awareness. First, you have to be aware that you are reacting. Sure, that ice cream cone was good, but did you eat it simply because it was good, or because your boss stressed you out when he put you on the spot in front of the board? What about buying that new dress? Did you really need the dress, or was it to try and recover after the nasty phone call from your sister?

To change behaviors, you must first be aware of them. Then, next time, you can say, "Wait a minute, I don't need that ice cream. I'll walk around the block instead." When you respond to stress, you invite your mind to take control of the situation. You stop and think before you act. The stress may not go away, but it will not gain control over you. Only you have the power to say no to the stress roller coaster. With practice, you, too, can become better at responding, rather than reacting to stress.

Busting Stress Is a Journey

No one manages stress perfectly every day. Some stressors kick even the most highly trained health-care or mental-health professionals onto the stress roller coaster. What is important to remember is that managing stress is a journey. Every day, in different situations, you will learn more about yourself, your stress, and how to relax and enjoy life.

Exploring your stress is only the first step in leading a happier and healthier life. But unless you manage your stress, it will continue to manage you. Keep up the good work, and continue absorbing all you can about stress and stress busting in your life. Everything you learn helps make you the expert on your life, and the master of your stress.

CHAPTER 6

A Guide to Your Personal Stress

Managing stress when it happens is a challenge, but figuring out what stresses you out and why can be an entirely new adventure in self-discovery. Though some things are stressful for everyone, individual stressors depend on a variety of factors based on your environment, upbringing, and personality. Explore what stresses you out, plot your breaking point, and delve into how your mind consciously and unconsciously manages stress as you continue the journey to mastermind your stress.

What Stresses You Out?

You really don't need anyone to tell you that you get stressed out. Most people have the insight to say, "That stresses me out." But do you know everything that is stressing you out? It's easy to categorize a car wreck, lost wallet, or screaming match with the ex as stressful. Some sources of stress, however, can slink under the radar screen and add to your overall stress, though you may not be aware of them. Common sources of undetected stress may include:

❑ Traffic stress and road fatigue
❑ Temperature of your environment (too hot or too cold)
❑ Difficult people at work, in the family, or at home
❑ Poor diet (fast food, unhealthy food, and eating too quickly)
❑ Untreated health conditions (your body may be overcompensating and wearing you down faster)
❑ Addictions
❑ Dehydration
❑ Lack of exercise
❑ Being in a rut (work, eat, sleep, but no play)
❑ Working too long without breaks

Remember, a stressor can be any internal or external source of pressure. The factors that stress you out depend on who you are, what you do, and where you live. Many people accept problems they encounter daily as a part of life, but over time the stress of dealing with those things can add up.

Discover Your Hidden Stressors

A good way to discover stressors that are normally acceptable is to answer the question, "What really bugs you?" Make a list and add these stressors to your list of known ones. Now, you can be on the lookout for these stressors, too, and make changes to eliminate them. Stressed out when the office is too cold to think? Bring a cardigan sweater to work and drape it around your desk chair. Stressed out when your spouse refuses to pull her share of the housework? Rearrange the budget to pay a cleaning person from your spouse's paycheck. Simple interventions can fight unnecessary long-term stress and keep you happy and better able to withstand a major stressful event when it occurs.

The Many Faces of Stress

Your home, job, daily life, and relationships are all common stressors, yet you live with them every day. Your environment includes where you spend most of your time each day. When you are uncomfortable or unhappy in your immediate environment, this is a source of stress. Is your home a safe, clean, and restful place? Are you happy with your living arrangements—living alone, with family, or roommates? Are you able to eat your meals in a pleasant, relaxing environment with adequate time to chew and swallow? If not, what can you change so home is a place where you want to be?

FACT

Signs of mild and moderate dehydration can be similar to symptoms of clinical depression: irritability, muscle weakness, poor concentration, fatigue, and loss of interest in life. Drink eight glasses of water a day, and keep your body and mind running in tip-top shape.

Life is busy. Most people have more things to do than there are hours in the day. If you're busy, your housework and home repairs may sit on the back burner, for months or even years. You don't want to think about the fridge that needs cleaning out or the yard that needs mowing, yet both can be stressors if you're planning a dinner party or trying to sell your home. Loud noises, rude neighbors, a difficult roommate, a leaky faucet, a dying air conditioner, and a mortgage to pay can make the home a landmine of stressors.

Stress in the Home

An ancient Buddhist proverb states that your home is like your heart. If your home is cluttered and messy, chances are your ability to connect with others in healthy relationships may be jeopardized as well. It's hard to return a dinner invitation when the house is a mess. Though different people have different definitions of what a "clean house" may be, keeping some level of organization is key to maintaining a comfortable home where you can relax and unwind for your physical, mental, and emotional well-being.

Another source of stress in the home is the expectations of others who live there. Do the kids complain about your dinner menus? Is your spouse slow on helping around the house? Does the dog yap at odd hours of the night and wake you up? Many things you may have shrugged away as "not important" or "no big deal" may, in reality, be wearing you down over time. They are a big deal; they bother you, and you are important. Many people avoid conflict, yet without sharing your needs with others, they may continue to walk all over you and leave you with more stress than you need.

Stress at Work

Work itself is a big source of stress, as the majority of those who work need the income and have no other choice. Even though you must work, you can choose how much stress your work will cause. First, however, you must be aware of what causes you stress at work to monitor and check those sources of stress. Besides the stressors of work itself—the boss, coworkers, productivity—there's also the work environment to consider. Do you sit all day in the same position staring at a computer screen? Is your desk in a basement or other space with no window? Is your work environment noisy, poorly lit, uncomfortable, or dangerous? All these factors contribute to work stress, yet you live with them every day.

Stress and Your Schedule

Your daily life can also be a landmine of unmonitored stressors. Are you more busy than you'd like to be? Do you have time to do what you really want to do, or is life continually hijacking you? Do you have obligations to your family, church, or other groups that don't fulfill you but take more of your time than you can spare?

Time management looks different for everybody, but before you can manage your time you have to decide what's important to you. Too many people live their lives, miserable from unfulfilling obligations to their jobs, families, and communities. Now, abandoning the kids and spouse because they are difficult sometimes may not solve this problem. Difficult family members may be draining, however, because they are feeling neglected and, believe it or not, actually miss you. Saying no to invitations and obligations that you really don't have time for is the first step in fighting the stress from an overbooked schedule and making time for what's really important.

Stress in Relationships

Relationships may be another source of constant stress. A healthy relationship means that both parties take from and give to each other. Even in healthy relationships, both parties go through difficult times and stress each other out. Perhaps your husband is going through heart trouble, your daughter's going through a piercing phase, and your sister has gotten divorced yet again. Dealing with other people and their drama can make your head hurt. Why even deal with it? Because you care.

Who cannot care when a friend or lover is upset? However, many people give up on marriages or friendships because the other person is difficult or stressful. If that person is constantly draining, this is understandable. But if you expect a relationship to be easy and always stress-free, then you'd be better off living in a vacuum.

ALERT

Signs your marriage may be in trouble include lack of intimacy, prioritizing the needs of work and children above your needs as a couple, fighting over nothing, and a breakdown in communication. If you see your spouse so rarely that you could send him a postcard from the office, stop and think, "Do I value my marriage?" If so, take a day off or plan a surprise date.

Relating to another person is challenging, and with the challenge comes stress. Accept this as fact, don't fight it. When you accept that a good relationship will have ups and downs, giving and taking, then you can plan for stress—even expect it—instead of fighting it. If you are going to invest in a relationship, whether it's with your partner, your child, or a friend, the relationship will be stressful at times. This is life.

When Relationship Stress Isn't Worth It

Relationships that are stressful all the time are another matter entirely. The griping friend who calls to talk about herself but never listens, the neighbor who forgets to return borrowed tools, and the sister-in-law who doesn't get the hint and stays for a month are the kinds of relationships that are just draining. If you are giving more than receiving and feel empty, frustrated, or exhausted after dealing with another person, your relationship with that person may be a toxic, or unhealthy relationship.

Toxic relationships are sources of continual stress because they are so draining. Dr. Judith Orloff, psychologist and energy healer, terms people who take more than they give "energy vampires" in her book *Positive Energy*. Energy vampires drain you of energy, compassion, and time because life is always all about them. They are the first violin, carrying the melody with everyone staring in awe, and you are a cello in the background, drumming out the beat so they can keep playing their tune.

ESSENTIAL

To combat the draining effects of an energy vampire, try the following simple meditation. Imagine a shield between yourself and that person, and let everything that person is sending at you bounce back at him. You remain safe behind your shield. Sure you may be there physically, but mentally you are safe within yourself. With time and practice, the energy vampire will have less and less of an effect on you.

When you try to carry the tune, or shift the attention to yourself, the energy vampire will retaliate, either with dramatic outbursts, mean words, or other forms of manipulative behavior. Life is really too short—and too full of fascinating, fun, and caring people—to deal with those who are constantly draining or hurtful.

How many of these energy vampires drain your time and energy? Do you recognize your boss, sister, or best friend in the description of an energy vampire? If so, stop and consider ways to minimize that person's draining effect on your life. You will see that person generate less stress as soon as you begin to set boundaries and say no. You may lose the relationship if the other person is unwilling to change, but in turn you will regain energy and time you can invest in relationships that will actually entertain, support, and sustain you. Isn't that a fair trade?

How Much Stress Can You Take?

All the stress from your environment and daily life can add up fast. Maybe you've noticed that some people thrive on constant change, stimulation, and a high-stress kind of life while others prefer a highly regular, even ritualistic kind of existence. Think of the people who have rarely left their hometowns and are perfectly happy that way. Most people are somewhere in the middle. They like to travel, to experience the occasional thrilling life event, but are usually pretty glad to get back home or have things settle back to normal (normal being the equilibrium where functioning is at its best).

Whichever type of person you are, the changes in your body that make you react more quickly, think more sharply, and give you a kind of "high" feeling of super accomplishment do not last indefinitely. The point when the stress response turns from productive to counterproductive is different for each person, but, in general, stress feels great and actually increases your performance until it reaches a certain turning point—your *stress tolerance point*. If stress continues or increases after that point, your performance will decrease, and the effects on your body will start to be negative rather than positive.

Your Stress Triggers

A stress trigger is anything that activates your stress response automatically. Any event, person, object, or even a smell or taste connected to a stressful event can trigger stress. The adrenaline starts pumping, sweat starts rolling, and you are primed for a fight. But wait, where's the emergency?

Stress Triggers More Stress

The way you reach your stress tolerance point, where stress begins to affect your quality of life, is highly individual. Everyone is different and therefore vulnerable to different stress triggers. If you experience more than one stress trigger or a certain stress trigger in the midst of an already bad day, you are likely to hit your stress tolerance point faster than a retired gentle-man lounging on a tropical beach. Of course, a sudden hurricane spotted just off the beach could give that gentleman a most unwelcome trigger of his own, much more stressful than your near accident, dry cleaning mix-up, and the realization that you bought expired cheese for family pizza night.

What's important to remember is that too many stress triggers can add up quickly. Just like the Sim with the green bar above her head, you need to keep yourself fueled and balanced. Be aware of what stress triggers have occurred as soon as they happen. Rate them on a scale of one to ten, and take actions to recover from them as quickly as possible.

If you have a difficult conversation with the ex-husband over the kids, pamper yourself with a bike ride or a Guitar Hero jam session. Let the stress go; do not let it fester and increase. When you've hit your stress tolerance point, your body, mind, and spirit are all in danger as the stress roller coaster careens ever nearer.

Your Stress Vulnerability Factor

Your stress vulnerability factor further complicates the picture. A stress vul-nerability factor is simply an area that causes you stress. Some people can handle upper level management but crumble when trying to manage their relationship with their teenage daughter. Others live for venting over coffee but sweat at having to balance the checkbook. Some can ignore criticism and other forms of personal stress unless it relates to job performance. Oth-ers may take all the criticism their friends and coworkers have to offer but will anguish for days about an impending dental appointment.

FACT

Getting enough sleep and eating a healthy diet are both key to boost-ing your resilience to stress. Make it a priority to keep your body and mind in the best physical condition, and you give yourself a better chance of handling whatever life may throw your way.

Every individual, due to personality, past experiences, genetics, and a host of other factors, will tend to be particularly vulnerable or sensitive to certain stress categories while remaining impervious to others. The stress vulnerability factor can determine which events in your life will tend to affect you, personally, in a stressful way, and which life events may not stress you out, even if they would be stressful to someone else.

Self-Evaluation: What Causes You Stress?

Your overall stress depends on how many stressful events have occurred recently (stress triggers), what events are stressful to you based on personality and other factors (stress vulnerability), and how much stress you can manage without losing the ability to function (stress tolerance). Use the following evaluation, in addition to what you already know about your personal stress, to map out what causes you stress.

Rate each event on a scale of 1 to 5, 1 being an event not at all stressful or that doesn't apply to you, and 5 an event that causes you stress, pain, or discomfort.

1. Your boss tells you that you have to fly out next week for a week-long conference in a city across the country. The company's providing a rental car, and driving to meetings will be mandatory. In addition, you'll have some free time to explore the new place. _____
2. The family member with whom you have the most unresolved issues calls out of the blue and tells you she is on her way for a surprise weekend visit, and is due to arrive at your door in five minutes. _____
3. A good friend you haven't seen in a while calls to ask how you are and you realize that it's your turn to organize an outing, but you've just been too busy. _____
4. You dread eating or postpone it all together because you aren't sure what foods are going to agree with you or how unpleasant it might be digesting or excreting them. _____
5. Your secretary just booked an evening meeting, and you won't be home tonight for the fourth night this week. _____

QUESTION 1 gauges the degree to which travel is a source of stress in your life. Traveling by car or plane are common routines for many people in this bustling modern world. Where do you fit in? Do you thrive on the energy from being in a hurry and on the go, or does it bother you? What effects, if any, does your body, mind, and spirit experience from a trip, especially one you haven't planned? Does flying or driving tire you out, or do you love it?

If you answered 1 or 2 on this question, it's likely that you love traveling and don't mind driving, even if it is nearing the rush hour. The adventure of a new restaurant or night life proves a welcome challenge. If you answered a 3, 4, or 5, you'd rather be at home with the dog than out in a strange new place. Maybe driving or flying are sources of stress, particularly when you don't know the terrain well. Planning trips ahead of time, switching to a career that doesn't require travel, or learning to meditate to minimize anxiety in a car or plane are good steps to manage travel stress.

QUESTION 2 explores how much power a toxic relationship has in your life. Does a family member really have the power to hijack your life, and you can't say no? Does the name or thought of a certain person, or your family in general, make you squirm? Is your worst nightmare dealing with the drama from another family member? Does your family put you down, use you, or constantly violate your boundaries? Unresolved family issues are a major source of stress and leave many people feeling helpless.

If you answered 1 or 2 to this question, congratulate yourself. You have healthy relationships with all your family members—a rare gift—and there's no chance any of them would inconvenience you by showing up announced. If you answered 3 or 4, you likely have someone in mind as the difficult family member. Brainstorm how to minimize that person's influence in your life, if you have not already done so.

ESSENTIAL

If a family member drives you crazy, try something revolutionary. Just say no. "No, I will not host the holiday dinner." "No, I will not let you move in with me." "No, missing my children's birthdays is not acceptable." By saying no, you not only set healthy boundaries for yourself, but you teach your family to respect you.

If you answered 5, it is likely that you are reactive to this family member; just the mention of this person's name stresses you out. If this is the case, explore why this person has so much power over you. Are there boundaries you could set? Are there unresolved issues between you that therapy or another form of counseling might heal? Be open to learning all you can about your relationship with this person, so that he stops being such as stressor in your life.

QUESTION 3 gauges how well you balance your personal and professional life. Do you make time for friends outside of work and family and enjoy hobbies such as golf, art, and embroidering that enhance your quality of life? If not, what gets in the way? If you answered 1 or 2, you are likely good at managing your time and always find time for your friends. You know how important it is to your mental, physical, and emotional health to have healthy relationships, and you enjoy time with people you love outside your family.

If you answered 3 or 4, you may have good social support but struggle to maintain it. Perhaps you forget to return social invitations, and have even stood up a friend because your life is too crazy. If your social calendar is a source of stress, stop and prioritize your life. Remember, life isn't just work. What have you really wanted to do lately with a friend: see an exhibit at the local art museum, go moose hunting, learn to scuba dive? It's never too late to go out and have fun!

FACT

A 2005 study by the Australian Longitudinal Study of Aging found that elderly adults with large and supportive social networks had lower anxiety and lived longer than adults who had few friends outside their immediate families. Don't wait until you're an octogenerian—make and keep good friends!

If you answered 5, just thinking about spending time with a buddy may be stressful simply because you don't have any. You may struggle to make and keep good friends. A move, a change in relationship status, and years of focusing on work and family may have left you lonely in your social life outside work and home. Having friends keeps you grounded, reminds you of your hobbies, and offers you support in difficult times. Dig out the phone book, call up a friend who's fallen by the wayside, or join a new activity to make a new one. A variety of healthy friendships is a sign of a healthy, balanced person.

QUESTION 4 explores how much stress food creates in your life. Do you eat a healthy, balanced diet and have a body that can digest your meals without causing you pain or discomfort? It may sound like an odd question, but many adults find elimination painful due to hemorrhoids or constipation from poor diet and dehydration. If you answered 1 or 2, you are either lucky and can eat whatever you want without digestive distress, or you eat a healthy diet of lean meats, fresh fruits and vegetables, whole grains, and minimal fats.

If you answered 3 or 4, you may experience stress from your diet at certain times. Are those times, by chance, triggered by stress? Were you eating out all week due to a busy work schedule, and now your body is hating you for it? Spend some time exploring whether there is a connection between stress and your digestive problems, and be extra careful not to compound a stressful day with food that upsets or clogs up your body.

If you answered 5, your body is screaming at you for relief from the stress you place on it by embracing the modern diet of processed fatty foods, syrupy sodas, and sugary sweets. Find a nutritional counselor, Google the latest version of the USDA Food Pyramid, and learn what to eat and what not to eat. Change your diet now before heart disease, diabetes, and stroke find you.

ALERT

According to a 2001 study by the Families and Works Institute, one-third of employees in the United States feel overworked or overwhelmed by the amount of work they have to do. If you are among them, finding ways to relax at work—taking breaks, keeping pictures of family and pets on your desk, hitting the company gym during lunch hour—may be key to reducing stress at work.

QUESTION 5 gauges how much time you spend at home. Is it stressful for you to spend most of your time on the road, or is it normal? If it's normal, then are you missing out on quality time you really need to unwind and enjoy your family and personal life? Many people sacrifice work and money for health and relaxation, but the costs can often be steep: anxiety, depression, obesity, and a limited social network, to mention only a few. If you answered 1 or 2, either you never have to work late or are never stressed out about having to work long hours. If working all the time has become a way of life, stop and check yourself. What, if anything, are you avoiding by being at work? Are you really living the life you want to live, working all the time? If the answer is yes, then you may be fortunate enough to have found a career that sustains and impassions you.

If you answered 3, 4, or 5, you may struggle to balance personal and professional life, but professional life always wins. Then how can you manage the stress of your job? Can you take breaks during the day and your entire lunch hour? Can you negotiate mornings off for late evenings? Is another career path really calling to you? The stress of poor work boundaries will compound over time, so if work seeps into your life two or more weeks out of every month, take action before your personal life becomes a casualty.

Coping Mechanisms

Now that you've explored what stresses you out the most—family, working late, diet—let's look at how your mind manages stress automatically. Modern psychiatry describes two ways that the human mind handles a stressor: a conscious response, known as a coping mechanism, and an unconscious response, known as a defense mechanism.

A child cries when she skins her knee. The crying is a coping mechanism, as the child knows she is crying. Common coping mechanisms for managing stress may include:

- Rescheduling events on a bad day
- An evening at home
- Sex
- Exercising
- Crying
- Scheduling a massage
- Smoking a cigarette
- Drinking a beer
- Eating junk food

What ways do you consciously manage your stress?

Coping mechanisms can be healthy or unhealthy. If you know you eat sweets after a stressful day at work, then sweets may be an unhealthy coping mechanism. Smoking or drinking can definitely be unhealthy coping mechanisms. Often, unhealthy coping mechanisms breed stress—cigarettes lead to health problems, excessive ice cream contributes to obesity.

Choose Healthy Ways to Manage Stress

Fortunately, you can teach yourself new and healthy coping mechanisms. Substitute taking a walk around the block for a square of chocolate. Punch a punching bag at the gym instead of spending the evening with ice cream and a movie. Try a massage instead of a night at the bar. With awareness, you can modify your behavior and choose ways to consciously manage stress that are healthy for you.

Defense Mechanisms

Defense mechanisms can be trickier to unearth, as they are ways your mind unconsciously deals with stress. Common defense mechanisms include:

- **Projection**—seeing your problems in someone else's life. That movie star must be single because relationships are impossible when you are really the one who believes relationships are impossible.
- **Displacement**—redirecting anger at a safer target. You snap at the dog because the commute was bad.
- **Passive aggression**—lashing out at another in indirect ways. You deliberately refuse the secretary her day off because she made you angry last week.
- **Isolation**—separating emotionally from a stressful or traumatic event. You describe a dangerous accident you witnessed without any emotion whatsoever.
- **Somatization**—expressing feelings of anger at another as physical pain or anxiety. You suffer from a headache after a difficult conversation with your mother-in-law.

These are only a few of many defense mechanisms. Defense mechanisms may make you feel better, as they release the stress, though some may harm your relationships. Do you see yourself or your loved ones in the above list? Have people pointed out other stress-related habits that you may be unaware of? If so, then take note. The next time you catch yourself doing the behavior, stop and ask yourself, "Do I really want to blame someone else for my bad day?" Remember, awareness is key to managing stress, but awareness is also key to managing stress in healthy ways without harming those around you.

Sigmund Freud, father of modern psychology, first termed the phrase "defense mechanism" in 1894 when exploring the basic human urge for self-protection. Many psychologists since have expanded his research, and the modern list of defense mechanisms is extensive.

What Is Your Stress-Management Pattern?

As you read the definitions for coping and defense mechanisms, which ones resonated with you? What does your mind automatically do to manage stress? Some coping mechanisms—such as an extra long workout after a bad day—can be healthy and you may want to keep them in your stress-management plan. You may want to substitute others, like lashing out at your family on a day when your boss is difficult, for a healthier coping mechanism. Make a list of the healthy techniques you already use to manage stress, and leave some room for new techniques that can make you even more versatile and efficient at managing your stress.

Managing stress is a lifelong journey that takes time, patience, and awareness. Now that you've explored what causes you stress personally, and ways you currently manage that stress, prepare for a new adventure: creating a stress-management toolbox you can use to fight stress anytime and anywhere.

PART II

Thrive with Stress:
Tools for a Balanced Life

CHAPTER 7

Tools for Stress Management

Managing stress begins with you. Know your stressors and stop stress cold by managing it as it occurs. A stress toolbox—a collection of proven stress-busting tactics—stops your stress before it stops you. Be creative and versatile as you collect your tools for managing your stress and remember—only you can control your stress.

The Stress-Management Toolbox

Every handyperson has a toolbox full of tools for simple repairs. Have you ever needed a wrench or screwdriver but the toolbox was a mess? When you can't find what you need for the repair, the repair is delayed. The faucet may continue to leak. The toilet seat may continue to wiggle. If the toolbox is neat and organized, however, you can find what you need and keep your home in efficient working order.

A toolbox is a handy analogy for your personal stress-management plan. If you have a collection of various stress-busting interventions handy and know what each can do for you as you begin to experience stress, you are ready to fix your body, mind, and spirit and restore balance to yourself so that a stressful event cannot mastermind you.

Case Study: Stopping Stress in Real Life

Following is an example of how a tool from the stress-management toolbox can be used to fight stress as it happens. Sandi, a stay-at-home mom and freelance writer, is struggling to make a deadline when her six-week-old baby begins screaming. Sandi feels her hands begin to sweat, a trigger for her that she is stressed. At this moment, Sandi's body is beginning to pump adrenaline and is blasting into red-alert mode. The deadline is next week. She needs the money to buy food for her family.

Since Sandi knows that the pressure of making a deadline and her baby's crying are both stress triggers, she pulls a tool out of her stress-management toolbox to fight her stress. She takes a big, deep breath and closes her eyes for a minute. "Everything will be okay," she assures herself mentally. After a few more deep breaths, Sandi feels focused and refreshed, even though the baby's still howling. She leaves her desk and picks up the baby, feeling irritated but no longer stressed.

Note that two elements made Sandi's use of stress management effective. She noticed that she was stressed before stress took over and she practiced a relaxation technique to take control of the situation. In Sandi's case, deep breathing and positive affirmations proved useful tools to manage her stressful situation before the stress roller coaster hit. Someone else may have found screaming along with the baby at the top of her lungs more effective. It's not what Sandi did that is important, but that she had a technique she knew was effective. Sandi had a habit to manage stress that worked for her, and she used it in real time to prevent stress from masterminding her.

Creating a Stress-Management Toolbox

A stress-management toolbox is simply a collection of habits and interventions that keep you healthy and resilient against the stressors in your life. If you don't have tools to fix stress, or a plan when you begin to feel stressed, stress can easily mastermind you. Creating a stress-management toolbox is easy, because most people already have some techniques they use to manage stress. Old tools work just as well as new ones.

ESSENTIAL

Walk the dog or pet the cat. Research indicates that pet owners have lower blood pressure and heart rate than people who do not own pets. Just stroking a pet is relaxing. In addition, pets offer companionship and a diversion from daily life. Take a break and spend some time with your pet. Your body will thank you.

Basic Tools of Stress Management

Every stress-management toolbox contains some basic tools to a healthy body, mind, and spirit. Do you have the following basic tools for stress management in your toolbox?

❑ Ability to say no to new demands on your time and resources.
❑ Healthy diet and exercise.
❑ Adequate, restful sleep.
❑ Supportive relationships with family and friends.
❑ Ability to leave work at work.
❑ Hobbies that you enjoy.

If these basics are not in your toolbox, stop and examine why. Don't you deserve quality time with the people you love, a healthy body, and a calendar full of activities you enjoy? Any other stress-management attempts will be futile, as they may fix a symptom of your stress but not a cause.

Developing Basic Stress-Management Tools

If you have trouble with any of the above basics, stop and begin here. It's impossible to fix a kitchen sink without a wrench, and it's impossible to manage stress if you lack basic tools in your toolbox that keep your body, mind, and spirit healthy. Like a gummed-up machine, the human body running on the wrong foods and lack of exercise cannot function properly, and it certainly can't resist stress. Helping your body run efficiently and effectively is a foundation for good health and effective stress management.

Right now, if you are not using all the basic tools for a healthy body and mind, you are a major cause of your own stress. Not caring for yourself is a red flag, inviting the raging bull of stress into your life. It's easier to resist stress when you can stop, think, and act. If you're just running from obligation to obligation, blindly on autopilot, without proper rest, fuel, and fun, you are just a sitting duck. Stress is coming, and it will find you.

Choose one or two of the basic stress tools to practice this week, and as you gain in confidence, add a couple more next week. Soon, you will begin to see a difference in your energy and mood.

Inventory Your Current Stress-Busting Tools

As you reflect on your life and how you already manage stress, what tools spring to mind? In other words, what do you do when you are stressed to make it stop?

Common stress busting tools may include:

- Working out
- Shopping
- Yard work
- Having sex
- Playing video/computer games
- Eating

- Drinking
- Therapy
- Medication
- Bubble bath with candles

ALERT

Smoking is the largest cause of preventable death worldwide today. A smoker will live an average of ten to twelve years fewer than a nonsmoker, and a smoker has a 70 percent higher risk of heart attack and a ten times greater risk of developing lung cancer than a nonsmoker.

Cleaning Out Your Toolbox

Now that you've explored the tools in your toolbox, figure out which tools you want to keep and which ones you want to throw out. Tools that keep you healthy and happy—workout routine, weekly coffee with a friend, Tai Chi class—are definitely ones to keep. Tools that have negative side effects, however, you may want to use with care or even throw out entirely.

Some tools can be healthier than others. An ice cream after a bad day at work may soothe you emotionally, but it rots your teeth and adds to your waistline. The ice cream tool may be one you want to save for a special occasion.

Smoking, drinking, or random sexual encounters may also be tools that you want to evaluate, if the long-term effects could be harmful to you. Sure, quitting smoking may add more short-term stress, but the long-term health problems may create even more stress. Any tool with negative effects on your life may be thrown out, or slowly eliminated over time.

The Stress Journal

Reading lists of possible stress-management tools may not mean much to you, if you don't know how to use them at the proper time. What good is a screwdriver if you can't recognize a screw? As you decide what stress-management tools to keep in your toolbox, you also need some awareness of stressful situations where these tools can fix your life and maintain balance in the face of stress.

Crashing with a movie on the couch after a long day may be one technique in your stress-management toolbox. However, if you knew exactly what made the day so long—that annoying client venting for thirty minutes, perhaps—using a tool immediately following the encounter, such as taking a walk around the building to let off steam, could have saved you time and energy, and may have even prevented an evening curled up on the couch.

A stress journal is a powerful tool to boost your awareness of what causes you stress and how you handle it. As you write and reflect on your stressors over time, you will begin to see patterns in your life and relationships. When you notice how the same person or event affects you, that awareness is a key step to managing the stress. Now you know when to practice a stress-management technique.

Case Study: The Importance of a Stress Journal

It's a lot easier to nip stress in the bud at the time than it is to stop the careening stress roller coaster mid-dive. Here's a practical example:

John can't understand why his wife Zeba always wants to talk when he gets home from work. He is so tired, listening to an explanation of her day is the last thing he wants. He wants to come home, go into the den, and doze until dinner. Seeing the hurt in Zeba's eyes as he walks past her to take a pre-dinner nap is very stressful for John, particularly as Zeba is "not in the mood" on nights when he takes a nap after work.

John begins to journal about this stressful situation. He identifies the stressor, needing down time after work, but as soon as he enters the door at home his wife expects him to be in family mode. To give himself some personal time, John brainstorms several options, including telling his wife no, taking a nap before his commute, drinking a coffee on the way home, or rescheduling his gym time. John decides that the gym time is the easiest and healthiest option for him and tries a proven stress-management tool. He reschedules time at the gym right after work and finds, to his delight, that working out wakes him up naturally, and he sleeps better at night.

John's journaling gave him the awareness he needed to mastermind a stressful situation in his relationship with his wife Zeba. John can go home to dinner and have the energy to be with his wife and actually enjoy her because he practiced a stress-busting tool at the right time.

ESSENTIAL

Let your creative juices flow, and decorate your own stress journal. Paint the cover your favorite color or create a collage of pictures of your favorite stress-busting activities. Any cheap college-ruled notebook can become a personal masterpiece to inspire awareness. Even if you don't have a creative bone in your body, give it a shot. Doing something different may end up surprising you!

Anyone can benefit from writing about a stressful situation. Brainstorm possible solutions to stressful problems. Experiment to find the tools that work for you. You, like John, may find the right tool at the right time to mastermind your stress in any given situation.

A Safe Venting Buddy

In addition to helping you figure out what tools are appropriate for which circumstances, a stress journal can also offer a safe place to let off steam. Journaling about that fight with your spouse may let out some of the frustration on the page and free up your time for other, more pleasurable activities. In addition, as you write you may even gain awareness about the fight or other stressful situation, that will help you be able to respond using your head rather than react using your previous patterns of behavior.

Map Out Your Stress Fault Lines

Just like fault lines from an earthquake, you have stress triggers in your life that can add up fast, compromising your resistance to stress until you experience a disturbance all your own. Learning what your stress fault lines are—those events and people that activate your flight or fight response—is key to masterminding your stress.

Stress Fault Line Activity

Take a page of your journal, and write "stress" in the middle in bold letters. Then draw a line through the word, reminding yourself that stress will not win. Then take different colors and draw lines coming out from the word "stress." Each line represents a person or situation that causes you great stress if not adequately managed. Common stress fault lines for many people include:

- Family
- Romantic relationships
- Health
- Finances
- Work

Be as specific as you can when identifying the events and people that trigger major stress with you. The more specific you are, the better able you will be to find a stress-busting tool personally tailored to keep each stress fault line in check.

Case Study: Mapping Out Stress Fault Lines

Here's an example of how mapping out a stress fault line can be beneficial. Cynthia, a single mom of two teenagers, knows that money is a big financial stressor, particularly that time of the month when the bills are due but there is still a week until she is paid. Cynthia labels "week bills are due" as a fault line in her journal. She knows, from previous study, that this one week alone is when most of her life goes wrong due to the stress of her finances.

As Cynthia examines what to do, she brainstorms ways to minimize her stress during the week the bills are due. She decides to say no to new obligations and social engagements that week, as they usually entail spending money driving or eating out that she really doesn't have. She has a talk with her children about not asking for money or expecting anything fancy during this week, as she's stretching her paycheck. She also decides to open a separate savings account and put the money she needs for bills there, untouched, until the bills become due.

Cynthia finds, by practicing these three stress-management tools, that the fault line "week bills are due" becomes much more manageable and, over time, causes her much less stress than it had before she examined it and used stress-busting tools to manage it.

Set Your Stress-Management Goals

As you look at the stress fault lines in your life, it's easy to feel overwhelmed. So much to work on, so much to improve, and so much to do. Take heart: there's plenty of time to manage each fault line in your life, and you may just find that by managing one, the others lessen or even go away.

Manage Stress Fault Lines to Manage Stress

To begin, prioritize. Which fault line is the source of the most stress in your life today? If you have trouble answering clearly or decisively, ask a trusted confidant or your spouse for an opinion. When you've determined a specific fault line, begin there. Ask yourself the following questions, and reflect in your journal or aloud:

1. Why is this event/person so stressful?
2. Do I have the resources to manage the stress generated by this event/person myself? What resources, if any, would help me make a better decision in regard to managing this stressor?
3. What can I do to make this event/person less stressful (short term and long term)?

When you've explored several options to manage the situation, set a plan for using your short-term stress-management tools. What tools will you use today or this week to manage this fault line?

After you've explored short-term tools for the situation, examine possible long-term tools. Do you need additional assistance—a finance class, a book or online research, or consultation with a mental-health professional—to help you manage this stressor in the long term? Create a plan to obtain the resources you need to mastermind the stress in this area of your life.

Managing Stress Is a Lifelong Process

In time, you may find the first stress fault line managed and can return to the page in your journal to explore another fault line. Another area of your life could also act up—the mother-in-law just has to call—and suddenly you're off, brainstorming ways to manage this fault line. Be flexible and open to what your stress management needs are, before stress erupts and takes over your life.

You will never have all your fault lines fixed, but over time you will develop a system to keep them all in check. As long as you are aware of what your stressors are and have a good idea where they originate, you are well on your way to responding to any stressful situation that arises. Just keep your head and reach into your toolbox.

Explore New Ways to Manage Stress

Managing your stress is a lifelong journey that takes patience, flexibility, and discipline. You may think you know everything about yourself, and have a tool ready for any stressful situation that presents itself, but life is full of surprises. Explore new tools to add to your toolbox that can keep your body, mind, and spirit healthy and stress free. Some tools you may want to add to your toolbox could include:

❏ Meditation
❏ Tai Chi
❏ Karate
❏ Massage
❏ Kickboxing
❏ Cooking from scratch
❏ Hiking, camping, or another nature-based activity
❏ Mindful eating
❏ Enjoying a pet

As you can see, your toolbox can contain many tools to fight stress before, during, and after it happens. Be creative and open to new tools. Ask your friends and family what works for them, and experiment.

ESSENTIAL

Stress-management coaches are trained professionals who motivate and guide others in managing their stress. Jill Rheaume, a stress coach trained at the Spencer Institute, recommends three tips for finding a qualified stress coach: credibility (is the person trained by a sound institution?), experience (has the person survived and managed stress personally?), and passion (does this person love helping others bust their stress?).

Be Spontaneous to Bust Stress

Try something new and different and totally unlike you. If you're a sedentary person, join a hiking group. If you have grandchildren, take them ice skating. If you have trouble settling down, try out a yoga class. Not only will you have fun and learn something about yourself, but you might just find a new tool for your toolbox.

Even with a versatile toolbox of stress-management techniques, is it possible to make all stress go away? No, not as long as you are alive. It is possible, however, to manage your stress so that it does not manage you. As you continue the task of identifying your stressors and using the tools in your toolbox at the right time, read on to explore and expand your stress toolbox so that you are better able to handle whatever stress may come at you.

CHAPTER 8

Tools for a Stress-Resilient Body

Your body is a miraculous collection of cells that work together to keep you thinking, eating, loving, working, and dreaming effectively and efficiently. Neglect your body, however, and you decrease your resilience to stress. Practice the basic tools to a healthy body—sleep, exercise, diet, and relaxation—and you are well on your way to masterminding stress in your life.

Sleep and Stress

Who has time to sleep other than babies, the hospitalized, and those in rest homes? You do. Sleep is necessary for a healthy mind and body. Yet for many people, sleep is the first thing they cut out of their schedule. Sure, you may unwind from work and have some fun, but if you don't get enough sleep, you are making yourself vulnerable to stress. Common effects of too little sleep include:

- Dizziness
- Forgetfulness
- High blood pressure
- Blurry vision
- Irritability
- Muscle aches and pains
- Trouble speaking
- Tremors
- Nausea
- Weight loss or gain

All these effects increase the likelihood that you are not running at your full potential. Remember that the key to managing stress is keeping your mind alert and aware so stress doesn't manage you. If you are groggy and grumpy, you're less likely to stop and think, "Wait a minute, I need a break" than a person who's had enough sleep. Who knows where stress will take you after you've mindlessly boarded the stress roller coaster.

The Dangers of Sleep Deprivation

Long-term effects of sleep deprivation are startling. A study of 82,000 nurses and their sleeping habits, conducted by Harvard Medical School in 2005, has linked fewer than six hours of sleep a night to obesity, cancer, diabetes, and heart disease. Most surprising, the study concluded that people who don't get enough sleep have a higher mortality rate than those who do.

Why is lack of sleep so bad for you? Too little sleep puts your body in red-alert mode. Remember how the adrenaline's rushing and your body is waiting for the emergency when you are stressed? Indeed, there must be a real emergency, because you didn't get enough sleep. Missing out on sleep stresses your body out.

One of the easiest ways to reduce your stress is to make sure you get enough sleep every night. Not getting that shut-eye will start off your day in stress mode, with that roller coaster blasting full speed ahead. Getting seven to nine hours of uninterrupted sleep every night is essential for good health in adults. Sounds great, but what if you can't sleep those seven to nine hours?

ESSENTIAL

Lavender is an old remedy against sleeplessness. Lavender's name originates from the Latin "to wash," and the ancient Romans valued lavender for its ability to clean a worried mind and restless spirit. Try a lavender spray or satchel of dried lavender tucked inside your pillow for a sweet smelling and restful night's sleep.

If you have trouble sleeping at night, you are not alone. The Better Sleep Council, a nonprofit organization that promotes nightly rest and relaxation for good health, reports that 65 percent of Americans are losing sleep due to stress. For those with trouble falling asleep, the Council recommends the following tips:

1. **Make sleep a priority.** Schedule a bedtime. Turn the phone off. Hang a "do not disturb" sign on your door, and mean it!
2. **Create a bedtime routine.** Remember, as a kid, how someone bathed you, read to you, and tucked you in? Well, now it's time to take care of yourself. Brew a cup of chamomile tea. Take a hot bath. Read a chapter of a novel, or say some prayers if you're religiously inclined—whatever you need to do to wind down.
3. **Make the bedroom dark and comfortable.** Is your bed clean and comfortable? Are the windows adequately covered to avoid disturbing lights? Make some changes, so that just thinking about your snuggly bed makes you very, very sleepy.
4. **Change your sleeping arrangements.** Is your mattress large enough for you and your partner? Has your pillow been replaced lately? Examine your sleeping arrangements, and change anything that adds potential discomfort.

5. **Keep technology out of the bedroom.** That means no TV in bed and no computer nearby. Watching a movie or computer screen in bed wakes your mind up, so to wind down, turn off the screen. Better yet, keep it in another room to resist temptation.

6. **Exercise regularly, but not right before bed.** Exercise keeps your body running smoothly. It also helps you sleep because your body is fine-tuned that day.

7. **Limit nicotine and caffeine.** Both stimulants, these commonly available drugs wake you up. Avoid them in the later half of the day—or better yet—altogether.

8. **Avoid eating two to three hours before bed.** Digesting food takes energy, and that energy wakes you up. Make the bedtime snack a thing of the past.

Getting enough sleep is extremely important, not only for your health, but also to keep you strong against stress. Spend some time modifying your sleeping habits if sleep is a problem for you. If you still have trouble sleeping despite changing your habits, visit with a health-care professional, as sleep disorders are common but serious conditions. Be gentle, kind, and patient with yourself, and know that every little victory in the bedroom is also a victory against stress hijacking your life.

Exercise, a Whole-Body Stress Buster

Now that you've gotten sleep under control, you have a major and important tool in your stress-management toolbox. Now it's time to focus on another. Exercise, like sleep, is a basic human need. You must exercise for a healthy body. Why? You are a physical being, designed for a natural life, even though modern life is anything but natural. If you neglect your body's need for exercise, you add unneeded stress to your life.

The Dangers of a Sedentary Lifestyle

Too many people today live sedentary lifestyles, glued to a computer screen at work, slumped into a car seat for the endless commute, and then glued to a television at night. According to the U.S. Center for Disease Control and Prevention, one-third of U.S. adults and 16 percent of U.S. children are obese, and the number of overweight and obese adults has doubled since 1980. Health problems linked to excess body weight include:

- Type 2 diabetes
- Heart disease
- Cancer
- Stroke
- Gallbladder and liver disease
- Hypertension (high blood pressure)
- High cholesterol or triglicerides
- Sleep apnea and respiratory problems
- Arthritis
- Gynecological problems (infertility, abnormal periods)

FACT

Your favorite tunes improve your workout. A 2010 study from Ohio State University found that listening to music while exercising cleared the brain, so that participants found themselves enjoying their workouts rather than worrying about other obligations. Create a play list for your iPod and hit the treadmill.

No one needs the stress of disease looming large in their lives. The human body is designed to move, walk, think, and go, not sit and veg out. In the natural world, a human would scan the environment for potential problems and process solutions on the go.

Keeping the Human Body Healthy

Like any predator, a human has keen eyesight, a large brain, and a nimble body to ensnare prey. A predator that can't catch prey due to age or infirmity dies. Is your body nimble? Could it catch your dinner if your life depended on it? Thirty minutes of walking five days a week is the minimal exercise required to maintain your weight, according to the U.S. Department of Health and Human Services. Just think: the human body is designed to walk thirty minutes a day, minimum. If your body needs that much to get by, how much more could it use to be healthy?

Exercise Is Key to a Healthy Body

If you do exercise more than thirty minutes, five days a week, then feel free to skip this section. Exercise is an important part of your life, and you likely know why you keep it up. Exercise feels good, and you feel good when you do it. Keep up your exercise routine, and your ability to resist stress stays strong.

For those of you who would rather eat ice cream than hit the gym, keep reading. You must bust your sedentary lifestyle to truly bust your stress. According to the Center for Disease Control and Prevention, modern society promotes environments of overeating, unhealthy eating, and physical inactivity.

FACT

The U.S. government declared war on obesity in 2009 with community grants to fight obesity and inactivity at the local level. Even First Lady Michelle Obama is speaking out against childhood obesity, making obesity prevention the health-care trend of the new millennium. Be active to bust stress.

Does this means that the heavier you are, the more stressed you are? Not necessarily. Weight is a complicated issue, as there are many causes including genetics and disease. Whatever the reasons you are sedentary, exercise is a proven remedy against being overweight and obese. Anyone, no matter his body type, can exercise. If getting into the grove is difficult for you, here are some tips to get started:

- Include exercise in your schedule. Showing up with sneakers laced is half the battle.
- Look for ways to swap activity for leisure in your schedule. For example, instead of eating junk food and watching a movie on a Saturday, go out for a hike and a picnic. Park at a distance from the store to make yourself walk. Substitute the stairs for the elevator.

- Recruit friends and family to exercise with you. If you're having a good time, you'll forget what hard work it is.
- Start small and expand. Walking and swimming are easy places to begin. Over time, you may want to join a gym and even find a personal trainer.
- If your schedule is crazy, break up your daily exercise goal. For example, walk ten minutes three times a day when you don't have time for thirty minutes in a row.

ALERT

Adults who exercise regularly live an average of six years longer than those who do not. In addition, adults sixty-five and older who exercise daily are more likely to remain disability free than those who do not. No matter what age you are, begin a daily exercise plan to enjoy as much of your life as possible, now and in the future.

Make thirty minutes your initial daily goal, and increase from there. As you exercise regularly, you'll begin to notice the following benefits of physically working your body:

- **Improved mood.** Exercise releases endorphins, a hormone that makes you happy.
- **Weight maintenance.** Exercise helps you lose unneeded weight and maintain your present weight. You will also notice your body converting fat into muscle and literally changing shape the more that you exercise.
- **More energy.** Exercise delivers oxygen to your body and improves your heart's circulation, meaning that you can breathe more deeply and do more every day.
- **Enhanced sex life.** No, this is not a Viagra commercial. Exercise really does improve erectile function in men and increase sexual arousal in women. Exercise also improves your body image and flexibility, making you more likely to want to hit the sheets.

- **Better sleep.** Exercise works the tension out of your body so you can crash at night with no worries.

Now aren't these great reasons to exercise? An energetic, sexually fulfilled, happy, and awake person is much more resilient to stress than a slow, sexually frustrated, depressed, and tired one. Keep exercising, and you have another important stress-management tool at your command.

The Importance of Healthy Eating

Adequate sleep and exercise are two important tools for stress management. A third goes hand in hand with keeping your body healthy. Eat a healthy, balanced diet that minimizes fats, sugars, and chemicals. Why? What you put into your body affects what you get out of it.

Too many people consider fat, sugar, and chemically processed foods to be food groups, when in reality these foods are dangerous to your health and waistline. Sugary beverages such as soda and flavored coffees add excess calories and chemicals. Whole grains, fresh vegetables, and lean meats—healthy foods that provide essential nutrients—are absent from many diets.

The Food Pyramid Guide to Healthy Eating

When was the last time you studied the food pyramid? The United States Department of Agriculture's color graph shows what foods to eat and how much of them to enjoy for a healthy diet. The food pyramid is a handy reference guide to keep your diet balanced. Here are the recommended daily servings for a healthy adult:

❏ Three ounces of grains, at least half being whole grains (1 ounce equals one slice of bread).
❏ Two-and-a-half to three cups of frozen, grilled, or fresh vegetables (high on the colorful vegetables and low on the starchy ones such as corn and potatoes).
❏ One-and-a-half to two cups of frozen or fresh fruit. Avoid fruit with sugar added (sugary canned peaches) or fruit juices (high in sugar and low in fiber).

- ❏ Three cups of low-fat dairy products such as skim milk and low-fat yogurt and cheese.
- ❏ Five to six ounces of low-fat meat such as lean beef and chicken or beans.
- ❏ Five to seven teaspoons of oil from low-fat cooking oils, salad dressings, and nuts.
- ❏ Discretionary calories (465–610) above and beyond the required food groups. (Note that one can of Coke contains 140 calories and a standard Frappuchino 230 calories.)

Notice that sugar, coffee, and soda are not necessary food groups. While eating foods you enjoy can be a treat, eating sugary foods all the time can stress your body. Why? Not only are sugar and caffeine stimulants that give your body an artificial boost, but they are addictive. The more you consume, the more you have to consume for the same high. In addition, you rack up empty calories fast consuming such foods, calories that may stay around if you don't burn them off through exercise.

Avoid Empty Calories for a Stress-Free Body

Talking about empty calories, processed and fast food is full of them. Whenever you eat on the go, you pay for the convenience not just with money. Processed and fast food is packed with chemicals and hormones that pollute your body and mind. The more natural a food, the easier it is to digest as well. Montezuma's revenge doesn't just target travelers, as anyone who's had a "bad" meal out can attest. Digestive distress is often a byproduct of a diet high in fats, sugars, and chemicals.

ESSENTIAL

A healthy plate is a colorful plate. Limit white foods such as white bread, rice, and potatoes that are low in nutrition and fiber. Instead, be bold: choose orange for carrots, green for salad, yellow for lean grilled chicken, brown for a whole grain roll, and you are well on your way to meeting your daily nutrition requirements and keeping your body strong and healthy.

Self Evaluation: Is Your Diet Healthy?

Take a minute to examine your diet. Is it high in sugars and fats? What role does fast and processed food play in your diet? If the food pyramid is something you strive for daily, congratulate yourself. You are doing well in wielding a healthy diet as a tool for stress prevention.

If fast food is your friend and vegetables are something that happen to other people, stop and evaluate your life. Do you really want to be healthy and live as long as possible? Is preventing a stressed-out body important to you?

If the answer is yes, begin moderating your diet. It's hard to change any routine, particularly a diet that tastes good. Make gradual changes to your diet—for example, substitute wheat for white bread or skim for whole-fat milk—and over time you can modify your diet to be healthier.

Choose Healthy Stress Busters

Adequate and uninterrupted sleep, daily exercise, and a healthy, balanced diet are all key tools to managing your stress. All three keep your body running in tip-top shape and your mind sharp, so that you're better able to manage stress when it strikes.

Keeping yourself well-rested, exercising, and eating the rights foods can be a challenge. Life turns busy and crazy, and suddenly it's take-out pizza night and the gym is put on the back burner while you stay up late watching a movie. Slipping up every once in a while is fine, and human. Living life on the edge—gambling your body's health for time you think you can't have otherwise—is a recipe for disaster.

As you begin to manage your stress, take time to focus on the big three. Many stressful situations on a daily basis can be minimized or eliminated entirely if you get enough sleep, exercise, and eat well. Keep these tools in your stress-management toolbox, or add them if you don't have them already, to make your body a mean, lean, stress-fighting machine.

Vitamins, Minerals, and More

A healthy diet rich in fruits, vegetables, protein, and grains offers the daily allowances of vitamins and minerals you need to be healthy. The problem is that most people don't eat a healthy and varied diet daily to meet their specific nutritional needs. So, many people take a daily multivitamin, and others, especially women and the elderly, consume calcium supplements for bone loss.

Choose Vitamins with Care

Because the vitamin industry is loosely regulated, and research is sketchy about the vitamin and mineral needs of different people, it is best to check with a health-care professional about any vitamin and mineral supplements you may be taking. The following vitamins and minerals are recommended, in general, for certain age groups:

- Calcium for adolescents and senior adults, particularly women, to protect the bones
- Vitamin D for the homebound, elderly, and dark skinned to boost calcium absorption
- Folic acid for women of child-bearing age and those hoping to become pregnant to prevent birth defects
- Vitamin B-12 for the elderly, as the body stops producing this brain fuel with age

True, the right balance of vitamins and minerals contributes to good health, but there is no magic pill for a healthy body. In addition, overdosing on vitamins can cause liver failure, cancer, and even death. Don't add to your stress by thinking a multivitamin can cover for your poor diet. Focus on eating well and exercising as your top priority, and if good health doesn't follow, ask a doctor if vitamins and supplements may benefit you.

Herbs Offer Stress Relief

These days, herbal supplements are another popular tool for good health. Many people who cannot find relief for disease or pain through conventional medicine turn to a herbalist or other alternative-medicine practitioner for assistance. Frequently used herbs and natural remedies for common ailments include:

- St. John's Wort for depression
- Aloe vera gel for cuts and burns
- Cannabis (marajuana, pot) for pain relief
- Chamomile for sleeplessness and to reduce anxiety
- Echinacea for colds, sore throats, and to boost the immune system
- Ginger for nausea and motion sickness
- Parsley to aid digestion (yes, that's why parsley garnishes your plate)
- Peppermint for bad breath

FACT

During the Middle Ages, people seasoned meats with savory herbs such as rosemary, thyme, sage, and lavender for dishes that smelled as good as they tasted. Medieval Europeans also used herbs we consider sweet, such as cinnamon and cloves, especially to hide the flavor of old meats about to go off. For a blast from the past, try pork with rosemary or beef with cloves and enjoy your own aromatherapy meal.

Though the tradition of healing with herbs is ancient, the use of herbs for medicinal purposes has not been regulated by the Food and Drug Administration. Use herbs with caution, and at your own risk. Hopefully, in the future, the mainstream medical profession will grow to embrace herbs, and the many other forms of alternative medicine, that have brought relief and healing to so many hurting in body, mind, and spirit.

Massage and Reiki

Massage and Reiki are two other tools to relax your body that you may want to place in your stress-management toolbox if you have not already done so. Massage and Reiki release tension and relax the body, but in very different ways.

Massage Relieves Tension in the Body

Massage is a general term for any physical stimulation of the skin and connective tissue to release tension in the flesh and muscles. Though massage often has a sexual connotation, it is a legitimate professional practice for heal-ing and relaxing the body. There are many different types of massage avail-able, including:

- Swedish massage, the most popular type of massage, focuses on muscles and joints.
- Deep tissue massage uses greater pressure to release tension in the muscles.
- Aromatherapy massage combines scented oils or candles with mas-sage to promote relaxation and healing.
- Hot stone massage uses heated stones to release tension at various tight points in the body, loosening it up for the massage.
- Reflexology releases energy in the body's organs and systems by mas-saging areas of the foot connected to each body part.

Most people who experience a massage can attest to its relaxing prop-erties. Some massage, such as deep tissue, may hurt for hours or days after-ward, but then again the stress in your body built up over time, so it only makes sense that it may take a while to release it.

When seeking a massage, ask for the credentials of the person offer-ing the service. A massage therapist, also known as a masseuse, should be licensed or in the process of obtaining a license through the American Mas-sage Therapy Association or another credible organization. Many massage training schools offer discounted massage services to the public so that their students can gain clinical hours toward earning a license, so this could be a viable option for those on a limited income.

Reiki Heals the Body's Energy

Reiki is another tool to manage body stress. Reiki, or energy healing, is a Japanese healing practice that regulates the body's natural energy flow. The Reiki practitioner will literally lay hands on or above a client's body and regulate his energy flow, smoothing out any blockages and clearing out any negative energy.

Reiki is based on the idea that energy flows through all living things, including the human body. A person who is stressed or becomes ill literally has no energy or poor circulation of energy in a particular region or regions of the body. Reiki is designed to free up any energy blockages by stimulating the area of the body where the energy blockage occurs, allowing energy to flow freely once again.

Many people experience a sense of peace and hopefulness after a Reiki session. Though Reiki is not religious in nature, it is a spiritual practice that encourages the participant to tap into his life force energy and seek healing by nurturing the self.

Mrs. Hawayo Takata, who introduced Reiki to the West in the 1970s, explained that *Reiki* comes from two Japanese terms: *rei* is the spiritual wisdom intuitive to each human being known by the religious as God, and *ki*, or life energy, is the nonphysical energy that gives all living things life.

Individuals interested in meditation or chakra healing naturally gravitate toward Reiki. If you have chronic pain in a particular part of the body or feel a strong desire to release tension in your body but aren't quite sure how to do it, Reiki may be for you. Be sure to find a Reiki master or healer who is licensed or certified by a credible organization, such as the Reiki License Commission.

Mindfulness and Other Relaxation Techniques

There are as many different types of meditation in the world as there are trees in the forest, and who can count them all? If the term "meditation" is confusing to you, stop and take a deep breath. Seriously, that was it. Did you get it? If not, take another bigger and deeper breath. Close your eyes. Focus on nothing but your breath. Open your eyes. Believe it or not, you were just meditating!

Meditation, a Break from Reality

Meditation is any practice that alters your mind and checks you out of reality, just like taking that deep breath did. Technically, you can meditate while jogging, listening to music, or having sex. Any time an activity clicks your brain off, that is meditation.

Meditation is a practice of concentrating and deliberately freeing the mind. For many people, this is easier with music, scents, chanting, or candles. Meditation is extremely relaxing for the mind, but more on that later. Meditation offers the body, too, much needed rest and relaxation.

Any time you breathe deeply, you inhale more oxygen. As you inhale more oxygen, you give your lungs and heart more oxygen to circulate throughout your body. That oxygen helps your body run more efficiently, making you healthier and happier. A breathing meditation is one of the easiest ways to meditate. Stop. Catch your breath. Focus on it going up and down in your chest. As few as one big, deep breath can make a difference in the midst of a crazy and busy day.

Deep Breathing Reduces Stress

Ever heard the phrase, "I just need to stop and catch my breath"? The person is really saying that she has been so busy, she can't even breathe properly. She's panting, desperate for oxygen, instead of breathing deeply and letting in enough oxygen. The wisdom in this phrase is startling, because those who don't breathe are dead. Morbid, yes, but telling in a world where everyone runs around missing out not only on oxygen, but also on many other gifts life has to offer.

Catching your breath is a very simple tool to relax your body in the midst of a busy day. Think about the possibilities; instead of jumping into a new obligation or argument, take a deep breath first. Who knows what new insight you'll gain after restarting your brain. With more oxygen circulating, your body and mind can tackle any task more efficiently and effectively.

Enjoy Life Now with Mindfulness

Mindfulness is another easy form of meditation. Mindfulness simply means being aware of the present. Don't just smile at your spouse—notice the color of his eyes, his hair, the way his chin curves, the hair sticking out of his ears. Don't just eat your sandwich—notice the slippery meat, the salty pickle, the crunchy lettuce against your tongue.

Vietnamese Buddhist monk and meditation guru Thich Nhat Hahn teaches that mindfulness is enjoying life now. Hahn encourages beginners to start with an orange, a particularly juicy and sweet fruit. Smell the orange as you open it. Feel the peel against your hand. Savor the exploding juice inside your mouth as you take a bite. Think of nothing in the world but that orange. This, Hahn teaches, is peace.

FACT

All of the world's major religions incorporate some form of meditation into their belief system. Jesus Christ, the Prophet Muhammad, and the Buddha all meditated. One doesn't have to be religious to meditate, however. Many people practice meditation for relaxation.

Why is enjoying an orange peace? Peace is being content exactly where you are, and if you are truly enjoying a simple task like enjoying an orange, you are capable of enjoying anything. Remember that stress is your reaction to pressure generated internally or externally. Mindfulness hijacks any attempts at putting pressure on yourself, because all you are doing is focusing on an object and enjoying it completely.

Mindfulness meditation is easy, portable, and inexpensive. Be present with a favorite food, pet, or flower. Lie down, sit, or stand. What matters most is enjoying life right now.

How can this relax your body? Well, if you are enjoying an orange, or any object, you learn to appreciate your body. Your sense of taste, smell, sight, and touch are heightened and become more aware as you focus on an object. Over time, as you practice mindfulness, your senses become beautiful gifts that allow you to appreciate the world in simple ways daily.

Other Relaxation Techniques

Another relaxation technique helpful to body relaxation is a walking meditation. A walking meditation is simply a slow, deliberate walk. Instead of walking for exercise, where one chooses a fast pace to burn calories, a walking meditation is an intentional walk, as slowly or as quickly as you please.

As you practice a walking meditation, give yourself a certain amount of time, ten to twenty minutes, for example. Focus on the body, and be deliberate with every step. If desired, regulate your breathing to match your steps. You may be surprised how quickly walking in a slow way can relax you.

A simple breath meditation, mindfulness meditation, and a walking meditation may be effective tools to add to your stress-management toolbox, or they may not work for you at all. What is important is to try these, and other new ways, to reduce your stress, so that you have a versatile arsenal of tools at your disposal for the next time stress strikes your life.

Nurture your basic stress busters, refreshing sleep, healthy diet, and exercise, and develop new ones, mindfulness meditation, herbal supplements, and vitamins, to keep your stress-management toolbox full and your body resilient against stress. With your body protected against stress, the next step in stress management is developing tools to keep your mind strong and flexible in the face of stress.

CHAPTER 9

Tools for a Stress-Resilient Mind and Spirit

The mind and body are intricately connected in the person known as you. The mind, your body's central processing unit, commands all you say, think, and do. It's impossible to nurture your body without nurturing your mind, and vice versa. That being said, there are specific ways to nurture the mind and keep it strong against stress.

Pessimism Does Not Pay

Everyone knows a grump—someone who sees the clouds in a sunny sky and points out everything that could possibly go wrong in any plan. Your friendly, or not so friendly, neighborhood grump reminds you of the potential hazards at any given moment. Whether at home, at work, or on the other side of the bed, your nearest grump is a constant source of potential worries and threats.

A grump is constantly primed for stress. Bad things may or may not happen, but a grump is ready either way. Being in a continual state of red alert is hard on the body. If you're always looking for something to stress about, you are always stressed. A study of ninety-nine Harvard University students over a thirty-five year period demonstrated that those who called themselves "pessimists" at age twenty-five had poorer health at age sixty-five than those who called themselves "optimists." All that worry takes its toll!

Be Positive to Bust Stress

When you are constantly seeing dirt, you miss the flowers. Optimistic thinking focuses on what's going well in life—the beautiful, the fun, and the well-done rather than the ugly, boring, and potentially hazardous. An optimist sees a glass half full, as the saying goes, and even puts a flower in it. Why? Seeing life as beautiful and fun increases not only your happiness, but the happiness of those around you.

ESSENTIAL

Cognitive behavioral therapy transforms negative self-beliefs into positive, life giving ones. Though nothing can substitute for therapy with a trained professional, trying cognitive therapy at home may just brighten your day. Choose a negative thought or belief about yourself, such as "my butt is fat," and replace it with a positive one, such as "I love how I feel when I exercise, and my body thanks me for it, too!"

Ever notice how humor is contagious? Someone starts laughing, and even if you didn't hear the joke, you start chuckling despite yourself. Positive thinking is like laughter. The more you seek happiness, the more you'll see it.

So if you are a pessimist, always searching for the clouds, stop and ask yourself if this is really how you want to live your life—constantly seeking out things to stress over? With work, family, friends, your finances, and your health in the midst of a crazy, busy world, isn't life naturally stressful enough without looking for potential stressors on the horizon?

If the answer is yes, consider adding positive thinking to your stress-management toolbox. Seek one positive word, image, or development every day. Surround yourself with inspiring people and activities who make you feel good about yourself. Practice smiling in the mirror.

Positivity can be a stress-management tool when dealing with a stressful person or relationship as well. If someone else is whiny or preaching gloom and doom about something that isn't that big of a deal, point out to him that life isn't that bad. You're still alive. Take great comfort in the soap opera complex—your life could be much, much worse, like the drama of a primetime soap where your mother's really your father who is also broke, sleeping with your husband, and possessed by demons. There, don't you feel better?

Meditation for Peace of Mind

Positive thinking is an important stress-management tool, but there are others to consider as you develop your toolbox to fight mental stress in your life. Meditation is a timeless practice that offers instant peace and relaxation. Meditation literally restarts your conscious mind, freeing it from all the clutter and worry of daily life.

Everyone has experienced the frustration of a stalling computer, usually when a deadline looms large. Often, if you restart the machine, it comes back running efficiently and effectively. Too many programs open, too much data to load—the poor little computer was overwhelmed!

Think of your mind as that computer, constantly juggling your work, friends, family, health, constant stimuli from your environment, and all the others stressors on your list—just thinking about it is exhausting! Now imagine restarting your mind, literally turning it off in the midst of your busy life, and then returning to your day, revived and refreshed. This is the gift meditation can offer to you.

Benefits of Meditation

As you meditate, you give your body a blast of relaxation. Heart rate and breathing slow down, blood pressure normalizes, and the spread of oxygen throughout the body increases. Immune and brain function also improve, as does inspiration and creativity. Research has even proven that people who meditate long term have better luck kicking bad habits like smoking, drinking, and overeating. There, isn't that reason enough to add meditation to your toolbox?

How to Meditate

Think you're a person who can't meditate? Many people try and fail at meditation, simply because they do not listen to their bodies. Perhaps they try a type of meditation that hurts them or bores them, when a simple modification such as adjusting the body could make the process click. Perhaps they can't focus when all they need is a guide, such as an object to hold or new setting to aid in concentration. Perhaps the silence bugs them, when a relaxation CD is all they need to succeed.

Listen to Yourself to Meditate

The reasons people can't meditate are many, but all obstacles can be overcome with experimentation. Explore different types of meditation and remain open to finding a type of meditation and a setting for it that fits your needs, personality, and schedule. Practicing meditation that works for you reaps the benefits of this stress-busting practice.

Common meditation practices to consider as you discern if meditation may be right for you include:

- Breath meditation (focusing on your breathing)
- Walking meditation (focusing on your steps)
- Guided imagery meditation (listening to an audio recording or live instructor telling you what to imagine)
- Mantra meditation (focusing on a word or image to clear the mind)
- Transcendental meditation (resting in silence)
- Mindfulness meditation (focusing on your environment)

Breath meditation is simply catching your breath. Focus on breathing deeply—in and out, in and out, in and out—at your own pace. This meditation is particularly useful at work, in the car, or other places where you need a quick pick-me-up.

FACT

The word "meditate" originates from the Latin, meaning to remedy or solve. Meditation, in the Eastern tradition, involves letting go and seeking a deeper sense of self. Funny how the Latin meaning holds true today, because Eastern-style meditation remedies or solves anxiety if practiced regularly.

A walking meditation is simply a slow, reflective walk where you focus on your steps. This type of meditation is particularly enjoyable on a sandy beach, in an autumn glade, or other natural environment where you can enjoy your surroundings. Try it to your favorite slow songs or a recording of blues or classical music.

A guided imagery meditation invites you to imagine yourself doing something relaxing, sometimes in another place or other times, for healing purposes. Audio CDs are readily available to practice this type of meditation. All you have to do is get in a comfortable position, hit "play," and follow the directions.

QUESTION

What if I just can't sit still when I meditate?
Yoga, a series of meditative exercises focused on the breath, helps many people meditate who have trouble fidgeting during conventional meditation. Other active forms of meditation include any of the martial arts, Tai Chi, Pilates, and even conventional sports like biking, hiking, or swimming. Add meditation to your exercise routine, and make meditation both active and fun!

In mantra meditation, you simply repeat a word or phrase to clear your mind. Select a word or short phrase with personal meaning to you, one that is inspiring. Sit or rest comfortably, close your eyes, repeat the word or phrase, and focus on it so that all your other worries disappear. Over time, you may repeat the mantra less as your concentration improves.

Transcendental meditation requires resting alone in silence. Some people take naturally to this practice, while others need something to do. Try holding a stone or other object to see if touch aids the process, or likewise try staring at an image or color to see if sight aids relaxation.

Mindfulness meditation involves being present in the immediate environment. Sit on a park bench and stare at a tree, enjoying its color, leaves, and the way it sways in the breeze. Eat your favorite meal slowly and carefully, enjoying every single bite. How you practice mindfulness meditation will depend upon your particular interests and desires, but take any activity, slow it down so that you notice and enjoy every step of it, and you are experiencing mindfulness.

Tips for Succeeding with Meditation

No matter which meditation practice attracts you, the following tips will help you get started and stay meditating:

1. **Position the body comfortably.** Sit, stand, lie down, whatever is comfortable to you, but find a position where your body doesn't distract you. If meditating in a group, do not think that you have to position yourself exactly the way everyone else does if it will hurt your body. Be assertive and do what works for you.
2. **Create a ritual.** Designate a space your meditation spot—your favorite bench in the backyard, a chunk of your bedroom, the toilet—wherever you can get away. Decorate with candles, pillows, and rocks to make your meditation space a place where you want to be, if desired.
3. **Give yourself permission to experiment.** Try several different types of meditation before giving up, and make modifications as needed to make the practice work for you. Enroll in a meditation class or seminar, and browse books on meditation to peak your interest. Remember, you are the expert on yourself; you just need to learn what works for you.
4. **Make regular time for meditation.** Add it into your schedule. Find a morning, evening time, or set a goal that at some point in the day you

will meditate. Begin with five minutes a day, and work your way up to fifteen or twenty minutes a day. Over time, you may choose to meditate every other day, several times a week, or on an as needed basis. To begin, however, practice daily until you get the hang of it.

5. **Incorporate meditation into your current spiritual or religious life, if applicable.** Experiment with ways to meditate according to your faith tradition, but also know that having spiritual or religious beliefs is not necessary to meditate successfully. Rather, including meditation in your private prayer or devotional life increases the likelihood that you'll keep meditating.

Begin small—five minutes a day staring at a picture of a beach or focusing on your breath—and practice the tips for beginning successfully. Over time, meditation may become a powerful tool to help relax you in the midst of a busy day and decrease your vulnerability to stress.

Daily Meditation Is Insurance Against Stress

Think of a daily meditation practice as insurance against mental stress. Health insurance protects you against the costs of health care. Regular meditation protects you against the costs of stress. How? Meditation builds you up, giving you reserve energy so that you are better able to cope with stress. Every day that you meditate—particularly on days when life is going well and stress is minimal—you add relaxation into your energy bank so that the next time stress strikes, you will be prepared.

Therapy for Stress Relief

You can ease stress on the mind by meditating and thinking positively. Some of the ways the mind approaches stress, however, may benefit best from therapy. Before you decide that therapy is not for you, take a look at the connection between therapy and stress reduction.

Therapy Increases Stress Awareness

According to a 2010 study in the *Journal of Experimental Social Psychology*, people seek therapy for the following reasons:

- They do things without knowing why and feel bad (guilt)
- They experience anxiety or sadness and do not know why
- They experience confusion when other people have strong feelings about something they did, and they have no idea why

Note that all three reasons stem from a lack of awareness. It's certainly stressful not to know what's going on inside your head and in the important relationships around you.

Remember how some people are reactive to stress—just a phone call from a family member, a memory triggered by a daily event, or a certain food can freak them out? An event occurs in their life, and instantly they are riding the stress roller coaster. Their minds simply are not able to stop and take control of the situation, due to a lack of awareness.

FACT

The annual "Stress in America" study for the American Psychological Association in 2009 found only 4 percent of Americans saw a therapist for stress, down from 7 percent in 2008. Watching television (38 percent), eating (28 percent), smoking (17 percent), and shopping (15 percent) were the main tools Americans used to manage stress that year.

Nothing boosts awareness quite like therapy. A good therapist can balance compassion with insights that change the way you think about yourself and the world around you. Any stress trigger that incapacitates you and completely ruins your day could be explored and even resolved with therapy.

Therapy Gives You Control over Your Life

Confusion is a product of not knowing. No one likes feeling out of control. Most people will do anything possible to avoid looking like an idiot, particularly when it comes to their own minds. Confusion is often a great place to begin therapy, as another person, particularly a trained professional, can help you make sense of the confusion and find relief for your stress.

Common Types of Therapy

Okay, so you are stressed and decide to seek therapy. Common types of therapy beneficial to managing stress include:

- **Family systems therapy.** A family systems therapist will explore relationships between you and your family to help you understand the stress inherent in your family. You will also learn ways to change unhealthy behaviors toward your family that cause you stress and pain. Most family and marriage counselors use this technique.
- **Cognitive behavioral therapy.** A cognitive behavioral therapist encourages the client (person coming to therapy) to share the reason she is in therapy. The therapist then examines behaviors that cause the problem and explores healthier behaviors that address and eventually solve the problem. Cognitive behavioral therapy is practical and focused on forming new habits to better manage life.
- **Jungian psychotherapy.** A Jungian psychoanalyst delves into a client's unconscious, looking for reasons unknown to her that cause unwanted behaviors and feelings. Dreams, fantasies, and strong emotional responses are examined for clues to the workings of the unconscious mind. Effective in healing depression, anxiety, and other emotional disorders, Jungian psychotherapy greatly increases emotional wellness and encourages the client to become aware of how her mind operates.
- **Biofeedback.** A therapy that focuses on listening to the body, biofeedback helps the client learn to relieve pain in specific parts of the body. Biofeedback is helpful in healing stress-related illnesses such as asthma, headaches, irritable bowel syndrome, and high blood pressure.
- **Anger management.** Anger management therapy or courses teach the client how to become aware of her anger and express it in healthy ways. This type of therapy may be especially helpful for people who tend to be physically, verbally, or emotionally abusive when stressed.
- **Group therapy.** Alcoholics Anonymous, Co-dependents Anonymous, and a depression support group all offer environments for sharing and support in mental healing. Benefits of such groups include mentoring, resources, and accountability.

Note that therapy will not just make the stress go away overnight. Using various techniques to increase your awareness, a therapist may increase your stress in the short term to do so. Not only will the therapist encourage you to talk about painful events such as what brought you into therapy and relationship challenges, but she will share insights about you and your behavior that may also cause pain.

FACT

Different types of mental-health professionals offer different services. Therapists and counselors are both licensed for various types of talk therapy. A psychologist counsels, though she also administers tests for mental-heath disorders. A psychiatrist is a medical doctor of the mind who offers testing, limited therapy, and medication to relieve mental illness.

Good therapy may cause short-term pain, but long-term gain as well. You will obtain the awareness you need not only to lead a healthier and happier life, but to respond in full control to stressful situations around you, rather than letting stress mastermind you.

Does Your Stress Really Need Therapy?

Some people love therapy, because they have someone to talk to. Others find therapy useful for intensely stressful chapters in their lives—divorce or loss of a child, for example—but have no need for it in daily life. If therapy is new for you, or you are not currently in therapy, consider the following questions as you decide whether therapy is a stress-management tool for keeping your mind healthy:

- Is there pain, confusion, frustration, anger, or sadness in your life that blocks you from living the way you want?
- Do you have a diagnosed DSM mental-health condition such as obsessive compulsive disorder, generalized anxiety disorder, or bipolar disorder that is currently untreated with either meditation or counseling?

- In the last year, have you experienced the loss of a spouse, your mobility, or a job; a reduction in the size of your family due to a move, the economy, or members leaving; or a major health diagnosis such as cancer, that you just can't get over?
- Do you use alcohol, drugs, food, or any other substance as your default method for coping with stress?
- Are there any particular events or people in your life that instantly stress you out so much that you can't function?

If the answer to any of the questions above is yes, seeking therapy may benefit you. A professional therapist can offer you a safe place to explore whatever is blocking your awareness of certain areas in your life, as well as refer you to other mental-health resources that can further reduce your stress.

Religion as a Stress Buster

Religion and spirituality are sources of strength and comfort for many believers worldwide. Whether you are Jewish or Ba'hai, Celtic pagan or nondenominational Christian, organized religion offers several benefits for mental health, including:

- Social support from a group of believers.
- Rituals, or repeated activities to connect with the divine, that give life meaning and purpose.
- A sense of tradition and connectedness to the past, present, and future.
- A source of hope in the face of death and other difficult life events.

Many mental-health professionals agree that religion can be a source of stress reduction if a person finds comfort from his beliefs and enjoys relationships of mutual trust and love found in a religious setting. Though religious activities can sometimes be stressful—power politics, belief structures that are negative or harm others—if your religious tradition or spiritual practices offer you calm and peace in the midst of a stressful world, keep the faith tool in your stress-management toolbox.

Hope Connected to Religious Belief

Dr. Jerome Groopman explores the connection between faith and healing in his 2005 book, *The Anatomy of Hope*. Groopman wonders at how patients with hope, a mixture of religious belief and optimism, beat the odds against terminal cancer more frequently than patients who relied on science alone. Hope, according to Groopman, is a key ingredient to healing and living a healthy life.

ESSENTIAL

Increase hope in the world around you by doing something kind for someone else. Send your spouse flowers, fix the kids' favorite meal, give a friend a hug, or write a thank-you card to someone who's changed your life. Even the most simple ways you say "I appreciate you" make a difference.

Hope is a process of seeking the best outcome in any given situation and believing it's not only possible, but probable. Whether or not hope is rooted in your religious beliefs, it may benefit you in any given situation. Seeking the positive in life draws you out of the mess of the present and inspires you to take action now, that a better world for you might be a reality rather than a dream.

Religious/Spiritual Tools for Stress Management

If you are currently religious or spiritual, take some time to examine if your beliefs and practices help you manage stress. If not, why not? Are you attending the wrong mosque, church, temple, coven, or synagogue? Is nurturing your relationship with your concept of the divine something you wish you did, but never have time to do? How can you connect with your concept of the divine in order to find hope in your life?

If you are not religious, explore the ways that you connect with your concept of life's purpose. Explore what gives you hope: your family, friends, garden, personal achievements? Are you enjoying these people and activities as much as you'd like to? Why or why not?

Seeking hope and meaning in life, with or without religion, is an important tool to improve mental health and wellness. Be creative, examine your personal beliefs, and practice them daily, so that hope, not stress, prevails.

Nature, the Original Stress Buster

Silence is rare in modern life. Traffic lumbers by, the air conditioner clicks, the cell phone buzzes, the refrigerator hums, and the kids bicker. Modern life is loud and distracting. According to a 2006 report of the World Health Organization, thousands of people worldwide die every year due to heart attacks triggered by noise-related pollution. In the midst of noise that's anywhere from annoying to deadly, the peace and quiet of nature is a welcome gift.

Nature Connects You with Yourself

Ever notice how taking a walk along the beach, snowboarding down a snowy peak, or smelling the crisp autumn leaves refreshes you? Nature, the original stress buster, connects you to your natural state, as a creature of the world. The wind brushes against your skin, the clean air fills your lungs, and the bright colors of trees and flowers dazzle your eyes.

The nagging partner, the leaky faucet, and the dented fender on your car from the accident at the grocery store seem like a distant dream compared with a mountain peak or the throbbing surf. For the human mind, constantly bombarded with stimulation from modern life, nature's slower pace offers a welcome break.

Nature Restarts the Mind

Like meditation, time spent in nature restarts the mind and cleans it of stress and worry. Whether a day hike through the forest, a scuba-diving vacation, or a picnic at the park, time in nature slows down life and gives your mind time to recover from the stresses of daily life.

Nature, an Easily Accessible and Effective Stress Buster

If nature's so good for you, why aren't you out there? Almost every country or region has varying terrain—forests, prairies, mountains, and bodies of water—to rejuvenate those weary from modern life. Spending time in nature can be as simple as a cup of coffee in your backyard or a jog through the nearest park. Many state and local parks offer free admission and priceless natural beauty. Open your eyes, explore the world around you, and keep your stress at bay.

ESSENTIAL

Nature sounds may soothe your mind both in the backyard and in your bed. Recordings of gently falling rain, ocean waves, crickets chirping, frogs croaking, and brooks bubbling help many who suffer from insomnia and anxiety fall asleep and stay asleep. Experiment with various recordings to find a nature sound that helps you get the sleep you need to be healthy and resilient to stress.

If nature is a tool that you'd like to develop for your stress-management toolbox, explore ways that you can routinely enjoy nature in your daily life. What natural places are available in your area and price range? How can you change your habits to enjoy nature more—picnics outdoors instead of pizza and movie night? How can you bring nature into modern life—a houseplant on the desk at work, fresh flowers in the bedroom weekly, adopting a puppy from the humane society who needs multiple outdoor walks daily?

Nature is one of the many ways to relax a mind frazzled from the stressors of modern life. Along with positive thinking, meditation, therapy, and hope, nature offers those eager to manage stress multiple options to fight mental stress. As your mind struggles to balance all the demands on your time and energy, give it the break it deserves. Take time out to relax and rest your mind and spirit, and you are well on your way to masterminding stress in your life.

PART III

Stress and Modern Life

CHAPTER 10

Stress and Money

Money may be the root of all evil, but it is also the fountain of life. Money equals food on the table, a roof over the family's head, and adequate health care. Whether you struggle to feed your family or fret over your family's trust, financial stress affects you. Learn how money stresses you out and develop tools to manage your greatest money fears to mastermind financial stress in your life.

What Is Financial Stress?

Financial stress is the pressure money puts on your life. It sounds so simple, but the reality is much more complicated. Though everyone's financial profile may differ, every adult has the same basic needs that only money can buy:

- Affordable housing (rent, mortgage)
- Affordable transportation (car, public transport)
- Food and other consumables (everything from apples to zoo trips)
- Health care
- Savings, for the dreary days after a surprise layoff or other emergencies
- Retirement, so you don't have to work forever

When these basic financial needs, or others important to your security, are not met, enter stress. The stock market is down, what have I lost? The car broke, how am I going to get to work? My daughter needs braces, can I afford this without putting it on the credit card?

Money Equals Security

For many people, money is an instant stressor. That's because money equals security. Without money in today's world of supply and demand, where would you be? Homeless? Living in a family member's spare room? Lose money and you don't just lose your home, car, and other assets, you lose your sense of identity in life. What would your friends think? What would you do to entertain yourself? Who would you be without the means to make money for yourself?

If you are stressed out by finances in your life, you have every right to be. Life costs money. Gone are the days when families told stories by the fire at night or friends shared wisdom while peeling vegetables from the garden. Today, coffee with a friend costs money. Families watch television or shop at the mall to bond, which also costs money. Eating necessitates grocery shopping with money—is there anything you can do anymore that doesn't cost money?

Life is expensive, and getting more and more expensive by the day. If children, elderly parents, or a homebound spouse rely on your paycheck to eat, sleep, and stay alive, the pressure is on. For the majority of people, masterminding financial stress is a daily challenge that looms large with that pile of bills.

Self-Evaluation: What Is Your Financial Stress?

Everyone has the same basic needs that only money can buy—shelter, food, and medicine top the list. What in particular stresses you out, however, may depend on various factors including your current financial portfolio, your and your family's needs, your personality, and your financial savvy.

FACT

If you worry about money, you are in good company. According to a 2007 survey by the American Psychological Association, 73 percent of Americans named money as their number one source of stress. This is not surprising, considering that the cost of living is going up while many sources of income, such as salaries, Social Security, and even welfare checks, remain unchanged or increase at a much slower rate.

To determine your major financial stressors, rate the following questions on a scale of 1 to 5, where 1 is no stress and 5 is maximum stress.

1. The credit card bill comes in the mail. _____
2. Your car breaks down on the way to work. _____
3. You sit down to pay bills at the end of the month. _____
4. Your child tells you he or she wants to go to college. _____
5. Your spouse needs major surgery. _____
6. Your retirement fund earnings are down this quarter. _____

QUESTION 1: "The credit card bill comes in the mail" gauges how much debt is a source of stress in your life. If you answered a 1 or 2 to this question, either you have enough money to cover your credit card balance every month, or you completely ignore the fact that you are in debt. Option 1 is healthy and to be applauded; the average American owes at least $8,000 in credit card debt according to a 2001 survey by the Federal Reserve. Option 2 means you are in denial and may be interested in managing debt stress when you wake up and realize you are sinking into a financial hole.

If you answered a 3, 4, or 5, debt is running your life ragged. The credit card comes, and you instantly react. "How am I going to pay that," or even worse, "Do I have enough left on this one to buy food this week?" Your day is ruined. Thinking and planning a budget may be outside your skill set, or simply impossible due to a lack of income or bills beyond your current means. Tackling debt stress is a good place for you to begin in order to manage your financial stress.

QUESTION 2: "Your car breaks down on the way to work" explores how well you plan ahead financially. Cars break down. They are machines. Does your budget already cover potential expenses from your car breaking down? If you selected 1 or 2 for this question, you have an emergency fund available to meet sudden expenses. You have six months' expenses, perhaps more, stashed away for just such a rainy day as the one in the scenario. Though being late for work, dealing with the tow truck, and calling a cab are stressful, they are nothing compared to the nightmare "How am I going to pay for this?"

If you chose 3, 4, or 5 for Question 2, an emergency fund may be wishful thinking. Sure, it sounds like a good idea, but you're living paycheck to paycheck and nothing bad is going to happen to you. Well, it just did, and unless you have money in your account already to pay for it, your stress may be high.

If a credit card is your emergency fund, the stress may be even higher as you continue to rack up debt from charges that an emergency fund could have covered, had you had the foresight or discipline to save up. If the car is stressful, imagine the stress if you lost your job or had a serious accident and became unable to work. The purpose of an emergency fund is to protect you and your loved ones so that a costly emergency doesn't break you. Saving and planning for the unexpected may be a stress-management tool you can develop to best relieve your financial stress.

QUESTION 3: "You sit down to pay the bills at the end of the month" examines how much financial stress you experience living within your means. If you answered 1 or 2 for this question, you can pay the bills at the end of the month. Sure it's irritating to see how much you paid for fuel and food, but hey, you are above water. You have a budget in place where you and your loved ones can meet all your needs, including recreation and leisure, and still come out in the clear. You cut corners and have things you want that you just can't afford, but overall you are satisfied with having your needs met.

If you answered 3, 4, or 5, you may struggle to pay your bills every month. Just thinking about how you are going to stretch that paycheck to the last penny may keep you up at night, and rightfully so. Without money, where will you live and what will you eat? Is a credit card filling in the gaps every month so your family can have what you think it needs to be happy, or are family members' basic needs, such as healthcare, going unmet due to lack of funds? If your income is less than the cost of your needs, exploring how to live within your means, increased income due to a job or hobby, or financial counseling may be tools to best bust your financial stress.

ESSENTIAL

Ever have a piggy bank as a kid? Ah, the satisfaction from those clinking coins within! Every penny saved brought you closer to the toy truck, bike, or shiny pair of roller skates. Grownups need a fun fund, too. Find your childhood piggy bank, or create your own using a large tin or jar. Throw all your loose change into the bank, and when it's full, do something fun—visit an amusement park, or something practical— transfer the money to savings.

QUESTION 4: "Your child tells you he or she wants to go to college" explores your financial planning skills. If you answered 1 or 2, you either have your child's college in your financial portfolio or you're not saving for your kid's college. Either way, a college-bound child is not a major source of stress for you.

If you answered 3, 4, or 5, your child's mention of college made you sweat. Yeah, it's important, but how are you going to pay for it? Do you have long-term, as well as short-term financial goals in mind? Creating a financial portfolio and making financial goals for your family may be a key tool for you to reduce your financial stress.

QUESTION 5: "Your spouse needs major surgery" examines how well you are covered in the face of medical costs. If you answered 1 or 2, then you have health insurance plus the money saved to pay what the insurance company won't. Sure, your beloved's condition is troubling, but you know you can fight with insurance and have money to cover the expenses, plus you make enough to cover the time you'll spend without her income while she recovers.

If you answered 3, 4, or 5, your spouse out of commission is a major source of stress for you and your family. You may rely on her income to pay the bills, and now it's gone. Even worse, you may be one of the many uninsured or underinsured wondering how on earth you will ever pay the hospital bills. Exploring ways to meet your family's medical needs—with health insurance or an emergency fund—may be key to managing your financial stress.

QUESTION 6: "Your retirement fund earnings are down this quarter" looks at how much your investment and retirement planning stresses you out. If you answered 1 or 2, you've either diversified your investments, so that a dip in one fund is irritating but not life ending, or you are not actively saving for retirement. Wait a decade or two, and you may be blowing the dust off this book, desperate to relieve your growing fear of having to work until you drop dead.

ALERT

If you don't have an emergency fund already, it's time! Automatically deposit a certain amount each month before you're even tempted to spend it elsewhere. Deposit unexpected and extra income, such as a tax refund, Christmas bonus, or inherited money there before you have a chance to spend it, too, and before long, you're ready for the financial worst.

If you answered 3, 4, or 5, you take your retirement more seriously. Perhaps you've been saving for years and watch your funds like a hawk, determined to live your final days in comfort. If this is the case, stop being so hard on yourself. If you will have what you need to live the retirement you dream of, even with market fluctuations, stop and give yourself a break. Increase your savings, diversify, and let go of your obsessive desire to control.

If your retirement stresses you out because you put it off or have saved too little, then you have something to worry about. Increase your savings, take a part-time job, or cut expenses; do something to get your retirement fund where you want it. Does the teenager really need a new car? Can the husband live without a big screen TV upgrade? Focusing on prioritizing your finances may be the best way to relieve your financial stress.

As you reflect on the results of this quiz, take note of any questions with an answer of 4 or 5. These are the areas that you could reap the most benefit if you reduce stress there immediately. Read on to explore various types of financial stress and ways to manage these stressors in your financial life.

Debt Stress

Whatever you owe that you cannot repay with your next paycheck qualifies as debt. Debt is a woe to many financial lives. Common sources of debt include:

- Car payment
- House loan (mortgage)
- Student loans
- Medical bills
- Health insurance
- Credit cards
- Personal loans

If you have any of the above debts and making the payments for your debt choices is difficult or impossible, debt stress is a part of your life. If you have debt but are not stressed about paying it off, wake up and smell the coffee.

Debt, the Anchor Around Your Financial Neck

The more debt you owe, the more crippled you are financially. Your credit score drops, and with it your ability to acquire more credit to buy a car or home. In addition, the interest on that debt compounds, meaning that a television you bought on credit today could cost you hundreds of dollars more by the time you get around to paying the credit card off.

Credit card use is rampant and destructive to many people's financial futures, as evidenced by the U.S. government's regulation of the industry. Since 2010, credit companies must inform lenders of fees before they change, pay the highest interest balance first, and avoid hidden fees. Still, these regulations mean little if people continue to rack up high-interest debt they cannot pay, leaving their children with nothing but debt.

ALERT

Paying the minimum balance on a credit card could cost you dearly. For example, paying the minimum payment of $200 on a $7,000 credit card debt at 11.9 percent interest will take you forty-four months and cost you $1,641 in interest. Double your monthly payment and reduce your stress. Not only is your debt gone in half the time (twenty months) but you will pay less than half as much in interest ($721).

If you spend more than you make, you are not alone. Many people sign off on the best house, the best car, and the best of everything on credit. In his books and popular speaking series, financial guru Dave Ramsey openly shares his family's story of living the good life on debt.

After going bankrupt, Ramsey started over living a life within his means—driving the car he could afford, living in the house he could afford, and learning to say no to himself and his family for purchases he could not afford. He inspires others to run away from debt, like a gazelle running away from a cheetah, so that they can live happy lives without debt stalking them.

Say No to Debt

Saying no to a nice house, new car, and fashionable clothes is never easy, particularly when you or a loved one want the good life. Who doesn't? The other option, saying yes to something that racks up interest, may just cost more than you can afford. Do you really want to be paying thousands of dollars in interest? What if you lose your job, and suddenly your assets are seized? Living in debt may offer you luxury now, but in an uncertain world anything is possible. Stop the debt cycle, and start living in the present instead of selling your future plus interest.

Since the economic downturn of 2009, many people have explored ways to cut costs as they plan for the worst or try to recover from lost savings and employment. Being thrifty is becoming trendy, so take the opportunity to join the crowd. Stop racking up debt you cannot pay, and begin to live within your means.

Live Within Your Means

Buying a smaller house, choosing a modest mode of transportation, shopping the sale racks, selecting quality used furniture, eating out less—there are many ways to cut costs now and stop the cycle of debt. Explore where you and your family rack up the most debt, and create a plan for minimizing it. Then explore ways you can save money now, so that more money can go toward paying off the debt you have and living the life you want now.

Unemployment Stress

What if you don't have the income to get out of debt, or worse, you are acquiring debt to pay for food and shelter due to unexpected unemployment? Unemployment is a financial stressor for many. If you have no income, how do you manage your finances? Even if you have planned for the unexpected and have an emergency fund, what do you do when the money is gone?

In today's uncertain job market, many struggle to find work. As more industries move overseas, and more employers chose to downsize and reduce full-time employment to part-time, a full-time job with benefits that guarantees a middle-class life in the Western world is on the line.

As younger people join the work force, they find themselves underqualified as older, more experienced workers desperate for work fill jobs beneath them. Educated people with no work experience inflate the market, and some experienced workers find themselves laid off so that someone who costs less can take their place.

Unemployed and Underemployed Stress

Many people seeking jobs hit walls of frustration, as they lack the connections, qualifications, or means to land a job they desperately need to meet their financial responsibilities. Depression, anxiety, a sense of hopelessness, and suicidal thoughts all plague the unemployed, and the longer unemployment lasts, the worse it gets.

Underemployment is another serious stressor for many. The underemployed work at less than their full capacity. Perhaps they work part-time when they need full-time jobs to pay their bills. Perhaps they have a job below their educational level and experience. Underemployment can be a struggle for many, as they work to feed their hunger for financial stability, yet do not earn enough to pay for the life they need or want.

Ask for Help to Bust Employment Stress

If you are unemployed or underemployed, you have every right to worry about your future. Make sure your basic needs are met: food, shelter, and health care. If your family and friends cannot help you, seek public assistance from community resources such as Social and Rehabilitation Services or faith-based assistance from your religious community, if applicable.

Nothing is harder than asking for help, particularly if you are a responsible person on hard times. Remind yourself that it isn't you, it's the economy. Be positive and vocal about needing a job. Shout from the mountaintops, "I need a job" with any form of networking available to you.

Singaporean Gilbert Goh founded the nonprofit organization, transitioning.org, as an online resource for the unemployed in 2009. The website offers support groups, resources for the job search, and free counseling services so that no one has to bear the stress of unemployment alone. According to Goh, 500 visitors a day find comfort from the website's resources.

Persistance Is Key to Finding Work

Englishman Mark Wheeldon is a classic example of how persistence pays off in the job hunt. Wheeldon braved the pouring rain with a sign pleading for a job in July 2010. Three hours later, a man hired Wheeldon, impressed by the unemployed man's dedication. Though Wheeldon's method may not work for you, keep trying and seek out all possible and legal money-making opportunities available to you.

If your employment fears are based on what you hear on the news or related to a friend or family member who has hit hard times, but you are not yourself unemployed or underemployed, stop and breathe deeply. Maybe your stress is a sign to increase your own nest egg so that, in the event you join the ranks of the unemployed, you are ready. Nothing busts worry about the future quite like squirreling money away for a rainy day.

Healthcare Stress

Healthcare, like food and shelter, is a basic human need. As the cost of living increases, so does the cost of healthcare. Though the United States passed the Affordable Care Act in March 2010 to reduce healthcare costs and insurance premiums, the country waits to see how it meets the needs of all Americans seeking adequate, affordable healthcare. According to the Centers for Disease Control, 15.4 percent of Americans have no health insurance, and over 60 million had gaps in their insurance due to unemployment and other reasons. Even in countries where healthcare is nationalized, such as the United Kingdom and Japan, the cost of healthcare is steadily increasing.

Health Insurance Stress

Even if you have health insurance or adequate healthcare coverage, health care is a financial stressor. Not only do you worry when a loved one is ill, but you worry about how much the insurance will actually pay as you're running from doctor to test to hospital room.

Everyone with health insurance knows that it is not worry-free. How many times do you have to haggle with your insurance about why they are not paying for this last round of tests? What do you do when your family doctor is no longer in your network, meaning that you are charged extra to see her? It can be extremely irritating to pay for health insurance and pay for your medical care until you have reached your deductible.

To further complicate matters, many health insurance plans are paying for less than ever before. Hospital stays, which used to be covered, are extra on many low-cost plans, and having a baby and seeking counseling are luxuries on most plans, rather than necessities. Whenever you or a loved one is ill, the medical bills for tests, doctor's visits, medicines, and hospitalization can add up quickly, and those medical bills can cause major stress. Maybe the medical bills have piled up from a long-term medical condition such as cancer or the long-term illness of a loved one. Or even more frustating, sometimes insurance won't pay for a necessary medicine, or you have to foot the bill until you can claim the item.

Given all the problems with healthcare today, it's no wonder health care can cause stress. Between insurance, bills, and actually being sick, heathcare is a stress trigger for many, and rightfully so.

Speak Up

The good news is that you don't have to just sit there and become a victim to your heath insurance plan, your medical bills, or your illness. Many patients and healthcare advocates are fighting back, encouraging everyone to be more assertive with their health care.

Healthcare For All, a nonprofit organization, encourages assertiveness to fight healthcare stress. On their website (*www.assertivepatient.org*), "The Assertive Patient: A Guide to Speaking Up When You Are Dissatisfied With An Experience," the group teaches people to ask questions, challenge medical staff who do not listen to their needs, and file formal complaints against any injurious hospital or medial practitioner.

Does it sound strange to question your doctor about tests, costs, or medicine? Many people, particularly in the West, act as though doctors are gods, to be obeyed implicitly. This attitude can cost you more than just money, it can lead to more tests, more prescriptions, and even a mistake in your care.

You Are Your Own Best Healthcare Advocate

A doctor or any other member of the medical team provides you with a service, quality health care. You'd question a mechanic about fixing your car. Why is challenging a doctor so different? Ask the doctor why this pill is necessary, and if it comes in generic. Interrogate the receptionist whether they take your insurance before you make an appointment. Though you may be sick and worried about an ill loved one, this is your money. Fight for it.

Practice assertiveness in all aspects of your and your family's healthcare, and you are guaranteed to save money. You may spend more time arguing and clarifying than you would if you just passively paid the bill. But then again, nothing beats stress quite like winning a good fight and receiving a discount or arguing yourself out of an expensive test you really can't afford.

QUESTION

Why does healthcare cost so much?
Factors such as rising costs, unregulated industrial standards, and everyone's desire to stay alive contribute to high health costs in the United States. Experts agree that until the industry changes, and consumers are educated about their medical choices, healthcare costs are likely to remain high.

Stress of the Uninsured

For those of you without health insurance at all, the thought of becoming ill is an added burden. All the basics—cancer screenings, dental visits, and yearly checkups—may have passed you by because you don't have the money. Many people with financial troubles will prioritize other family members' care, particularly children or the elderly, above their own. If you do not take care of your medical needs, however, you may be the next source of financial healthcare distress for your family.

You may think you cannot afford health care, but can you afford to die? In order to prevent possible life-threatening conditions, the average adult needs basic medical care yearly including:

- Blood pressure checked
- Cholesterol checked
- Dental exam
- Vision exam (every two years if your eyesight is good)
- Current immunizations
- Testicular exam (men)
- Pelvic exam (women, with Pap smear every two years)
- Colonoscopy (if history of colon cancer)

- Prostate exam (if history of prostate cancer)
- Breast exam (if history of breast cancer)

If you think avoiding the doctor is thrifty, you are gambling with the most important asset you have—your life. Sure you may not have the money, but if you die of a preventable illness, what good is money then? Plus your loved ones will stress and grieve your loss. So, the least you can do for everyone's stress level is to go to the doctor.

Many community organizations sponsor screenings and checkups for free or reduced rates to low-income individuals. Free clinics are also available in many communities to meet these basic healthcare needs. Even if you have health insurance, you still need to be checked for the above conditions. Do not be too proud to take care of the only body you have. Be assertive about meeting your basic health-care needs, and you are well on your way to minimizing health-related stress in the future.

Investment Stress

No one wants to work until they keel over onto their desk. Retirement motivates many people to save for the future, and investments are a key part of that nest egg. Wherever your money is—a 401(k), a 403(b), mutual funds, stocks—your heart will be also. When the market drops, so does your mood.

QUESTION

What is the best low-stress retirement fund?
The best retirement fund depends upon your personality. If you like to take risks, a diversified investment portfolio may be for you. If you'd rather play it safe, your company's retirement plan may be the best option. To bust your retirement stress, make sure that you put enough into the fund monthly so that you can afford the retirement of your dreams.

Stressing about investment returns is normal, considering what investments represent. Your hard work and your future rest in your investments, so it's only natural to be concerned. What if you lose your money? With the rapidly changing economy, many fret about how their investments will weather the storm.

Investing safely, diversifying, and educating yourself about your investments are all tools to bust investment stress. Do you know what you have invested in and how it is doing? Are your investments diversified—spread out across the market—so that gains in some funds may compensate for losses in others? Are you informed about the status of your investments and able to go to bat for them, moving them at will if needed?

If you, or your trusted financial broker, has these skills, take heart. You are doing the best you can in the current market, so stop worrying. Many people do not have investments, or aren't even worried about them because they lack basic financial resources such as full-time employment and health care. Congratulate yourself on your financial prowess, and go out and enjoy the life you've worked so hard to build up for yourself.

Is Financial Counseling for You?

For severe financial stress, a good vent with a therapist may be the best stress-busting tool for you. To mastermind your finances, however, a financial counselor will better suit your needs. Financial counseling is not just for individuals facing foreclosure or bankruptcy. Benefits of financial counseling include:

- Debt management
- Creating a budget
- Solutions to current financial problems
- Assistance financing a home or other major purchase
- Educational information about retirement and investments

A financial counselor can not only help in setting up a budget, getting out of debt, and managing your retirement, but she holds you accountable, so you actually make a financial plan and stick with it. Look for professional counselors affiliated with a nonprofit or other accredited organization motivated by your financial health and not their own.

If professional one-on-one time is not for you, there are other financial assistance options. Many financial institutions offer courses or free consultations to members. Take a financial planning class or ask a frugal but wealthy friend or family member for tips. Online courses and literature from a finance whiz, such as Suze Orman or Dave Ramsey, could be another possibility. Explore what is available and affordable, and get started. It's never too late to get your financial house in order.

ESSENTIAL

Instead of focusing on what you don't have financially, focus on what you do have. Be grateful for your family and friends. Focus on the relationships in your life, rather than your possessions. Cultivate an attitude of gratitude, and you may just find some of your financial worries disappear on their own.

Five Golden Rules of No-Stress Money Management

Just as food, sleep, and exercise are necessary to a healthy body, five basic financial goals are necessary for a healthy financial life. Not only do they keep financial stress at bay, but they can actually prevent future worries about your money. The foundations of a sound financial life are not easy to achieve right away. Yet, over time, these five golden rules of no-stress money management can help you mastermind your finances, and your financial stress:

1. **Live within your means.** In other words, don't spend more than you make each month. Don't use credit unless it is absolutely necessary. If you don't have the ready cash to go on a shopping spree, don't go on a shopping spree. Of course, to accomplish this rule, you need to know exactly how much you actually make.
2. **Conquer your debt.** Make chipping away at those high-interest debts your top priority. Debt may not be something you can hold in your hand, but neither are a lot of the things that cause you chronic stress. Just knowing you've got huge debts is enough to activate the stress response in some people. First, purge the debt. Then, start saving. Even as you start to pay off your high-interest debts, you'll feel as though a black cloud is lifting from over your head.

3. **Simplify your finances.** Set up a simple system for financial management. Go through a single bank for all your transactions. When possible, have your paycheck automatically deposited into your bank account, and have payments made automatically or make them online so that you don't have to run to the bank all the time. If you invest, go through a single firm. If the thought of investing stresses you out, don't do it.

4. **Know your money.** Know how much you earn. Know how much you spend. Know where all your money is. Know how much your investments are earning you. Know (and trust) your broker. Or, if you invest on your own, keep track of everything you do. Keep your checkbook balanced and your bank statements reconciled. You'll never have to get stressed out because you don't know whether a check will bounce, whether your investments are earning or losing, or how much you have saved.

5. **Plan for the future.** Save. Save. Save. The short-term sacrifice of buying something you don't really need and probably won't use very much, the decision not to do the expensive remodeling or get the really high-profile SUV, the decision to move to a smaller and more manageable house, to stop eating out so much, to spend more time at home, all in favor of saving, is well worth it in many ways. Your life will be simpler. It will be easier. You'll have a nest egg. All that adds up to a lot less stress.

Add these golden rules to whatever other financial tools you are already using that work for you, and you are well on your way to beating money stress in your life.

FACT

The U.S. Department of Labor and Statistics estimates that the average consumer spends 34 percent of the family income on housing, 17.6 percent on transportation, 12.2 percent on food, 10.8 percent on investments and retirement, and 5.7 percent on healthcare. Other top expenses include entertainment (5.4 percent), clothing (3.8 percent), and education (1.9 percent).

Tools to Transform Money Stress

Practice the five golden rules—live within your means, conquer your debt, simplify your finances, know your money, and plan for the future—as a foundation for healthy finances. Target your specific sources of financial stress—debt stress, retirement stress, unemployment stress—and voila!, you have a plan to bust financial stress in your life.

Whether credit card debt drives you crazy, or you're trying to send your kids to college, stress does not have to win. Bust financial stress by planning ahead, being positive, and making sure you and your family have the security you need to live comfortably, if not as royalty, then at least as people with enough to eat, somewhere to sleep, and access to the medical care you need to be alive and thrive.

CHAPTER 11

Stress in the Workplace

Work is work! The people, the boss, the repetition—just thinking about it can stress you out. It doesn't have to, though. Set boundaries at work, say no whenever possible, and choose relaxation at key times to keep work stress at bay. With time and practice, you can mastermind work stress and maybe, just maybe, leave work at work!

When Work Stress Rules

Nothing's worse than work following you home at the end of the day. Whether you crash in front of the TV, too tired to even think, or you can't enjoy your family, or worst of the worst, you end up finishing work at home, work never seems to end. What's the point of life, you may wonder, when all you do is work? Good question!

Work, like stress, can only control you if you let it. Remember why you work: to have a life. Even if you love your job, it's healthy to step away from it for a while. What about your family, friends, and even your pets—they miss you when you're not around. Not to mention your body and mind, they would rather be exercising or meditating than sitting at a desk, jabbering into a BlackBerry, or staring at a computer screen.

Self-Evaluation: What Stresses You Out at Work?

The first step to masterminding work stress is to learn what, exactly, stresses you out at work. When you have determined your workplace stressors, you can then find tools to bust the stress and get on with life. Use the following quiz as a guide to determine your work stressors. Rate each question on a scale of 1 (not at all stressful) to 5 (extremely stressful).

1. You are trying to concentrate at work, but you just can't tune out the sound of your coworkers chattering as they gossip about their weekends. _____
2. Your work environment is too hot, too cold, too loud, too damp, too uncomfortable, or too dangerous. _____
3. You dread lunch, breaks, and social time simply because you don't want to deal with your coworkers. _____
4. You try to leave for the day, but your phone just won't stop ringing. _____
5. Your boss calls you into her office. _____
6. You never have time to eat, drink, or go to the bathroom while at work. _____

QUESTION 1, those distracting coworkers, gauges the health of your work environment. If you answered 1 or 2, it's likely that your coworkers don't spend too much time talking while they are working, or that it doesn't bother you. A manager walks by, and everyone gets back to work. Everyone talks a little, everyone gets work done, and no one is working more or harder than anyone else.

FACT

According to the 2009 American Time Use Survey of the U.S. Bureau of Labor Statistics, 40 percent of men and women with a college degree or higher did work at home after hours, compared with 10 percent of men and women with a high school degree. If you find yourself doing work at home, it's especially important to find ways to rest and unwind to prevent burnout.

If you answered a 3, 4, or 5, it's likely that your coworkers aren't working when they are supposed to, and it's stressing you out. If you can't work because they are talking, you may just be the only one working. Are you pulling the weight for more people besides yourself? Are you an outsider simply because you work instead of gossip? While getting along with your coworkers makes working easier and more fun, being the one who does all the work is miserable, irritating, and unfair. Setting boundaries and expressing your concerns to management may be ways to manage stress in an unhealthy work environment.

QUESTION 2, your physical work environment, addresses your personal safety and comfort at work. If you answered 1 or 2, you are physically comfortable at work. You have achieved a comfortable balance of sitting and standing during your day, the work space is clean, safe, and well lit, and you do not worry about getting hurt at work.

If you answered 3, 4, or 5 to this question, your physical work environment may be a source of stress. Is work too hot or too cold? Is your work space poorly lit and uncomfortable? Are you experiencing physical pain or suffering at work? If the answer is yes, explore ways to address these particular concerns. Being assertive, making changes to your work environment if possible, and taking breaks may be ways to relieve stress from your physical work environment.

QUESTION 3, dreading social time at work, gauges how much your coworkers cause you stress. If you dread social time because your coworkers are two-faced, manipulative, and overall unpleasant, just the thought of the company BBQ gives you a headache. If you answered 1 or 2 to this question, congratulate yourself. Though you may have a coworker or two that you don't like, which is normal and healthy, overall you get along with your coworkers and find working with them pleasant.

If you answered 3, 4, or 5, your coworkers stress you out. Maybe they pick on you. Maybe they are jealous of you for having more education than they do. Maybe you don't take enough time to socialize, or maybe you just don't like them. Setting boundaries and taking breaks may be tools to help manage stress from your difficult coworkers.

QUESTION 4, the phone that never stops, explores your job's demands upon you. If you answered 1 or 2, you either can control the demands of your job, or constant interruptions, even when you are not on the job, simply don't bother you. Congratulations! Most people would love to have your job, or more specifically, the boundaries you've created to manage your job.

ESSENTIAL

Many people ignore their vacation time or wait for a big, exciting vacation. When you're stressed out and need a break desperately, take a vacation day. Explore a park or museum in your home town, stay at a bed and breakfast nearby, or take your grandson to the amusement park. Life's too short not to take a vacation when you need it, if you're fortunate enough to have a job that gives you vacation time, that is.

If you answered a 3, 4, or 5, you just can't leave work at work, and it's causing you stress. The phone won't stop ringing, so you stay late. That report didn't get done, and you took it home. Your boss expects you to be working all the time because she does. With no personal life, rest, and fun, you are setting yourself up for disaster. Actually taking a vacation in the Bahamas or just having a picture of the Bahamas on your desk are both excellent ways to fight the job that never ends. Setting boundaries and saying no may be other tools essential in busting this particular work stress.

QUESTION 5, your boss calling you into her office, explores how big of a stressor your boss is. If you answered 1 or 2, congratulate yourself. You have a healthy relationship with your boss, and you two understand each other. Though she may stress you out occasionally—that's what bosses do—for the most part you do your work well and don't have problems with the boss.

If you answered 3, 4, or 5, your boss is a serious stressor. Does she change her mind constantly? Does she change deadlines at the last minute or lash out at you for things you don't do? Not every boss is perfect, but some are better than others. If you have a bad boss, you will have stress. Setting boundaries, being assertive, and taking breaks to refresh after a difficult conversation can all be key to managing boss stress at work.

QUESTION 6, do you have time to eat, drink, or go to the bathroom at work, gauges how well you meet your basic human needs at work. Most people, if they are lucky, work forty hours a week and eight hours a day. Everyone needs to eat, drink, and go to the bathroom during that time. If you answered 1 or 2 to this question, you work in an environment where you have time to meet your basic human needs in relative comfort.

With an answer of 3, 4, or 5, however, you may be stressed simply because you can't meet those basic needs. Does your boss pressure you not to have breaks? Do you choose to work through your lunch hour to get work done? Whether you or your work environment causes the stress, it's time to change. You're a human being, after all, with the need for a sandwich and a drink of water, at the very least. Focus on taking your breaks, all of them, eating and drinking when needed, and remember that work may be work, but you still have to stay alive in the midst of it.

Go back over each question, and pay special attention to those where you answered a 3, 4, or 5. Begin with the topic that causes you the most stress, and record the others in your stress journal for future attention.

Setting Healthy Boundaries at Work

At work, it's easy to let your boundaries slide when you're cramped up in a small space with others, tired and over stimulated, or constantly bombarded with new demands from the customers and management you serve. It's extremely likely that any workplace stressor is caused by poor boundaries between yourself and those around you.

ALERT

A 2003 study conducted by the Stress Research Institute of Sweden found that people who repressed work anger had a greater chance of a heart attack than those who didn't. Keeping work stress inside can literally kill you! Go to the gym after work, scream (quietly) in the restroom down the hall, or learn to say no—whatever you need to do to let go of your anger.

Boundaries are fences between yourself and the people around you that keep you and your energy secure. When a boundary is violated, you experience irritation, anger, a sense of hopelessness, and an energy drain. When a boundary is reinforced, however, you feel empowered and good about yourself. Try this guide to set healthy boundaries at work:

- Take all breaks and lunch breaks, and actually enjoy them
- Prioritize your schedule
- Learn how to say no nicely
- Reposition your body periodically if you perform repetitive tasks
- Advocate for your own needs and for the needs of those you manage
- Schedule times to drink water and go to the bathroom into your day
- Train your coworkers to respect you by doing what you say you'll do and challenging them when they try to pawn their work off onto you

Increase Relaxation at Work

Relaxation and work may be two words that just don't go together in your mind. Well, get rid of that negative perception. Most people spend the majority of their adult lives at work, and life's too short not to enjoy yourself, at least every time you have a break.

Many people daydream about vacation when they desperately need a break from work. Well, why not plan mini-vacations in the midst of your work life? Here are a few examples:

- **Take your lunch break at a nearby park.** Fold out a blanket, lie down on the grass, and watch the clouds until your break is over.
- **Set your clock to enjoy each of your breaks every day.** No matter how busy you are, take your break. Walk around the building, have coffee with a friend, or enjoy a crossword puzzle. Be creative—what do you really enjoy that you can do in ten minutes? Ten minutes of reading a romance novel is better than no romance novel at all.
- **Personalize your work space.** Bring in houseplants, family pictures, and other personal symbols that remind you why you are working. Make your environment comfortable for you so that you're more likely to want to be there.
- **Practice meditation.** Easy meditations, such as a body stretch or a guided imagery on your last vacation, can get you through a boring hour, plus no one has to know as long as your eyes are open.
- **Learn when to tune out.** Some meetings are important, but for the most part the discussion is nonrelevant. Learn when to focus your attention at work, and when to zone out. Office gossip at the beginning of a meeting may be a great time to let your mind wander, plan your week, or imagine yourself somewhere wonderful, like a tropical beach.

Brainstorm other ways that you might relax more at work. Invite a friend at work to be your mini-vacation buddy, so that you actually stick to one relaxation technique at work daily. Over time, you may find that work isn't such a horrible place to be, after all.

Say No to Difficult People

Ever notice how demands on your time pile up when you're already busy or working toward a deadline? Saying no to new demands on your time at work is key to managing work stress. "How can I say no," you may wonder, "when I have to keep my job?" It's not that you say no, but how you say no. Try the three steps to saying no:

1. Awareness
2. Openness
3. Assertiveness

Awareness is the first step to saying no. You, and only you, can admit to yourself that you're pushing your stress tolerance and cannot handle any more triggers. Are you overwhelmed by your current project, exhausted from staying up all night with a sick child, or remembering how this person likes to pawn her job off onto you? Whatever your reasons, just the fact that you want to say no is a good enough reason to do so.

ESSENTIAL

Good customer service representatives are friendly but insistent as they interact with customers: friendly to keep the person listening, but insistent to communicate the company's policy or products. Be friendly but insistent as you fight to protect your most precious commodities, your own time and energy.

Openness is the next step to saying no. Some requests, such as a phone call from the boss or an important client showing up in person, mean that you have to say yes. Other requests—the boss needing someone to run an errand, a coworker drumming up support for the company BBQ, the secretary wanting to chat—can go on the backburner, or disappear altogether. Now that you've decided whether or not you can refuse the demand on your time, it's time to act.

Assertiveness, the third step in saying no, puts you firmly in control of your choice. If you say no pleasantly and explain why, you're more likely to get your way than if you become nasty or put the other person down. Be honest about your reasons and word your statement with an apology, the reason you said no, and a timeframe when the person can get back with you. "I'm sorry. I have to get this report done before I go home today. If you ask me tomorrow, I can give you an answer." Kill them with kindness, and when they come back next time, you'll be better able to deal with it.

How to Leave Work at Work

Leaving work at work is a challenge for many. With more demands on your time, it may be harder and harder to just say no. In addition, in a tough job market, you don't want to give your boss any reason to let you go. The drive to perform and excel is powerful, yet if you have no life outside of work, just the stress of work, then what is the point?

Some people love making money, and taking their jobs home is part of life. Great for them. For the majority of people, desperate to leave work at work, why do they take work home? Explore the following questions to increase awareness about this significant work stressor:

1. Does your boss know you take work home? Does he encourage it and expect it?
2. Are you competing with others in your office to keep your job or prove yourself?
3. What are you losing when you take work home; what are the effects on your family, spouse, and health?
4. Do you schedule time off—weekends when you have plans—and communicate to others you are not to be disturbed during those times to compensate for those times that you take work home with you?
5. Do you take work home to avoid other problems in your life—loneliness, depression, or family conflict?

Now that you have some awareness about why you take work home, explore some ways to manage it. Could you prioritize your time at work to finish the project there? Do you really want to pay for your present position with loss of family and relationship bonding? Could treatment for depression or grief make you want to live life again, rather than hiding behind work? Explore tools at your disposal to control work's effects on your life, and if nothing works, consider the possibility of seeking employment elsewhere, before the stresses of a job that never ends take their toll on your health.

Avoid Emotional Eating at Work

Work can be boring, as everyone who works can tell you. Whether you stand up for hours at a factory, type documents for hours on a computer, or make tacos all day at a fast-food joint, work's monotony can get to you, fast. Take comfort, though, that you're not alone.

A cup of coffee, chocolate from the vending machine, or other uppers such as a cigarette may be how you manage stress. If you find that you crave unhealthy foods after a stressful event, such as a conversation with an upset boss, you may practice emotional eating at work. Emotional eating is unconsciously choosing a target food to soothe unpleasant feelings of fear, sadness, or unworthiness.

ESSENTIAL

You could be a major cause of your boredom at work, according to *Harvard Business Review* blogger Susan Cramm. If you run on autopilot, ignore your energy needs, and just slide by at work, then you are making your life boring! To bust boredom at work, Cramm recommends exercise, a healthy diet, performing daily tasks in new ways, professional goals to achieve, a hobby in your private life, and getting enough sleep.

Though there is a difference between a person with a compulsive eating disorder who cannot stop eating once he starts, and someone who goes for a candy bar to break the mid-afternoon grind, both eating habits are unhealthy. Spend some time observing your eating habits at work. Do you eat the healthy foods you would eat at home? What food choices do you make at work that are unhealthy, and why do you choose those foods when you do? Practice substituting other stress-busting tools to manage your stress, such as a walk around the office or a glass of ice water, instead of the bag of potato chips. Your body, and waistline, will thank you.

Sanctuary in the Workplace

Finding rest and peace at work can be a challenge. Do you have a special place you can go for a time-out on those rough days? If not, what options are available—a nearby park, an indoor waterfall, the restroom? As little as twenty minutes of silence does wonders for your stress level.

A U.S. service woman stationed in Germany would visit churches for a place to relax and unwind while she was on duty. After she got transferred to Afghanistan, she could find no such sanctuary for a break from her very stressful job. Within a few months, she was honorably discharged with post-traumatic stress syndrome. Explaining her stress to family, she said that it was too dangerous for her to go out alone to the mosques, and losing her sanctuary literally broke her spirit.

Few people work jobs as stressful as this veteran, yet anyone can benefit from taking some time out in the midst of their job, wherever they might be. Where is your sanctuary from your job? If you don't have one, find one to connect with some good old-fashioned peace and quiet.

Breaks

A meal break is required by law, and other breaks depend upon your employer and line of work. In today's fast-paced world of cell phone and e-mail communication, work can even follow you to the gym, the grocery story, and the urologist's office. With a mobile office comes mobile work hours, and only you can stop the many ways work encroaches on your time.

ALERT

While many people work second jobs to increase their standard of living, working two jobs decreases family time and opportunities to enjoy life, in addition to adding more stress to life. Consider carefully whether you need the extra income badly enough to sacrifice your personal life and relaxation for it.

Taking breaks not only increases your productivity, but it also gives you much needed rest and relaxation. The Novia Scotia Public Services Commission launched a program entitled "Let's Do Lunch" in 2010. The program's slogan—relax, refocus, reenergize, refresh—encourages managers to model relaxation in the work place, including taking and enjoying a daily lunch break. Inspired by a University of Toronto study that found employees who took a lunch break outside of work experienced increased productivity and work satisfaction, the program hopes to make the lives of Novia Scotia's working class as pleasant as possible.

You don't have to live in Canada to take your lunch break or turn your work cell phone off for dinner with the family. Only you have the power to take your breaks. Whether you have a half hour or an hour, spend the time relaxing, enjoying your food, and remembering why you work: because you love being alive!

Tools to Transform Work Stress

As you've explored the causes of workplace stress in this chapter, you've encountered several tools to manage your work stress: say no to new demands, set boundaries on your precious time and energy, and take your breaks. Though many stressors of work won't change, you do have the power to change your perception of work and how much you let work take over your life.

As you continue to manage your work stress, remember that you have great power in busting stress. Only you can take a lunch break, enjoy a vacation day in the middle of February, share a daily joke with your coworkers, and take a meditation break mid-morning. It's never too late to say no to work's neverending demands and say yes to meeting your needs to be a happy employee and person.

CHAPTER 12

Stress in Relationships

Whether you're single or married, a parent, or a mentor to others, relationships are a part of life. No man is an island, and even famous poet John Donne, who first penned that quote in the seventeenth century, struggled to maintain his marriage. If your relationships bother you, you're not alone. Explore ways that relationships stress you out, as well as tools to manage that stress as the quest to mastermind your stress continues.

Stress and Love

Love has inspired some of the greatest works of art and literature. Why? Love's exciting, everyone wants to be in love, but no one wants the dark side: life after the honeymoon when the other person's flaws become oh-so-apparent.

Love is stressful not only because everyone wants it, but because society tells us what it should be like. We put pressure on ourselves and believe that our love life should be this or that—anything but a real relationship with a real person who has quirks and makes mistakes.

Valentine's Day is the epitome of love and all our expectations surrounding love: love is glamorous, sweet like chocolate, and beautiful like a rose. When your love life is neither sweet nor beautiful, then, is something wrong? It must be the other person's fault, right?

According to the Wright University's "Seven Year Itch Study" of 500 Midwestern couples over a ten-year period, a couple's satisfaction with the marriage declined significantly for four years after the wedding, and then stabilized only to be followed by seven more years of dissatisfaction. Most modern couples never stick around until the seven year itch, however, with divorce rates at an all-time high.

Why is divorce so prevalent? Marriage is hard work, and people don't put in the time. Granted, dealing with an abusive spouse is not something anyone should have to deal with. Many people bail, however, just because the marriage gets tough. Well, life is hard. Children, money, hard work, and the stresses of life all too often take their toll on people's love lives.

ALERT

Americans for Divorce Reform estimate that 40 to 50 percent of American marriages will end in divorce. Buck the trend and keep the flame burning with effective communication, shared commitment, and lots of physical intimacy.

If love causes you stress, examine your expectations of it. How do you think your significant other or potential significant other should act, and is this realistic for a human being? If you're in a relationship to try and change the other person, you might as well leave now. If you're in a relationship to grow with someone else, then you'll be doing your share of the changing, too. Adjust your expectations of love, and you may just find the pressure you put on your love life disappears. No one is perfect, so why expect your lover to be?

Stress and Intimacy

No one may be perfect, that doesn't mean that you can't make suggestions occasionally. A significant area for improvement in most relationships is in the bedroom. Sex, like eating, drinking, sleeping, and exercise, is a basic human need, yet many people ignore their sexual needs and let society or their partner dictate their sexual desires to them. Though sex is still a taboo topic for many people, research has shown that couples who communicate their sexual needs are more satisfied in their marriages than couples who do not.

Ask and You Just Might Receive

If you have sexual needs, and they aren't being met because your partner doesn't know about them, then that pressure builds over time. Just thinking about sex can be stressful, because you can't or don't talk with your partner about it. Even worse, your partner may begin to feel rejected because she knows something is wrong, yet you don't talk about it. Holding in your needs is stressful for you and everyone around you.

Timing, Timing

Another source of stress in relationships is when one partner has a greater need for sex than the other. The stereotype is that the man desires sex and the woman is not in the mood. Even in same-sex couples, there can still be one person with a greater need for sex, or one person who just isn't in the mood. Timing can be a great source of intimacy stress.

Each relationship is unique, and no stress-management book can solve your problems in the bedroom. Rather, start with your greatest source for sexual satisfaction—your partner. Begin a conversation about what's going wrong in your sex life, and what you'd like changed, and encourage her to share, too.

Brainstorm tools to decrease sex stress—scheduling two nights a week, using direct commands during lovemaking, getting a toy for the partner with an insatiable appetite—to solve the challenges you face, and put them into practice. Experiment with different tools until you've minimized the sources of stress. The health of your sexual life is a direct reflection of the health of your relationship, so keeping life hot is key to relationship bliss.

ESSENTIAL

In an interview with WebMD, sexologist Dr. Ava Cadell recommends creating a wish list of three experiences that would spice up your sex life and sharing them with your partner once a month. As you and your partner exchange lists, you not only learn what the other person desires, but you get your own needs met, too. It is a win/win situation with no room for stress and plenty of room for fun.

Self-Evaluation: What Relationships Stress You Out?

If you are in a romantic relationship or married, your significant other surely knows where your buttons are. For those singles out there, and for healthy people with relationships outside their romantic attachments, any relationship can be stressful, as you well know. Take the following quiz to pinpoint the type of relationship that stresses you out the most. Mark the following questions on a scale of 1 (not at all stressful) to 5 (extremely stressful).

1. Your significant other does not answer your phone call when you randomly call during the day to ask about dinner plans. _____
2. A holiday dinner is at your house next month. _____
3. A certain friend calls for a chat, and you know it will take a while. _____
4. You just can't say no to people, even if they've hurt you before. _____
5. You wish you had more friends and experience loneliness on a regular basis. _____

Question 1, your partner hasn't returned a phone call, gauges the health of your primary relationship. If you answered 1 or 2, you know your beloved is a busy person with a separate life. You give your partner space and trust he will get back to you when he has a chance.

If you answered 3, 4, or 5, your romantic relationship stresses you out. Either you don't trust your partner because you can't let him exist separately from you, or your partner has done something to lose your trust, such as having an affair or other form of irresponsibility. Explore ways to build up trust in your romantic relationship such as counseling, open communication, or shared experiences, so that you stop trying to micromanage your partner.

Question 2, a holiday dinner is at your house, explores how stressful your family is to you. If you answered 1 or 2, you may be excited about seeing your family though somewhat concerned about cleaning up the house and preparing the food. Indeed, a little stress is normal in the face of hosting a meal for people you love.

If you answered 3, 4, or 5, your family stresses you out. Is it all of them together or one particular relation—an evil sister, an abusive uncle, your poorly behaved niece—who makes you want to run screaming from your own home? Hosting a holiday meal is enough work without worrying about how you're going to stay sane in the company of this person. Brainstorm ways to minimize the damage from your family: practice saying no or challenging inappropriate behavior in your head, give yourself permission to take a break at some point during the meal, or schedule a massage the day after the event. If just thinking about a family member maxes out your stress at a 5, consider therapy to help you understand why this person has the power to make you reactive and lose your mind to stress.

Question 3, a friend calls for a very long chat, explores the health of your social ties. If you answered 1 or 2, your friends who call needing support don't stress you too much. Healthy relationships involve give and take, and next time you may be the one calling for a long chat.

If you answered 3, 4, or 5, you may experience unhealthy social ties. Does that friend always ask for support but never offers any? Do you dread his calls but feel guilty about not wanting to "help" him? Do you find yourself the strong one, always listening to everyone else's problems while no one cares about yours? If any of these are the case, it's no wonder you're stressed. Experiment with setting healthy boundaries with this draining friend, seek out and spend more time with friends who will support you, and consider exploring with a trusted therapist why you need so desperately to be needed.

FACT

University of Chicago psychologist John Cacioppo reports, after extensive research, that friends are essential to good health. Lonely people have a greater risk for depression, alcoholism, high stress, sleeplessness, and heart trouble. Most astonishing, lonely people are less likely to recover from a major illness, and many doctors admitted that their lonely patients get lower quality medical care than patients with a fan club by the bed.

QUESTION 4, you just can't say no to people who've hurt you, examines your assertiveness and self-esteem. If you answered 1 or 2, setting limits with those around you, particularly those who've used you or don't value you, is normal for you. Why hang out socially with the coworker who steals your ideas? Why invite your son's friend's mom in for coffee when she spreads lies about your cleanliness throughout the church? Sure you may experience a little stress when you say no and do the opposite of what the other person wants, but aren't you worth it? Life's too short to deal with hateful, draining people who just want to use you and those you love.

If you answered 3, 4, or 5, you have trouble saying no when people who don't care about you try to use you. Sure, it's stressful saying no, but it's even more stressful being around people who put you down and don't appreciate you. You know how busy your life is with work, family, and your other obligations. Don't you deserve to spend time with people who actually care about you and support you? Learn some assertiveness skills, familiarize yourself with the energy vampires in your life (there are more than several, probably), and practice saying no ahead of time to bust the stress of giving in to unpleasant people in your life.

QUESTION 5, you experience loneliness and would like more friends, explores the health of your social network. If you answered 1 or 2, you have a healthy social network in place: you do different things with different friends, have work friends, gym friends, couple friends, and friends through the kids. Your social schedule is full, and you are satisfied with it.

If you answered 3, 4, or 5, you experience stress from a lack of social support. Maybe you've moved recently and haven't had time to make new friends. Maybe you've gone through a divorce or other life change, and lost some buds as a casualty of the change. Maybe you've put work first, and you can reconnect as easily as a phone call or e-mail. Whatever the reason for your loneliness, it is stressful. The best way to make new friends is to enjoy your life. Select a social activity that you enjoy and put your heart into it. Passion is contagious, and soon you may find others drawn to you.

Reflect on which question causes you the most relationship stress today and write that topic in your stress journal. Brainstorm tools to manage that stressor, and put them into place. In time, after you manage the first stressor, you may return to this quiz and work on another relationship stressor. That's great! Flexibility is key to masterminding your stress, in your relationships and anywhere else in your life.

Honesty, the Relationship Stress Buster

Life is short, as everyone knows, and between work, family, and friends, there's barely enough time in the day to do what you want to do. That's why honesty is one of the best tools for busting relationship stress. If you are honest with yourself, you can figure out what's really important to you. Then, if you love yourself, you can prioritize those things and people that matter and cut back on those things and people that don't. Voila! You're spending time doing what you want, and you're no longer stressing because you're not constantly doing what other people want.

Sound cold and uncaring? What about doing unto others as you would have them do unto you? Well, if you have unlimited time in the day, then great. Be everything to everybody, but very soon even you may run out of energy. Prioritizing your relationships simply means you're aware of where you want to invest your precious time and energy, and you're committed to doing so. As you honestly reflect on your social ties, consider the following relationships that are necessary to keep you healthy and balanced:

1. **Significant other** (if you're single, you may be just fine without this person, and good for you!).

2. **Close family** (children, parents, pets)—those you care for financially and emotionally.

3. **Soul friends**—those who know you like family, thoroughly understand you, and stand by you no matter what. Whether these people are biologically related to you or not, they are your real family.

4. **Social friends**—people you hang out with to have a good time, shopping friends, golfing buddies. They know general information about your life and family, but you're not that close.

5. **Family**—people biologically related to you who you see at holidays and other family events. Some may be soul friends, but others may not be due to their uncanny ability to drive you crazy.

6. **Social acquaintances**—people you know from your social life at the synagogue, zumba class, or senior center who remind you that you belong, even though they don't know you beyond a superficial level.

FACT

Dependent personality disorder is a mental-health condition that affects .05 percent of the adult population. The dependent individual cannot make his own decisions, seeks constant attention and care, and constantly changes his personality to fit in wherever he is. More common in women than men, people with this condition will do anything to stay in a relationship and exhaust those around them with their neediness.

Make a list of the people you invest the most energy and time into, and put them in the appropriate categories. Note that the closer to the top of the list, the more energy and time that relationship needs to be healthy. Relationship pressure comes when you're not spending enough time with a person to maintain that relationship. If you spend more time with your social acquaintances than with your partner, your relationship may be headed for trouble.

Boundaries Are Key to Healthy Relationships

Boundaries are fences that protect your precious time and energy. Each category of relationship in your life serves a different function. Like layers of an onion, each keeps you healthy and protected from loneliness. Your partner meets your intimacy needs. Your children or elderly parents meet your nurture needs. Your soul friends meet your need to be understood. Your social friends encourage you to have fun. Your family reminds you where you've come from, and your social acquaintances connect you with the community around you.

Each relationship category in your life requires attention, but the closer the person is to you, the more attention that relationship needs. When a relationship isn't getting the attention it needs to survive, stress occurs. If you spend all your energy with people you are less close to—social acquaintances, fun friends—but ignore your teenage daughter living with you, your relationship with her may be stressful simply because she needs more time with you (though she'll never admit it). Another example: if you don't nurture your soul friends, you may end up paying a therapist to listen to you because no one else cares. Therapists are great and caring, sure, but nothing can beat a true friend.

Another form of relationship stress occurs when you put people in the wrong category. Still trying to get your mother to love you and be your soul friend, even though all she does is put you down and talk about herself? All that energy you've wasted over the years, just because you wanted your mom to actually be a mom. Maybe it's time to put Mom in the family category, humor her, and spend more time with Aunt Linda who really does listen to you and make your day.

ESSENTIAL

Struggle with family members who take more than they can give? Pull a role reversal, and treat them the way they treat you. Forget their kids' birthdays, make dinner conversation all about you, or show up to their house unannounced. Either you'll shock them into awareness or they'll avoid you.

Being honest in your relationships and withdrawing energy from some people to reinvest it in others may sound cruel, but it saves you stress in the long run. You invest your limited energy where it matters most. Sure some people may call you names for not being as close as you used to be, but they may just be jealous that you have time to enjoy the people who really matter now that you know who they are.

How to Avoid Energy Vampires

You may find, as you begin to manage your relationship investments, that some people resist you when you try to withdraw time and energy from them. They may need you as an audience and source of attention. These people, who take more than they can give, are a major source of relationship stress. Relationship expert Dr. Judith Orloff calls these people "energy vampires" because they literally drain the blood of a healthy relationship— your precious time and energy—right out of you.

Keep Vampires at Bay

A sensible person who wants to minimize relationship stress keeps energy vampires at bay. Whether it's a sister who has to tell you everything but never listens to you or a coworker who's always looking for an audience, place these people in the lower categories of your relationship priorities. Why? They drain your energy and time, but give nothing back.

Here's an example. In a healthy relationship, the attention and care you and the other person exchange is 100 percent; you input 50 percent, and the other person inputs 50 percent. You hustle around to make dinner for your spouse—input 50 percent—and he helps with the dishes and then surprises you with a long backrub—input 50 percent. But when you do something nice for an energy vampire, such as listen or nod—input 50 percent—she doesn't return the favor. In fact, she keeps taking until you have given twice as much as you've planned—input 100 percent—while she has offered you nothing.

The 50 Percent/50 Percent Test

Begin to analyze each of your relationships to see how much you're putting into it, and how much you're getting out of it. Calculate the percentage in your head, and maybe even keep track of it. One day your best friend may call upset over her partner's new car purchase and you input 80 percent while she only gives 20 percent, but the next week your kid is sick and she takes him to the doctor for you—input 80 percent while you give 20 percent with the thank-you hug. That relationship is fair and healthy. An energy vampire consistently takes more than she gives.

You may find, during your research, that you are yourself an energy vampire in some relationships. While this awareness can be embarrassing, it is truly a gift. You can practice being a caring spouse, friend, or daughter yourself, and the balance in that relationship is restored.

Just Say No

Now that you've noticed people in your life who stress you out, it's time to stop the power they have over you. No one likes change, and the people who are your stressors are no different. Many people have no clue they are energy vampires, but until they change, you simply don't have time to be their host.

ALERT

Abuse is behavior designed to control another person. An abuser creates a power dynamic where he dominates another person physically, emotionally, sexually, or psychologically. When the victim says no, the abuser lashes out more to regain control. Anyone concerned they are in an abusive relationship should seek help from a therapist, social services, or law enforcement, depending upon the severity.

There's no better way to assert a boundary with a stressful person than to say no. Granted, there are many ways to actually say no besides the obvious and direct approach. Here are some creative ways to assert a boundary without saying the two-letter word:

- **Time freeze.** Your mother-in-law is calling, again, with a demand to see the kids tomorrow night. By not responding immediately, you're letting her know that her whims are not top priority and that you will get back to her on your terms. This leaves the ball in your court, so you have an upper hand in the situation.
- **Mirror effect.** Your coworker drives you crazy pulling your wardrobe apart. Give her a taste of her own medicine. "Wow, I saw shoes like

that in a bad 80s video," lets her know what it's like being on the other side of her. Chances are, she'll stop the behavior.

- **Change plans.** Break the pattern in a relationship you're trying to change, and take the offensive. Your best friend's spilling details about your sex life at the gym. You can't imagine life without her, yet she can no longer be trusted as a soul friend. "Let's go shopping this weekend," is a great offensive, if you've decided to make her a fun friend instead of a soul mate. If the person nibbles, then the transition is complete. When she tries to get you to bare your soul, laugh and comment on the handbags. Repeat until she gets the picture.
- **The schoolteacher stare.** When your son cusses at the dinner table, there's nothing like a schoolmarm stare of old to melt the cold of his teenage rebellion. Make eye contact. Wipe all expression from your face. Count to fifty or until he breaks eye contact. When he asks, "What did I do?" explain clearly, now that he's listening.
- **The deep freeze.** If a friend suddenly becomes unpleasant, and you don't need that negativity in your life, turn on the deep freeze. Limit contact, don't return calls, and completely remove any warmth from your end. He will get the picture. Best to use as a last resort, as this approach can lead to bad feelings.

If none of the above work, nothing sets boundaries quite like a good old fashioned no. "No, honey, I'm making dinner now." "No, Dad, I'm not going to come over now." "No, Lisa, I can't go out for coffee now." If saying no is still scary, practice in front of a mirror or with a trusted friend. Learning to say no is key to busting stress of any kind, including relationship stress.

Seize the Day: Relieve Relationship Stress

Cackle with a friend over a Jim Carrey movie. Snuggle with the spouse. Relationships can make all of life's other problems go away in an instant of connection. Yet with the demands of so many relationships, investing energy in the right places is important.

Know what your relationship stressors are, be honest in all your relationships, learn to say no, and do not be afraid to let your relationships grow and change as you do. Some relationships last only for a short time, and others for a lifetime. A wise person manages relationship stress by putting his heart in the hands of those who are also holding out theirs and have proven worthy to hold his.

Remember that any relationship takes time and work. Invest in the people who make you happy and resilient to stress, say no to the people who create more stress without giving support in return, and you are well on your way to masterminding relationship stress, today and always.

Stress and the Family

Relationships are stressful, but relationships with the family can take stress to a whole new level. Why do the people closest to you drive you so crazy sometimes? What would it be like to not dread time with the family? Learn why your family stresses you out, how to break family patterns of stress, and practice awareness in your family relationships as the journey to mastermind your stress continues.

Is Your Family Stressed Out?

Have you noticed a pattern with your family: you can be having a great day, suddenly one of them contacts you, and you're stressed. It's like an infection, as soon as you answer the phone, you're sick with stress. Whether it's your teenage son, your bossy brother, or the mother-in-law you just can't stand, they have the power to stress you out.

Is your family really stressed out, or do they just have a knack for stressing you out? If your family always manages to trigger your stress, you are not alone. Funny how the very people you love the most can also drive you the craziest.

If your family instantly stresses you out, you react to them out of habit. Remember the two ways to respond to stress: responding to stress, where you make a conscious decision to act, and reacting to stress, where stress takes over and you instantly lose your mind to it? You have a mind. You're aware. Why, then, can your family have so much power to stress you out? The answer: you give it to them.

Family Systems Theory

Family systems theory, a psychological concept used in family counseling, suggests that each family functions as a unit, or system. Each individual member has roles within the system that he or she must perform for the unit to function normally, and the entire unit is designed to protect the family unit from stressors of any kind. "Don't rock the boat," is the default operation pattern to maintain a stable family unit.

Your Family, Your World

Family therapist Maggie Scarf describes how family systems work in her ground-breaking book, *Intimate Worlds*. Scarf argues that families can only maintain a certain level of stress to function normally. If one person becomes too stressed, he unconsciously passes that stress throughout the system.

This is why you can be going about your day-to-day business, then the phone rings, and suddenly, your blood pressure is through the roof. A family member connects with you to literally share the stress throughout the system, so that everyone can bear a little of the burden. Great for the family system, perhaps, but not great for your daily stress load.

Family Stress: An Example

Doesn't being a good son, husband, brother, or lover mean being supportive? Sure it does! However, there's a difference between being a loving and kind family member who chooses to be concerned and a family member who's sucked into other people's stress and reacts to it by getting even more stressed.

ESSENTIAL

Quality family time is important to develop and grow as a family. Whether it's the holidays, Sunday dinner, a family reunion, or a backyard BBQ, make time to make the memories. The food may go fast, but the memories will last forever.

Here's an example: Tina's sister Sara calls, devastated that her teenage daughter Shelly has been using drugs again. Tina listens to Sara, as she always does. Tina used to offer suggestions—take Shelly to counseling, have a family intervention, set consequences for Shelly—but Sara doesn't listen. All Sara wants to do is vent and whine. When the two hour phone call is over, Sara thanks Tina and says that she feels so much better. Tina has a headache and wishes her sister would call sometime that wasn't an emergency.

Notice how Tina answers Sara's call because she cares. Tina does what she always does, listen until she gets a headache. Sara does what she always does, vent. Shelly, the teenage daughter, does what she always does, use drugs. In this cycle of family stress, nothing ever changes. Tina answers the phone and she's sucked into her family's stress. She even has the headache to prove it!

Dare to Say "I"

Tina thought of the family system, the "we," when she let her sister vent and give her a headache. How could Tina be kind and concerned, but not take on all the family's stress? Set a boundary. Thinking "I" puts the focus back on you, so you notice what's happening to you and respond, rather than react, to the stressful scenario.

The Stress Cycle of "We"

The family unit functions because everyone thinks collectively and puts the "we" first. Tina thinks "we" when she answers Sara's stressful phone call and absorbs Sara and her daughter's stress. Maybe Tina is the older sister, who always takes care of Sara. Maybe the only relationship Tina has with Sara is that of supportive listener. Whatever the case may be, Tina and Sara are stuck in a cycle of "we," and the stress from that "we" gives Tina headaches.

Say "I" and Bust Stress

A therapist trained in family systems theory would encourage Tina to put herself first. In Tina's case, the therapist would ask Tina why Tina puts Sara's needs above Tina's own and encourage Tina to use "I" statements to set boundaries with Sara, so that Sara's phone calls no longer blast Tina's day full of unwanted stress. An "I" statement to Sara might be, "I'm tired of hearing about Shelly's drug problem when you won't do anything about it. If you want help taking her to get help, let me know. Otherwise, I don't want to hear about this topic. Thanks."

Using "I" statements separates your needs from the needs of your family, and also separates your stress from the stress of your family. If you keep "I" in mind, you can monitor your own stress level and say no before your stress level gets too high. Though family members may object to "I" versus "we" thinking, in the long run it will greatly reduce your own stress level when relating to your family.

How Can You Say "I"?

Take a moment to reflect on a recent family situation that proved very stressful to you. Write down what happened, and pinpoint the exact place where you reacted, rather than responded to stress. Practice using "I" statements with this family member the next time she begins to stress you out, and when the opportunity arises—which it undoubtedly will—be bold.

Communicate your needs, resist the family drama, and be kind yet firm. You can care without being stressed out of your mind.

Tools for Changing Toxic Relationship Patterns

Even the most loving families can dump their stress onto others unintentionally. In a toxic pattern of relating, the family members do not communicate their needs directly and take individual responsibility for themselves, they just pass stress and responsibility on to someone else in the system. If you automatically feel stress or drained dealing with a member of your family, it's likely that a toxic relationship pattern is at work.

Stress and the Drama Triangle

Family systems therapists use a drama triangle to describe how toxic roles work in the family system. One family member is the persecutor. She does something that causes stress within the system. A second family member is the victim, the person hurt by the persecutor. A third family member is the rescuer, or the person who makes the victim feel better.

In the case of Tina, Sara, and Shelly, Shelly, the teenaged daughter is the persecutor. She is using drugs and worrying her mother, Sara, who is the victim. Sara subsequently calls Tina so that Tina can rescue her from Shelly, which Tina does by listening to Sara vent for two hours.

Each family member takes turns serving each other, and sometimes they even switch roles in an attempt to manage the family stress. If Tina calls Shelly and chews her out for using drugs, Shelly may complain to Sara about Aunt Tina's call. Sara listens to Shelly until she's exhausted, and the roles are reversed. Tina becomes the persecutor who's picking on Shelly, Shelly the victim, and Sara the rescuer who made Shelly's problem go away. Everyone's stuck in a script, and no one is honest and real with each other.

If this scenario sounds all too familiar, don't get discouraged. Honest communication is the remedy for the drama triangle. Say "no" to the person trying to victimize you, persecute you, or rescue you. When the triangle is broken, each member becomes responsible for himself and his own problems. Instead of everyone's stress, you experience just your own. Isn't that better?

Be Aware and Break Free

Breaking up a drama triangle takes patience and practice. The first step is awareness. Do you know when someone's trying to victimize you, persecute you, or rescue you? Anytime a family member won't let you be yourself but tries to control you, that's a good indicator that the drama triangle is at work.

ESSENTIAL

Many people experience stress because they do not assert themselves. Other people dictating what you do, say, or believe is certainly stressful. Learning assertiveness can be stressful at first, mainly because others in your life are shocked that you've changed. With time and practice, though, assertiveness becomes easier and the stress of being a doormat decreases.

Whether your most stressful family members are your kids, your in-laws, or your own siblings, setting boundaries and refusing to think as "we" sets you on the path to avoiding family stress. You can love and care about your family without sharing in their stressors. Only you have the power to say "I," and until you train your family members to respect your "I" they will expect the same "we" they've always known.

Family Vacation: Dream or Nightmare?

The traditional family vacation—mom, dad, and kids—is often a source of stress. The American Psychological Association proves what every parent knows: more time with the kids is stressful. The association's 2006 study found that parents experienced a 53 percent increase in stress when school ended for the summer. Just imagine the statistic for parents stuck in an airport with their kids!

The Many Vacation Stressors

Even if your family doesn't include children, you still have the stress of dealing with your spouse and other family members. You may chuckle,

Chapter 13: Stress and the Family

but everyone knows that you can get sick of anyone if you spend too much time together. A poorly planned family vacation can be just such a nightmare.

FACT

A survey of vacation habits on Expedia found that only 34 pecent of Americans took all of their vacation days, a shocking percentage given that Americans generally receive only thirteen vacation days, less than Japan (fifteen), the United Kingdom (twenty-six), and France (thirty-eight).

Why do family vacations go sour? The stress around family vacation has many sources. Just a few include:

- Adults hit a vacation burned out or tired already.
- Family members sit in a car, train, or other source of transportation for longer than normal.
- Eating out and new cuisine upsets the body's usual dietary habits and digestion.
- Adults don't plan out the vacation ahead of time, and when a hotel is booked, a restaurant is bad, or the trip takes longer than normal, irritation spreads like wildfire.
- Many families spend the entire vacation together crammed in a hotel or other small space, when they don't usually spend so much time together at home.
- Some family members do what they think other families would like rather than planning activities that everyone will enjoy or that appeal to the wide array of interests within the family.
- Family members have different expectations and conflict arises when everyone's expectations are not met.

With so many potential stressors, it's no wonder a vacation is stressful. Given the purpose of a family vacation—creating memories and fun as a family—it's important to manage as many of the above stressors as possible, so that your family vacation can be everything you hope for, and more.

Family Cooperation

A major stressor during the family vacation, and indeed any family activity, is discord within the family. Why are the kids fighting and complaining? Just like all human beings, children complain when their needs aren't being met. Sure, the kids don't need ice cream every two hours. But skipping the largest zoological park in the country because it's not on the parents' schedule, may not be the best choice for family bonding.

Family Meetings Bust Vacation Stress

A family meeting before the vacation may be key to reducing vacation stress before it even starts. Family meetings are organized discussions where every family member contributes her opinion on a topic. Invite each member of the family to share any concerns about the upcoming vacation as well as one or two activities she would like to do on vacation.

After everyone has had a chance to talk, the facilitator (an adult) begins a discussion about how the family can compromise so that everyone is happy. The adult needs to explain the reasoning behind the decision aloud, so that no member feels as though her voice was ignored. Perhaps the compromise is that everyone gets to have her own "day" of the vacation where she chooses the activities and the meal.

Compromise for Vacation Harmony

Whatever the compromise, go over it and make sure each family member agrees to it before ending the meeting. Type up the compromise, and have each family sign it. If and when children, or even your spouse, complain about wanting to do something different, remind her of the terms of the agreement and that an activity she will enjoy is scheduled soon.

Life is too short not to enjoy time with the family, even if they do drive you crazy. Set healthy boundaries, be honest, and listen to your needs as well as theirs. Practice effective communication and compromise. Success in busting family stress rests well within your grasp. Managing family relationships takes time and awareness. The more you practice with the tools, the more you mastermind family stress with them. Keep up the good work, and remember, you have the power to bust your stress.

CHAPTER 14

Stress and Technology

Technology improves our lives, but is it also destructive? What if the texts and e-mails never end? It's so easy to plug in and end up missing the most precious gift you have: your own life. Explore ways to make technology a tool to enhance your life rather than take over your life as the journey to mastermind your stress continues.

The Blessings and Curses of Instant Communication

Thinking about your sweetie? He's a text message away. Yearning for a good murder mystery? Three clicks, and it's yours at the local library. Instant communication can certainly make life easy. Just like the drive-in at a fast-food restaurant, so many goods and services are literally there, at your fingertips, for your viewing and listening pleasure.

Isn't technology great? You don't spend days doing laundry, like your grandma did, or worry about your kids dying of preventable diseases. Technology has improved the quality of life for those who have it, but technology is also creating a new world, a world of infinite possibilities.

Take a Break

In this world of infinite possibilities, anything becomes possible. Unfortunately, human beings just can't keep up with constantly, rapidly changing technology. Technology is a major source of stress for the busy modern person. If the technology in your life is stressing you out, you are not alone.

FACT

The International Telecommunications Union of the United Nations reported in 2009 that more than half of the world's population pay to use a cell phone, and more than a quarter of the world's population have access to the Internet.

Drs. Michelle Weil and Larry Rosen, authors of *TechnoStress: Coping with Technology*, estimate that 85 percent of the population is uncomfortable with technology. Why the discomfort? Technology is invading our lives as text messages, video games, and social networking sites bombard us continuously with no end in sight. People are overloaded.

You take breaks from work, but when do you take a break from technology? Sure it's great to talk to your mom on vacation, but when your cleaning lady, your lawyer, and your boss can all reach you, and do, where's the vacation? Stress is pressure, internal and external, and when that cell phone buzzes or beeps, there's pressure.

Can You Turn Off the Phone?

The average person plugs into technology daily. He has no choice. The work-place isn't just four walls anymore. E-mail, cell phones, pagers, and chat are reshaping what modern people know as work. Yet how are the human body and mind to keep up?

The Computer: Stressor or Savior?

The computer has revolutionized work and life. You access your bank account, feed a virtual dragon, headbang with Bon Jovi, and chat with your boss—all from the comfort of your home. Want to tour the Taj Mahal or play checkers with a new friend in Uzbekistan? Anything you want is there, at your fingertips. All you have to do is log-in.

Computers versus the Body

Computers aren't just changing our personal lives. In many professions, you're expected to know and use a computer. If you stare at a computer all day at work, you know all too well the telltale signs of computer stress: headache, eyestrain, cramping hands, achy back, and fuzzy brain. Exces-sive computer usage is also linked to the following repetitive stress injuries, common among sports athletes and computer users:

- Tendonitis involves inflamed tendons—the flesh that holds bones to muscles.
- Carpal tunnel syndrome is a condition in which the tunnel-shaped space between the bone and ligaments of the wrist swells. This condi-tion irritates nerves going into your hands, causing numbness, pain, and tingling sensations.
- Epicondylitis, also known as tennis elbow, is a sore and uncoopera-tive elbow.
- Ganglion cyst is a liquid filled lump on the wrist from a leaking joint or tendon.
- Radiculopathy is a cramped disk in the neck, caused by tilting the head during phone use.
- Reflex sympathetic dystrophy causes dry, swollen, and painful hands with limited muscle control.

What do you do to prevent such conditions when you have to be on the computer all day at work? Breaks, breaks, breaks. Not breaks from what you're supposed to be doing on the computer, but breaks from the computer itself. Despite company policies banning web surfing and social networking sites, Facebook, e-mail, and online sites give many of the employed breaks. Though these breaks may be fun, they're not actual breaks from the computer.

Breaks Save You from Computer Stress

The Mayo Clinic recommends the 20/20/20 rule for computer eyestrain, but it will work to relieve all computer stress. Stop using the computer every twenty minutes and look at something twenty feet away for twenty seconds. Better yet, every twenty minutes file, clean, or return a phone call without looking at that computer screen, to give your body and mind a much needed break.

ESSENTIAL

Stuck at your desk? Give your head a quick massage. Close your eyes. Place your hands, palms up, in front of you. Sink your head into your hands, and gently massage your temples and forehead with your fingers. Then massage your eye sockets with your palms. End the massage by breathing deeply three times. All that relaxation really can come from the discomfort of your office desk.

A breathing meditation in the restroom could restart your mind and refresh your body. So could walking around the office and delivering a message in person rather than by e-mail. You can't burn nearly as many calories in your inbox as you can on foot. Be creative as you explore ways to bust computer stress, and refuse to let technology fatigue win.

Technology Boundaries at Work

Ever wonder if work's ever going to end? If you do, you're not alone. Traditionally, a full-time job consisted of eight hours a day, with a meal break, and forty hours a week with two days off. Today, thanks to technology, many employees find themselves bombarded with demands: answer the company cell phone, finish that report online after hours, sign into the company website. Do the technology demands of work never end?

With more demands at work, an employee either finds himself bombarded with demands from e-mail, phone, and fax at work or, even more challenging, he may work in a field where he has to have a "mobile" office.

Mobile Office Nightmare

The cell phone commercials glamorize the mobile office. A tan bikini babe lounges on a tropical beach while telecommuting via BlackBerry. The realities of the mobile office are much bleaker: employees are expected to be available at any time because technology permits it. If you're supposed to be available all the time, and you haven't learned to say no, you're a prime candidate for stress. Remember what happens when the personal boundaries that keep you healthy and well are violated—pressure!

Manage Technology First

Managing time with technology is a major stressor for workers, whether in a building or in a virtual office. The mobile professional, in particular, will have to set boundaries and learn to turn the technology off, mainly to preserve his own sanity. Consider the following questions as you explore how to manage your time with technology at home and at work:

1. How many hours do you have to spend using technology, such as a computer or cell phone, for work? How many would it be if you organized your time better?
2. How many hours do you currently spend using technology for pleasure—surfing the web, watching movies, or texting? How many hours do you really need to spend, and how many do you spend just wasting time?
3. If the time is five or more hours a day—the maximum recommended before your health is affected—how can you decrease your time online?
4. What health effects, if any, are you noticing in connection with your technology use?
5. What hobbies or people have you lost in your life thanks to surfing the web, playing on Facebook, or watching TV?

Even if you don't have to be online for work, it's likely that you're plugged in more than you need to be. How often do you answer the cell phone while driving, or making dinner, or trying to have coffee with a friend? "It's the kids." "It's the boss." "I have to take this one." Everyone has good reasons to answer the phone or play online.

FACT

Scientific research has been unable to confirm the urban myth that cell phone use causes brain cancer. You are more likely to hurt yourself driving while talking or texting than you are to get cancer from a cell phone.

Only You Can Bust Your Technology Stress

If you complain about technology invading your life, ask yourself—what's stopping you from pulling the plug? Every cell phone has an off button, as does every television and every computer monitor. The technological device can run forever as long as it's charged and electricity flows. Only you have the power to turn it off.

A wise history teacher at a small university in the midwestern United States insists that students place their cell phones and other handheld electronic devices on her desk while they are taking tests. "Your network is not invited to take this test with you," she instructs the students. Even though the university has a policy prohibiting electronic devices in the classroom, she cannot get her students to turn their phones off during class. Rather than keep beating a dead horse, she simply confiscates the phones.

How sad that a future generation of Americans cannot even make it through an hour college class without checking Facebook, returning a text, or surfing the net. Like a science fiction movie, they cannot function without their technological brain extensions. Only you can turn off your phone, wait on the e-mail, and ignore the temptation of losing an evening surfing the web. Try it, and though you may experience stress from changing your habit, in the long run you may just find that you have a life to live that technology can enhance, rather than dictate.

Television: Watch Life Pass You By

Television is everywhere: the living room, the bedroom, the doctor's office, the computer, and the airport. Everyone's watching. Nielsen's Report, a survey of TV, web, and cell phone use, found that Americans watched an average of 151 hours of television a month, or five hours a day, in 2009. Why? TV's so relaxing. No demands on your time and energy—just sit back and watch life happen on the screen.

The Easiest Stress Buster

Is watching your favorite show on DVR a stress buster? Sure it is. But so is walking around the park, playing with the dog, and enjoying a romantic dinner with your partner. If all you do to bust stress is watch TV, though, you are severely limiting your versatility in the face of stress. One power outage, and there goes your stress buster!

ALERT

The American Academy of Child and Adolescent Psychiatry warns that children who watch a lot of television have lower grades, read fewer books, exercise less, and weigh more than children whose parents monitor their children's viewing, turn the television off during meals and family time, and encourage kids to watch only a few favorite shows every week.

Use TV in Moderation

The average American watches five hours of television a day. That's enough time to exercise, start a hobby, work a part-time job, learn sky diving, and make several new friends in a month! Television is fun and helps you unwind, you may argue. Sure! Excessive TV—more than four hours a day—is also linked to a slew of negative consequences, including:

- **Unhealthy eating and even obesity.** Junk food and TV is a unhealthy duo.

- **Violence in children.** Children witness murders, violence, and negative language on TV and video games that they would never encounter in other places.
- **Sleeplessness.** Watching TV before bed wakes up your brain, so it's harder to calm down and fall asleep.
- **Cardiovascular disease.** Long periods of sedentary activity are bad for your heart because you don't use your muscles to burn fat, which then clogs your arteries.
- **Fewer friends and less contact with family members.** Maintaining relationships takes time, and if you're watching TV all the time, you're not keeping up with the people in your life.

So TV is dangerous for your health and inhibits your ability to have a life full of activities and meaningful relationships if it becomes your primary leisure-time activity. Sad but true—too much of anything is bad for your health. Watch TV in moderation, choose healthy movie snacks, or invite friends over for a favorite show so you're not just shut away in front of the tube, living a fantasy while missing your own life.

Watch TV in Moderation

You love TV. You'll miss it. This isn't the end, just a new beginning where you explore other ways to bust stress, too. The best stress-management toolbox contains a variety of stress-busting tools. Choose one favorite show, and then spend the two hours you'd normally be watching TV exercising or preparing a healthy lunch for work tomorrow. Flexibility with your stress-busting tools increases the chance that you'll be able to manage your stress before you reach your stress-intolerance point.

Realities of Long Distance

Technology connects the globe more closely than ever before. A new friend or love is a phone call or a click away. Everyone knows someone who's had an online romance, and some people even move around the world to be with their true love or take the perfect job. Though this is great for some people, the reality is that long distance relationships—or long distance anything—can create stress for you.

Stresses of Long Distance

Why is long distance stressful? First of all, you must have technology to sustain it. If your cell phone dies, there goes the conversation. Second of all, you must travel for true intimacy. Whether the client wants a personal briefing, or an online flame is serious, you'll be racking up the miles and jet lag.

Besides the commute and reliance on technology, other stressors from a long-distance relationship of any kind include:

- Dream versus reality. It's easy, with only chat and phone calls, to make the potential lover or job better than it actually is.
- Cost. It's cheap to have a movie date in your city, but really expensive to fly across the world to get some loving.
- Isolation from social support. Though a new friend or flame across the world is great, time you spend with her cuts down on time you spend with your real friends, the people who can laugh at your jokes, host a birthday bash, and visit you in the hospital if you're sick.

ESSENTIAL

Social networking sites such as Twitter and Facebook offer ample opportunities for online social interaction. To keep yourself balanced socially, make an online friend and offline friend, too. If an online friend lives nearby, plan a real experience together such as dinner out or a concert. You may just find that you have even more to talk about online.

Looking Everywhere for the Right Job

Another source of long-distance stress is the job hunt. Many people, particularly professionals with a particular skill set, must apply nationally or even internationally for a job that fits their training and education. While moving to a new city is exciting, it is also stressful. Living alone in a strange place increases your chances of anxiety and depression, and creating a social network for support takes time and effort.

Other people are working online or as freelancers to make an income, thanks to the wonders of technology. The benefits of working at home are many. While stressors are unique to each individual, common stressors here include generating enough income to make a decent living, communicating with clients via technology, setting one's own schedule, and using and keeping the technology to make the business run smoothly.

Living life long-distance takes time and effort. With discipline, the modern person can do anything she sets her mind to. Just be careful to keep lots of stress-management tools handy for those days when the stress of driving, lack of Wi-fi signal, or a miscommunication with another person online threatens your sanity.

E-mail versus Face to Face

If you're ever fixed your TV remote on chat or learned of a work meeting via text message, you know that written electronic correspondence is here to stay. Whether it's e-mail, chatting, or texting, the written word conveyed via technology has definite positives and negatives. Like other forms of technology, there's also the availability challenge—the technology's available, so why aren't you?

FACT

E-mail began in the 1960s, when computer scientists first figured out how to run two programs on the same computer at once. The first e-mail could only be exchanged between users using the same computer, however.

Pros and Cons of Electronic Communication

With the flurry of e-mail correspondence at both home and office, it's hard to keep it all straight. You may have to answer and keep track of e-mails as part of your job, a formidable task in and of itself. Chatting and texting, in general, are more informal modes of communication. Yet bosses and organizations are beginning to offer, and require, both as standards of communication.

E-mail, chat, and texting have definite advantages. Instant or near instant communication, a record of the conversation, and convenience, to name a few. Thanks to the latest hand-held devices, you can e-mail, text, and chat from anywhere you can hold your phone.

Disadvantages exist, too. Other people, particularly those at work, may expect you to be as available as the technology. In addition, miscommunication can happen when a word or meaning is misunderstood. Unless you can look into a person's eyes, it's hard to really understand him.

Flexibility Is Key to Surviving

If your boss insists that you use chat, and your college-aged grandkids only text you, what's to be done? Like any form of technology that offers flexibility and mobility, make it work for you. Say no, sit on messages that can wait, educate others around you about your technology boundaries, and ask your boss if you're really being paid to read messages after hours. As with any form of instant communication you, and only you, have the power to turn it off.

Does Work Ever End?

Life is busy—perhaps busier than ever before with the many benefits and intrusions of technology. "Does work ever end?" you may sigh at the end of a long day. Only you have the power to make it end. Get offline. Turn off your cell phone. Say no to technology invading your life, and yes to a break.

If your seven-year-old got irritated and tired from watching all the *Star Wars* movies, what would you do, give him caffeine and tell him to watch them all again? No. It sounds so simple when referring to a child. Why is it so difficult to say stop in your own life?

The kind parent would encourage the seven-year-old frazzled from technology stress to take a break, have a snack, maybe even share a story before bed. As you explore ways to manage technology stress, indeed, any kind of stress, pretend that you are that kind parent setting a boundary to keep a very important person energized and stress-resilient: you!

ESSENTIAL

Enjoy a historical or cultural event from the comfort of your own computer. Take an online tour of the Taj Mahal, wonder at the Sistine Chapel, and relax on the Florida Keys. Who says vacationing has to be expensive?

Seize the Day: Transform Technology Stress

Technology enhances modern life, but it can also fill life with unwanted stress as the phone beeps, the inbox fills, and others scream for our attention via our electronic brain extensions. Yet hope is not lost. Be aware of the many ways that technology affects your life. Use technology as a tool to enhance your work and play, and say no to it when it's stressing you out and bogging you down. Limit your television time, take breaks from the computer, guard your personal space, choose real people over online ones, and invest more in your real life than you do in your avatar.

Only you can chose to pull the plug when the demands of technology take you to the brink of burnout. Better yet, unplug yourself before you're even stressed. Give yourself permission, and follow through. Then, and only then, is technology in its proper place, as a tool at your disposal rather than a menace stressing you out.

PART IV

Stresses for All Ages: What Causes Stress in Different People

CHAPTER 15

Stress and Children

Children are full of boundless energy and excitement, most often when you really wish they'd take a nap. What could possibly be causing them stress? Plenty. Life's gotten busier and more complicated for everyone, including the kids. Today's child develops more quickly, uses more technology, views more violence, and has a greater chance of losing a parent to divorce than ever before. Learn to see the signs that your kid is crying out for stress relief, and model savvy stress busters for her as the journey to mastermind your stress continues.

What Stresses Kids Out?

A "kid" is developmentally anyone who can walk but hasn't entered puberty. So, kids encompasses everything from toddlers to the teenager, right? Recent studies show that girls are entering puberty earlier than in previous generations; age seven is the new twelve. Why are kids growing up so fast?

Babies definitely experience stress, but they are pretty self-explanatory. When they're stressed, they cry. The older kids get, the less likely they are to cry, and that makes your job as a parent more difficult. Unless you teach your children to express their needs, or better yet ask them all the time "what's going on," you just won't know.

Growing Fast Equals Stress

Rapid changes in your child's growth and development certainly stress you out, and you're not the only one. Childhood is a life stage chock-full of growing: learning to walk, playing with others, reading, going to school, dealing with siblings, developing physically and socially, and watching Mom and Dad and any other adults around to see how they act. Just thinking about it will make you want to take a nap!

Parents Essential to Bust Kid Stress

The Nemours Foundation's KidsHealth (*http://kidshealth.org*), an online resource for children's health, polled junior users about stress and found out the following:

- 36 percent of kids worry about grades and school
- 32 percent find their families a constant source of stress
- 21 percent fret about social relationships, particularly gossip and teasing

The KidsHealth study also explored how kids manage their stress. Two statistics are startling. Twenty-five percent of children surveyed practice unhealthy coping mechanisms, such as blaming themselves, hurting themselves, or eating to feel better. Seventy-five percent also wished their parents would be more supportive by asking what's wrong, listening to them, and spending time with them.

Kids themselves know they are stressed and can even tell what's causing it sometimes. The next step is to encourage healthy ways to handle these stressors. Be the parent, grandparent, or other caring adult that 75 percent of kids want and need, the one who is there and cares.

ESSENTIAL

With a daily dinner check-in, you can keep track of your child's stressors and how she's handling them. Eat dinner together as a family, and encourage each member to share how her day went and anything that bugged her that day. If a child shares a stressor—someone stealing her lunch, a poor math grade—then you'll know how you can best support your child.

Self-Evaluation: Is a Child Stressed?

Though children, like anybody else, can often tell that they are stressed, they may not be admitting it to themselves or to you. Take the following quiz on behalf of an important child in your life, or better yet ask him to take it for himself, if he's willing. Rate each question between 1 (no stress at all) and 5 (maximum stress).

1. It's Sunday night, and you have school again tomorrow. _____
2. Your brother/sister always gets what he/she wants, and you don't. _____
3. You are happy with the friends you have. _____
4. You have enough time to do everything you want to do. _____
5. Your parents are there when you need them. _____

QUESTION 1, the weekend's over, explores how much a kid stresses about school. If your child is a 1 or 2, he isn't having any major problems at school. Sure, he may not always want to do homework, but he enjoys school and the friends he has there. He can understand his assignment and work with his teacher. No one at school puts him down or makes him feel worthless.

If your child earned a 3, 4, or 5 on this question, school may be a stressor. Any number of factors can stress out a child at school—lack of friends, bullying, conflict with a teacher or other staff, or a learning disability that makes understanding difficult, are all possibilities. Ask a child why he doesn't want to go to school, and if that doesn't work, speak with a child's teacher. Sometimes school-related problems are connected to something in the child's private life, so explore that option as well.

QUESTION 2, sibling jealousy, looks at how much stress siblings create in a child's life. If a child answered 1 or 2, he feels little to no jealousy toward his siblings and has seen the way that parents and other adults take time to treat each child with love and patience, even though the children have different needs. He feels loved and accepted for who he is. This child likely interacts well with other siblings, despite occasional bickering, and will even chip in and play with and care for the others.

If a child answered 3, 4, or 5, siblings can be a source of stress. This child may perceive that a parent favors another child besides himself or gives another child special treatment. This may, in fact, be true if a sibling has a learning or developmental disability, is younger, or needs more care for other reasons.

FACT

Research by North Carolina State University Professor Amy Halberstadt published in 2008 found that children jealous of their siblings had four triggers: the other sibling received a special gift, got more of the parent's time, earned the parent's alligiance in a conflict, and got more attention due to a special talent. Treat all children fairly, and nip jealousy in the bud.

Jealousy is also common for older children, who may feel neglected due to younger siblings. Often, a child stressed by jealousy is really just stressed by a lack of attention. Ask a child why he feels that his siblings get special treatment, and make special efforts to give that child attention, maybe even asking a grandmother or other kind adult to specially mentor this child if the parents are bogged down with care for other children.

QUESTION 3, satisfaction with peer support, gauges a child's friendships. A socially healthy child has a variety of friends from various places: school, family, sports and leisure, and maybe even online. If a child answered 1 or 2, he enjoys his social life and is connected with his peer group.

If a child scores a 3, 4, or 5, he may be lonely. Sadly, a move, personal interests, bullying, weight, and a child's socioeconomic status can all affect his ability to make friends. Ask the child why he doesn't have any friends, and support the child in activities that he enjoys where he will meet other children, as well as nurture any friendships he does have.

Confront any bullying or hazing at school, or other social arenas, that may be affecting a child's ability to connect with his peers, and notify the appropriate authorities. Teach your child that such behavior is not appropriate and that there's nothing wrong with him, just with the kids hazing him. Your proactive stance will let the child already struggling with a lack of support know that someone is on his side who loves him—you.

QUESTION 4, time management, explores how much a schedule stresses out a child. If a child scores a 1 or 2, he has time to do everything he needs to do: go to school, socialize with friends, participate in sports and cultural activities, bond with family, and practice any hobbies he may have. His parents let him be a kid and have fun, and he has a say in prioritizing his life.

If a child answers 3, 4, or 5, his schedule is driving him crazy. He may be participating in too many activities without adequate leisure. Parents or other adults may be pressuring him to achieve good grades, sports trophies, and contest awards. Whatever happened to having fun? While a spirit of healthy competition and achievement is great, a child is still a child. Offer him more say in his activities and encourage him to balance his goals with his play time. Childhood's already short enough without making kids grow up before their time.

QUESTION 5, your parents are there when you need them, explores how much parents stress out a child. If a child answered 1 or 2, he is either sucking up to Mom or Dad watching him take the quiz, or he really does feel loved and supported. Though Mom and Dad may work busy jobs and balance their own social lives with family obligations, they always make time for him, and he knows he can ask and receive their attention.

If a child answered 3, 4, or 5, a very important source of support may be lacking in his life—parents. Everyone's busy, and after a long day at work it's hard to turn "on" for the kids. Yet carving out quality time with them is extremely important, not only to teach them stress management, but to give them the love and attention they need to grow up healthy and well.

Review this quiz and record a child's highest scoring questions. Focus on the issue that creates the most stress now, and go down the list. If a child is interested, invite him to participate in brainstorming stress-management tools in his own stress journal. It's never too early to start masterminding stress.

ALERT

Many children will not tell their parents they are being bullied. Signs of bullying include damaged personal property, unexplained injuries, few or no friends, fear of school and other peer activities, taking an odd route home from school, lack of interest in school work, expressing physical symptoms to stay home from school, bad mood after school, and a low sense of self-worth.

Parents as Stressors

Some parents, knowingly or unknowing, neglect their children's needs. Drug addicts, the mentally ill, those awful parents that everyone sees on the news—they abandon their children, broken and hurting, in foster homes or with well-meaning relatives. But, you'd never be like them. You'd never neglect your children.

Stress of Super Parents

The negligent parent stresses out her kids. So does the micromanaging one. Experts agree that parents pushing too hard for a child's success in the classroom, the playing field, or even the social sector are setting up the child for failure. Andrée Aelion Brooks, author of the 1989 parenting guide *Children of Fast-Track Parents: Raising Self-Sufficient and Confident Children in an Achievement-Oriented World*, interviewed hundreds of children, parents, and child experts across the United States. Brooks concluded that too many extracurricular activities added up to stressed-out kids on the road to burnout.

Stop Super Scheduling Your Kids

How do you avoid overwhelming kids' schedules when good grades are connected with college scholarships, and various extracurricular activities are linked to good health and socialization? Moderation. Encourage a child to choose one or two activities she especially enjoys and offer a child a rare gift in the busy modern world: free time.

Creativity, a trademark of childhood, develops out-of-the-box thinking, personal freedom, and autonomy. It's also fun and cheap. As a child learns how to manage certain aspects of her time, she'll learn more about who she is and what she values. These are invaluable tools as she grows into every parent's dream: an adult who knows what she wants and goes for it.

Only you can loosen the reins on your superkid and give her the freedom to learn who she is and see if she can fly. Though you may struggle with doing so much less for her, she'll appreciate the time to goof off and be a kid. Who knows, you may just find some time for yourself to practice your own stress-management skills in the midst of the free time you find from trimming your child's schedule. It's a win/win for everyone involved.

Being Different, The Rejected Child

If your child has special needs, he may experience the stress of rejection, in addition to his other worries about fitting in and caring for himself. Though many children are open and accepting of others no matter who they are, others can be cruel and target a child due to something as major as a wheelchair or as minor as red hair.

Pain of Childhood Rejection

Rejection hurts, no matter what age you are. As a parent or other caring adult, you have an opportunity to heal a child's stressful feelings of rejection with love. Encourage relationships and social settings where a child is accepted. Find child support resources such as therapy, medication, and tutoring that help him lead life to the fullest. Most importantly, teach your child that though others may reject him, you never will.

Tools to Bust Rejection Stress

All children seek independence as they grow, but those who need their parents and other resources more than others experience a special pressure. Whether your child has dyslexia, attention deficit hyperactivity disorder, slight mental retardation, or another condition, you know only too well the extra time and energy you spend on him.

FACT

The American Academy of Child and Adolescent Psychiatry estimates that 1 in 10 school children has a learning disability. Classic signs include failing grades, inability to read, write, or spell, acting out, no concept of time, and poor memory.

It's easy, with all the extra demands on your time, to become stressed yourself. Both you and your special-needs child should practice the following tips to give you both what you need:

❏ Have a plan of care for your child, endorsed by the appropriate profession, that outlines your child's needs and how you are meeting them.
❏ Do not attempt to parent a special-needs child, or any child for that matter, alone. Compile a support network of family, friends, and professional resources to help you in times of crisis with your child or when you hit your stress-tolerance point and need a break yourself.
❏ Know your child's limitations, and do not push, criticize, or ridicule your child for something he is incapable of. Instead, praise what your child does well.
❏ Encourage your child to explore what excites him. Many children with a learning disability in one area may be exceptionally gifted in another, and all children have talent and passion for something.
❏ Teach other children in the home, if applicable, to understand the special-needs child's condition and offer support and encouragement where appropriate.

Parenting a special-needs child, indeed, any child, takes time, patience, and the wisdom to let go of what's not important and fight for what is. Though others may reject and misunderstand your child, give him the most valuable gift possible, your unconditional love and acceptance. Remember that you and your child are on the same team—both working for him to be the best he can be.

Teaching Kids How to Manage Stress

Have you ever joked with your parents by saying, "You taught me everything you know"? This isn't far from the truth. Kids look to you for guidance, modeling, and an understanding of how to navigate the highly complicated and potentially stressful modern world.

What is the best gift you can give to your child—besides your love, that is? Empower her to make her own choices and choose her own destiny. That power includes the ability to live a life free from the stress roller coaster and ravages of a body and mind worn down from the many pressures of life.

Start young. Encourage your child to decorate and use her own stress journal. Teach her to notice a stressor, and then use tools to manage it. You are the best model for this technique. If you're actively busting your stress and always seeking ways to enjoy life, it will teach her to do the same.

Seize the Day: Transform Your Children's Stress

Junior does not have to live as a slave to stress. If he has a caring parent or other adult to support him, advise him, and encourage him to enjoy life and be healthy, he's well on his way to managing stress for the rest of his life.

ESSENTIAL

Create special moments every day with your child. Eat breakfast and dinner together. Take the dog for a walk. Spend time on a nightly routine that includes laying out tomorrow's clothes, preparing lunch, and sharing a bedtime story. It's these little things that your child will remember.

Teach him the Big Five Tools for Stress Resilience: healthy diet, adequate sleep, water, exercise, and fun. Model them for him, so he knows how important they are. Help him brainstorm healthy stress-busting tools of his own like playing Xbox and practicing karate, and teach him how to practice one when he's feeling stressed. Throw in assertiveness, love, and a constant desire to monitor stress and bust it when you see it, and you've got a child ready for the stressors of college, marriage, and paying a mortgage.

Remember, your child is still a child. Watch how much you push him. Be there and care, but also give him freedom and free time to explore who he is. Whatever your child's stressors—bullies, depression, obesity, or a burning desire to be on *American Idol*—he can manage them the same way Mom or Dad does: with awareness, action, and a little bit of fun.

CHAPTER 16

Stress and Young Adults

Teenagers, people between the onset of puberty and the age of eighteen, have a bad rap for being difficult. "She's just being a teenager," with an eye roll, is a code between frustrated parents. Just to make life even more stressful, many young adults struggle for independence well into their twenties and thirties. With support, autonomy, and other tools, however, the young adult can be well on her way to managing her stress.

What Stresses Out Teenagers?

Sassy, rebellious, conflicted, defiant—sound like someone you love? It's a well known stereotype: teenagers are stressful. Ever wonder why? Actually, they have good reason to be.

Between hormonal craziness, body changes, peer pressure, the struggle for independence and identity, and major life choices such as college, career, and relationships, the average teenager has a lot on his plate. Add to that drugs, sex, and the uncertain future, and your teenage years truly do beg an aggressive stress-management approach. It's enough to stress out anyone.

The people who love a teenager the most often get caught in the crossfire of fear and anger as the teen struggles with the conflict within herself. Any well-meaning parent or mentor who's said the wrong thing at the wrong time knows that. If you're a teenager, knowing your stressors and working with a caring adult to manage them responsibly is key to busting stress now and always.

What Stresses Out Twenty-Somethings?

Traditionally, young people grew up, saved up, got married, and moved out. In recent decades, the trends have changed. More and more people live with their parents well into their twenties and thirties. Not only does this put pressure on parents, nearing retirement, but also on the adult children, seeking an independent life in a home that is not truly theirs.

There are several reasons that young adults are taking longer to be completely independent from their parents. Attending college and graduate school can delay an adult child from leaving the nest completely. Some adult children live at home to save money for the uncertain future. Some simply cannot find work to suit their education and wait, living at home, until the perfect job comes. Others are just comfy and don't want to leave.

The pressure of yearning to be fully grown up, with a good job, house, the perfect partner, and nice things, eats away at many in their twenties. Others have no qualms about bumming off of Mom and Dad and may need some motivation, such as a good job, significant other, or parental consequences, to help them grow up.

Whatever the reasons they're not ready for prime time, it's truly difficult for young adults to be stuck in two worlds: the world of parental or family support, and the world of independence and big dreams. Starting life takes work. Any adult can explain that it stinks. That's why so many adults wish they could be kids again. Work is hard. Marriage or another committed relationship is hard. Having kids is hard. While crashing at home or taking classes full-time may be comfortable, adulthood has to begin sometime.

FACT

According to Monster.com's 2009 Annual Entry-Level Job Outlook, about 40 percent of 2008 college graduates still live with their parents. Forty-two percent of the 2006 graduates surveyed live with their parents, too.

Many young adults waiting for that perfect job or enough money to move out don't realize that the good middle class life they're waiting for—with the big screen TV, eating out, nice clothes, and private Jacuzzi—is something their parents have worked decades to achieve. A nice house, good car, classy furniture, and great vacations take time to afford, for most people, anyway, unless they're living in debt or lucky enough to be independently wealthy.

By changing their expectations, life is hard and has to start some time, young adults reluctant to leave the nest for whatever reason can get the guts to fly. Maybe if Mom's lasagna just wasn't so good . . . .

Self-Evaluation: Is a Young Adult Stressed?

Whether you are a teenager or a twenty-something, you have stressors unique to your stage in life that may be negatively affecting you. If you're reading this chapter as a concerned parent or other adult, invite the young adult in question to take this quiz himself for the most accurate data. Mark each question between 1 (no stress at all) and 5 (maximum stress).

1. Your body's growing in ways or creating urges that make you uncomfortable. _____

2. Drugs, sex, and other forms of peer pressure just won't go away. _____
3. You wish your parents would just leave you alone. _____
4. You wish your boyfriend/girlfriend would change. _____
5. You dread thinking about the future, but know you have to plan for it. _____

QUESTION 1, your changing body and desires, gauges how much the normal hormonal surges and growth spurts during the young-adult years stress you out. If you answered 1 or 2 to this question, your body changing isn't a major source of stress. It may get you down sometimes, but you know it's a normal part of life. Even though most people think of teenagers as the ones with growth spurts, men continue to grow into their early thirties.

If you answered 3, 4, or 5 to this question, your changing body is causing you stress. Maybe you're uncomfortable that your body is growing so fast, or maybe your body's not developing as quickly as your peers and you feel left out. Insecurity is normal during this life stage. Healthy lifestyle choices like enough sleep, healthy diet, water, and fun can keep you balanced and reduce your risk of depression or anxiety. If your body's changes are difficult to deal with, visit a therapist or medical doctor for answers.

QUESTION 2, peer pressure for drugs, alcohol, and sex, explores a young adult's stress from his peers. If you answered 1 or 2, you either have set boundaries with others in your life who may be trying to get you to engage in risky behaviors, or you're engaging already but don't see any problem with it. Note that excessive drug and alcohol use is not only illegal for most teens, but it can cause unwanted health problems down the road, meaning more stress in the long run.

If you answered 3, 4, or 5, peer pressure stresses you out. Are you doing things to fit in that you wish you weren't? Are you desperate for friends and to prove yourself? Many young adults seek a sense of identity outside of themselves, in a peer group rather than from their parents as children do. Learning to see yourself as the source of your identity takes time and determination. While having friends is great and important for living a long and healthy life, doing whatever your friends tell you is just plain stupid. Explore your own interests and dreams, and find friends that pull you up and encourage you rather than dragging you down to a place you really don't want to be.

QUESTION **3**, you wish your parents would leave you alone, explores how much your parents stress you out. During the young adult years, breaking away from your parents is a normal part of life. Yet that breakup is tough, and means fighting and tears on both sides. If you answered a 1 or 2 to this question, your parents give you the space and freedom you need to do what you need to do. They're there when you need them. They still stress you out, but they know when to back off.

ESSENTIAL

Young adults are busy with school, friends, and activities. Encourage a young adult to take time for herself: a spa day, beach day, or another place where she'll have no demands placed upon her. Not only will this bust her stress, but it will also teach her to plan relaxation regularly, an essential life skill for masterminding stress.

If you answered 3, 4, or 5, your parents don't have a clue how much they stress you out. They get in your face, wanting answers, or they let you do whatever you want without checking in. You may be struggling with a major challenge—such as the pressures of sexual activity, college choice, and a possible career—and you'd like some support, but you can't talk to them because they'd go crazy and tell you what to do, or worse, act like they don't care.

If you parents aren't giving you the support you need, let them know it. Sit them down and explain that you'd like suggestions on a certain decision or problem, but that you will be making the ultimate decision. Most good parents will be thrilled that you're involving them in your life again, and your relationship may just improve. If your parents, sadly, don't care, don't give up. Find a teacher, grandparent, or other caring adult and try again. Some adult in your life wants to be there for you. You just have to find him.

QUESTION **4**, you wish your boyfriend/girlfriend would change, gauges how much a romantic relationship is stressing you out. Most young adults experience their first romantic relationship during this stage of life. It's easy to live in a dream world where that perfect person just needs to behave in a certain way and everyone's happy. If you answered 1 or 2 to this question, you are lucky to have a healthy romantic relationship. Though you and your partner may fight, you both listen to each other and struggle to love the other person for who they are.

If you answered 3, 4, or 5 you may be stressing because you have unrealistic expectations in your romantic relationship. You can't make another person fit a dream in your head. Maybe you're really with the wrong person, or worse, you're pushing the right person away by not letting him be himself. Despite the myth that true love is magical and effortless, maintaining a relationship of love is hard and messy.

It takes patience and direct communication to keep a relationship going. Your partner may drive you crazy. Only you can decide enough's enough. You can't change him; change the only person you can: you. Focus on your goals and interests. Find passion in your own life without the help of another. When you're excited about your own life, you can attract a partner who's attracted to the real you, not who he thinks you are.

QUESTION 5, dreading the future, examines how much you're stressing about your future plans. The young-adult years are full of life-changing choices: what college will you attend, what job will you have, who will you date, and when will you move out? If you answered 1 or 2, either you have good support in making life decisions or you just aren't thinking about them.

ALERT

Eating disorders are increasingly common among teenagers of both genders. Signs of an eating disorder include change in eating habits, negative body image, excessive exercise, continual desire to be thin, and superficial relationships.

If you answered 3, 4, or 5, your future's stressing you out. Maybe college looms ever closer, or ends soon with no job in sight. Perhaps your boyfriend's pressuring you to move in, but you're rather be independent for a while.

To make good decisions, simply consider all the possibilities, make a choice, and don't let the worry consume you. It's especially important to practice the Big Five Tools for Stress Resilience: healthy diet, adequate sleep, water, exercise, and fun. Life's too short to worry all the time, and the future's coming whether you're ready for it or not.

Now that you've completed the quiz, note the two or three areas where you have the highest score. Record the area that's bothering you the most right now in your stress journal, and begin brainstorming ways to bust that particular stress. Save the other stressors for another day, and be open to new stress-busting tools as you continue to manage your stress.

Parents as Stressors

Teenagers have many stressors: schoolwork, relationships, peer pressure, the future, and parents. A study of Baltimore teens by the Center for Adolescent Health, John Hopkins Bloomberg School of Public Health, found that 56 percent of teens named their parents as a major source of stress, along with romantic relationships (48 percent), friendships (52 percent), and drugs (48 percent). The only other stressor more prevalent than parents was school at 68 percent.

Why Parents Can't Let Go

How can the people who gave you life, raised you, and love you be so stressful? Oh, because they won't leave you alone. As teenagers and young adults grow up, they break away from dependency on their parents. This process, which psychologists call differentiation, involves developing your own values, personality, and life separate from your parents. Differentiation is a normal part of growing up. Those loving, caring people who gave you life and love suddenly become monsters who hold you down and cramp your style.

How a parent responds to a young adult breaking away affects how much he stresses out his fledgling child. If a parent becomes more controlling, demanding answers and information he used to get freely before the process of growing up began, he stresses out the teen, who will respond accordingly. Avoidance, anger, and other forms of rebellion are so common among teenagers because many parents try to thwart a young adult's natural desire to separate from the parents and become an independent person.

Why Parents Are So Annoying

A parent who is bossy and demands answers usually does so out of love. Imagine how hard it would be to raise a child who talked to you and did things with you, only to suddenly have that child avoid you and not want to spend time with you. Parents are people, too, and no one likes being rejected.

If your parent is controlling and demands to know about your life, treat her with compassion. "Mom, I'm fifteen. I love you. I appreciate that you want to know how today went. Right now, I'm busy, but we'll talk later, okay?" Set boundaries with your parents. Remind them you are growing up and masterminding your life now. Great ways to teach your parents who's in charge:

- ❏ Say "not right now." Set a time to talk that's convenient for you.
- ❏ Make a list of decisions on which you want your parents' input. Write down specific questions you have for them. This will keep them from running all over you and trying to take over the conversation.
- ❏ Repeat positive phrases of affection such as "I love you" and "I appreciate you wanting to help me out." This lets parents know you still care, and reminds them you're not rejecting them, just their continual intervention in your life.
- ❏ Thank your parents when they answer questions and offer advice that you've asked for. This positive reinforcement encourages them to work with you and not against you.

A young adult naturally wants to fly away from her parents. Just make sure you don't put your parents off, all the time. Making major life decisions is stressful, and you need all the support you can get. Parents have life experience, connections, and knowledge that they'd love to use to your advantage. There's no better advocate than loving parents as long as they know who is ultimately in charge: you.

The College/Job Myth

More teenagers and young adults are attending college in hope of a better life and a better job. The 2010 U.S. Census Bureau's "The Big Payoff: Educational Attainment and Synthetic Estimates of Work-Life Earnings" study found that a high school graduate earned an average of $1.2 million during his working life (ages twenty-five to sixty-four) while a college graduate earned $2.1 million.

The Costs of Education for Young Adults

The more education you have, according to the study, the more you'll make during your life. The average master's degree holder will earn $2.5 million, and the doctorate $3.4 million. The data confirms the hope of many young adults and their parents: education opens a door to a lucrative future.

The realities of higher education may include more money in the long run, but putting off life for school has unique stressors. Many young adults take out loans for their education and work part-time to make it through school, adding to their stress loads. In addition, many live far away from family support and have to find new networks of connection and support while away at school.

FACT

Adult children who return home are known as the boomerang generation because many of them left home once for college or a job only to return due to lack of work, financial challenges, or divorce.

College Doesn't Always Equal a Job

As college ends, the job search begins. Many graduates find themselves in an unexpected conundrum—they cannot find that long-expected dream job. Labor Department statistics from 2009 show a startling trend: unemployment for those with a college degree is the highest ever recorded, above 4 percent.

Even without a recession, some degrees make you more employable than others. A science, engineering, or technology degree can generate a well-paying job right out of college. Other degrees, such as those in the humanities, require additional training and sometimes work experience to reap the rewards of gainful employment.

School versus Life

Unlike school, where hard work and good grades equal success, potential employers often evaluate young workers based on criteria beyond their control. In some sectors, employers prefer experience over education. In others, such as the humanities, a young adult must receive on-the-job training (often out-of-pocket) to create a career for himself.

Still another roadblock is that many recent college graduates find themselves overqualified for certain jobs simply because of their education, though they may lack work experience. How do you get work experience when you appear overqualified for it?

There are no easy answers to unemployment for young adults new to the workforce or for anyone seeking a means of livelihood. Know that college isn't an instant ticket to an easy life and a good job, and expect to work for what you have. Prevent depression and anxiety with healthy life choices, and stay out of debt during periods of transition to keep yourself financially ready for whatever life has in store.

ESSENTIAL

The best way for a young adult to increase his likelihood of a job after college is to compile a resume of diverse activity that highlights his education, leadership experience, team collaboration, and work experience. A well-rounded candidate is much more attractive to a potential employer than one gifted in only one or two areas.

Depression and Suicide

As though finding a job isn't stressful enough, teens are also under pressure to stay mentally healthy and balanced, too. Depression and suicide are another area of concern for young adults and those who love them. According to the National Institute of Mental Heath, suicide is the third major cause of death for adolescents. Eight out of every 100,000 teens actually committed suicide in 2000. The institute estimates that for every teen who successfully committed suicide, there are ten who made attempts.

Reach Out to Bust Teen Depression

Whether a young adult knows a friend who's struggled with these serious issues of life or death, or you are the one suffering in silence, teen depression is no light matter. Being a teenager is stressful: growing and changing so quickly, dealing with drugs and alcohol, seeking the right friends, trying to plot your course in life, and striking out on your own. Though it may seem like you're all alone sometimes, reaching out for support is crucial to keeping yourself mentally healthy.

Act Against Teen Depression

If you or someone you love struggles with depression and thoughts of suicide, immediate action could mean the difference between life and death. Contact a counselor or medical professional if the person is not actually suicidal; if she is, dial 911. Depression is a serious illness that requires medical attention. Even if you think you can handle it yourself, statistics show that many teens who try end up losing their most important possession: their lives.

Most teens who kill themselves don't want to; they just don't know what else to do. A survey by the National Youth Violence Prevention Resource Center found that eight out of every ten high school students who committed suicide cried out for help in some way before the event. If you are crying out for help, keep crying until someone listens. Try your parents, another trusted adult, the school counselor, your coach—someone in your life who cares. Remember, you are only as alone as you choose to be.

ALERT

Though both teenaged women and men attempt suicide, young women are more likely to attempt suicide, while young men are four to five times more likely to succeed in killing themselves.

If the pressures of life are too much for you, share them. There are many adults out there, including your parents, who care about you and value you as a person, even if you don't value yourself right now. Managing stress is tough for everyone, not just teens. Know that you are not alone or weird for having trouble managing stress. That's completely normal. The depression and thoughts of suicide, though, are not normal and need urgent attention.

The Stress of Not Knowing

With the future looming large, there's a lot to worry about. The stress of not knowing what college you will attend, where you will work, where you will live, who you will marry, all these worries can add up fast. Anxiety, or persistent worry, can develop from excessive stress about something you can't immediately change.

While some teens choose medication as an option for their anxiety about the future, there are other ways to manage the unknown. Control what you can control: your life now. Create short-term, mid-term, and long-term goals. Short-term goals keep you rooted in the present as you strive to be the best you can be. Hoping to lose the freshman fifteen before you graduate? Fight senior year stress by joining a gym. Sure, you still have to apply for graduate schools, but right now you're hitting the punching bag and wow, it feels good!

When you worry about your unknown future, fight it with any and all stress-management tools at your disposal. If you've worked hard and planned ahead, you'll be able to make it as an adult. No one fails at growing up; some just do it happier and healthier than others.

Seize the Day: Transform Young Adult Stress

Teens and young adults have many stressors: the pressure of growing up and being their own people, finding gainful employment, living with love, and keeping mentally healthy. Reach out for support. Set boundaries. Have realistic expectations for your life, and practice the Big Five Tools for Stress Resilience: healthy diet, adequate sleep, water, exercise, and fun. Keep it up, and you are well on your way to managing stress for a lifetime.

CHAPTER 17

Stress and Adults

If you're reading this book, you know the power stress has over your life. With work, a home, family, finances, relationships, and your health, it's truly a miracle you get it all done. There's always room for improvement, though. Explore stressors unique to you and others adults close to you and gather new tools for your toolbox as the journey to mastermind your stress continues.

What Stresses Out Adults?

Life gets busier and busier for everyone, but especially for people age twenty-five through sixty-five. Though you're only as old as you choose to be, those lucky enough to retire have different stressors than younger adults juggling children, relationships, and a career.

FACT

A 2007 study by the American Psychological Association released startling statistics. Not only did nearly a third of adults (32 percent) surveyed describe their stress as extreme, but almost half (48 percent) said their stress levels have risen in the last five years. Note that extreme stress, or the maximum stress you can possibly have, has serious effects on your physical, mental, and emotional health.

What causes stress in adults? Increasing demands of technology, financial insecurity, children living at home longer, and the breakup of relationships are only the tip of the iceberg. In 1950, one parent worked to finance a middle class lifestyle, but in 2010 it takes two parents, and often three or more jobs between them, to finance a comparable lifestyle. If an adult loses a partner to divorce or death, her stress load increases even more.

Cheer up, it's not all gloom and doom. There is much you can do to mastermind your stress if you approach it from a viewpoint of power, rather than a viewpoint of powerlessness. You are only a victim to your stress if you choose to be.

ALERT

Divorce can be one of the most stressful events of an adult's life. Be as prepared as you can. Seek support, care for yourself, and grieve when you need to do so. Know that a divorce takes time and energy, and save yourself the stress of pressuring yourself to get over it.

Self-Evaluation: Is An Adult Stressed Out?

Knowing your greatest stressors is key to managing them and subsequently reducing your overall stress load. Take the following quiz when you have some free time to yourself to reflect in a journal about the results.

Mark each question between 1 (minimum stress) and 5 (maximum stress) depending upon your stress level right now:

1. You wonder how you're going to achieve a major financial goal, such as paying your bills, this month. _____
2. You are responsible for dependent children or parents and wish you had more help with them. _____
3. You often bring your work home with you. _____
4. You never manage to get time for yourself. _____
5. You wonder if there's more to life and feel urges to do something crazy and unexpected. _____

QUESTION 1, how you're going to meet your financial goals, explores how much stress you experience from financial concerns. If you answered 1 or 2, you either have your budget and finances under control or just don't think about your finances, even though your debt or retirement needs are not going away.

If you answered 3, 4, or 5, money is a serious stressor. Maybe you scrape by to pay the bills and have no money to invest in the future. Maybe you're a single parent trying to do everything, including manage a household, with less. Select an area of your finances that creates the most stress for you, like your monthly bills, debt, and college savings, and examine your budget. What ways could you cut corners to give yourself more flexibility? If there are no corners to cut, take in some additional income, such as freelance or part-time work. With discipline and patience, you can make your finances work for you. You may not have all the money you'd like, but you'll have a plan that stress can't bust.

QUESTION 2, your dependents need more than you can give, gauges how much your kids or elderly parents stress you out. If you answered 1 or 2, either you have no dependents or you have adequate support and resources

The Everything Guide to Stress Management

to love and care for those who need you. This is no small feat, considering that some adults must care for their parents as well as their children, sometimes in the same home.

If you answered 3, 4, or 5, caring for your loved ones stresses you out. Maybe you aren't making enough money to meet their needs. Maybe you are burnt out being a stay-at-home parent to a child or a full-time caregiver to a homebound senior. Whatever your reasons for stressing about your child or adult parent, remember that you're doing so out of love. Your kids and your parents wouldn't want you to suffer. Explore resources—such as in-home care for your senior parents or child care for your children—to give you a much needed break. Take special care to meet all your own needs in the midst of caring for others.

QUESTION 3, work that never ends, explores how much your job is stressing you out. If you answered 1 or 2, you either have healthy boundaries with work and know how to leave it where it belongs or you have a job you love that has flexible working hours, and you know how to balance your private life within that. Congratulations! Many people struggle to make their jobs work with a flourishing private life.

ALERT

It's easy to focus on work and forget to eat healthy and exercise. According to the U.S. Department of Health and Human Services, over two-thirds of American adults are overweight or obese. Excess weight increases your chance of diabetes, heart attack, stroke, breathing problems, and a difficult pregnancy. Though many factors contribute to obesity, poor diet and lack of exercise are chief among them. Avoid unwanted health stressors in the future and pay attention to your body now!

If you answered 3, 4, or 5, your job stresses you out. Maybe you physically bring work home, or maybe you can't leave the anxiety or anger from work at work, and stew about it during your time off. Whatever your reasons for work stress, explore ways to set boundaries. Practice saying no, learn what's important and what isn't, and schedule time to do what you want to do, so that you have something to look forward to in the midst of the daily grind.

QUESTION **4**, no time for yourself, examines how much your schedule stresses you out. Many adults juggle children, a romantic relationship, a home, a job, and their own needs in a constant flurry of activity. If you answered 1 or 2, you are able to balance your many obligations. Sure it gets tough sometimes, but you know when to schedule a massage or put off unnecessary obligations until the next time.

If you answered a 3, 4, or 5, your lack of time stresses you out. You're doing too much with too little time for you. Chances are, you may even skimp on the essentials like sleep and a healthy diet. It's not far from here to the stress roller coaster, where stress masterminds your time and energy. First of all, explore why you don't have enough time for yourself. Make time for yourself a top priority, even if it's just twenty minutes a day. Drop unnecessary activities, learn to say no, and be as driven in enjoying yourself as you are in caring for family and work. Surprise! You have more time than you thought you had; all it took was a little prioritizing.

QUESTION **5**, wanting more in life, gauges how much a mid-life crisis exacerbates your stress. Yearning for change and feeling dissatisfied are normal for those exploring their life's purpose halfway through it. If you answered 1 or 2, you may not be experiencing a mid-life crisis, or if you are, you don't find it extremely stressful. You understand that these urges are normal, and while they may be uncomfortable at times, you can manage them.

If you answered 3, 4, or 5, a mid-life crisis seriously stresses you. Are you in denial that you're approaching the mid-life mark? Do your urges encourage you to indulge in something you consider inappropriate, wrong, or just plain silly? You can be your own worst enemy, especially when it comes to doing something good for you. A mid-life crisis is a normal stage in the life cycle. As long as you don't want something illegal or harmful to another, indulge your fancies. Buy that sports car, as long as you can afford it. Ask your husband for more sex. You'll never know unless you ask.

After you complete the quiz, record your highest-ranking areas. Select one that generates the most stress in your life now. Record it in your stress journal, and brainstorm short- and long-term goals to manage it using tools in your stress-management toolbox. With practice and patience, you can mastermind this stressor and move on to the next one in your life.

Raising Kids and Staying Sane

Adults who choose to become parents open themselves up for a whole new world of excitement and pressure. Every stage of the parenting cycle, from trying to conceive to flying across the country for college graduation, has its own unique stressors. Whether you're eagerly expecting your first child or catching some rare time for yourself in the midst of a screaming houseful of them, you know how much work and sacrifice parenthood can be.

ESSENTIAL

Kids grow up so fast, and every moment with them is precious. Create a "Rainy Day Jar" for yourself and your child as a bonding project. Take two clean jars and strips of paper. On each paper, write something you love about the other person. Then, on a rainy or stressful day, your child can pull out a piece of paper and see proof he's loved.

Sure you love your kids and want them to have the best. What good parent doesn't? In the crazy business of masterminding your kids' needs, remember another very important person: you. Your kids may come first, but where will they be with a mom or dad who is sick with stress and unable to care for them?

Manage Your Kids, Don't Let Them Manage You

Set boundaries with all the stressors in your life, including your children. Reflect on a time that your child drove you past your stress-tolerance point. What happened? Did you lash out at the child and feel guilty later? Did you end up confusing the child with a cold tone or other dismissive gesture? Notice when your children are triggering your stress and record it in your stress journal.

Brainstorm tools to prevent taking out your stress on the very people you strive to protect. Ask Grandma to babysit once a week. Assign a daily nap. If you are a stay-at-home parent, take special care to prevent burnout. Plan activities outside the home away from the children, and find groups of other stay-at-home parents to share the load with socialization and reciprocal child care.

Teach Everyone to Use Stress-Busting Tools

If it's still weird to consider putting your needs above your child's, consider that you're doing both of you a favor when you prioritize stress management. Why? Stress management is an essential tool for anyone wanting a happy and healthy life, and it's never too early to start. Model for your family effective stress-management techniques, and practice family stress busters. Possibilities could include:

- ❑ Organize family leisure activities such as cycling, hiking, or visiting a site of cultural interest that promote healthy lifestyle choices.
- ❑ Have sit-down meals with conversation and a daily check-in of how each family member's day went.
- ❑ Encourage free time and alone time for each family member. Teach children to enjoy themselves and be creative during free time. Say, "Not now. Mommy needs a break" when your anger or anxiety is rising, and encourage children to do the same.
- ❑ Practice the Big Five Tools for Stress Resilience: healthy diet, adequate sleep, water, exercise, and fun, and advocate them to your children.
- ❑ Teach children to use a stress journal, write about their stressors to let off steam, and brainstorm tools to bust the stress, just like you do.
- ❑ Experiment with new ways to have fun and relax. Karate? Baseball? Find an activity that inspires your child's passion, and be the best cheerleader in the stands.

Now that you're teaching your children to manage stress and modeling good stress-management skills, you don't feel quite so guilty about focusing on yourself. Raising kids doesn't have to be the end of your life, but a new beginning of working together as a family to live healthy, fun, and stress-resilient lives.

Stress for Women

Women between twenty-five and sixty have stressors unique to their gender. Many choose to be mothers, while others share their nurturing spirit as bosses, mentors, friends, and lovers. However you express your womanhood, you have special pressures that you are wise to address.

Women's Special Stressors

Not only do women balance work, home, and a biological or social family, but they also care for their reproductive needs. Younger women make life-changing reproductive choices before menopause, and older women face physical and emotional challenges as their reproductive systems shut down.

FACT

In 1917, Anna Jarvis coined the holiday "Mother's Day" to celebrate the many contributions of women as mothers and mentors. Mother's Day, the second Sunday of the month of May in countries all over the world, still honors women from all walks of life. What better way to thank a woman who's changed your life?

Women, in general, also tend to have higher rates of anxiety than men, simply because many take others' problems onto themselves as caregivers. Researchers from The University of Arizona's School of Family and Consumer Resources studied the stress levels of 166 married couples and found that women experienced more high-stress days and fewer low-stress days than men did. Caring does, indeed, have a cost.

Too Much to Do, but No Time to Do It

Gone are the days when women would stay at home managing their household and children, at least in Western societies. Women are doctors, firefighters, and presidents. Despite progress in recent decades, women still make less than men and struggle with sexual harassment, domestic violence, and abuse. Yet women defy the victim role. The modern woman strives to do it all, and often in the midst of the quest she forgets the most important person to her continual health and happiness: herself.

Since women are more sensitive to stress than men, maintaining resilience is especially important. Try these tips to manage your stress and juggle your many obligations, including your health and happiness:

❑ **Prioritize your to-do list.** Many women overschedule themselves with children's activities, social obligations such as church or synagogue, work, or volunteering. Select a few activities you want to support whole-heartedly, and offer a kind but firm no to others.

- ❏ **Nurture friends for soul sharing.** Women relieve stress by talking, so schedule time with a friend or family member to vent that stress away.
- ❏ **Think of yourself.** Women, especially mothers, think of everyone else first. If you cannot think of yourself automatically, make a daily to-do list—healthy food, sleep, water, exercise, and fun—and check off each item when you've done it.
- ❏ **Keep up with your medical appointments.** Whether you need the doctor for birth control or breast exams, check in periodically about your health. Your family and friends really don't want to live without you.

You know, only too well, how many people depend on you for love, food, security, and care. As all women manage their stress, they should prioritize their number one source of energy and happiness: themselves. The reality is, if you don't, who will?

Stress for Men

Like women, men have special stressors unique to their gender. Young men struggle with the decision to marry and have children. Some men choose to be fathers, others leaders in the corporate sector, yet all struggle with autonomy and a sense of purpose in the world.

Men's Special Stressors

More men die in dangerous accidents than woman, due to their drive for adventure and excitement. Perhaps men's most significant stressor is their uncanny ability to shoulder responsibility in silence.

QUESTION

Do men have more stress-related heart attacks than women?
No. Heart attacks are the number one killer for both men and women. Women tend to get heart attacks later in life than men do and have different symptoms, but they, too, experience heart attacks.

Since the feminist movement, men don't have to be the sole provider anymore, but men are conditioned to silently bear their burdens alone, even though they do the dishes and change diapers. While women talk to bust stress, men keep it inside. This automatic response can have serious implications for a man's health and happiness, as well as that of those who love him.

Break the Strong, Silent Sterotype to Bust Stress

Pushing stress down can lead to health problems, including depression and heart conditions. Everyone knows of a man—someone's lover or father—who died too young of a sudden but massive heart attack. Sure, this could happen to women, too, but it's a stern warning to men: don't bottle up your stress.

Men have many obligations, including work, family, and relationships. Try the following tips to manage stress effectively:

❑ **Be aware of what's stressing you and do something to release it.** Take a break, hit the gym, tell your partner, but do not sit on it in silence and let it fester.

❑ **Nurture social ties.** Don't get stuck in the work/family grind with no fun. Go golfing. Catch a game. Take your friends. Male bonding is good for you.

❑ **Communicate openly with those who love you.** Many women worry when their men are silent. Explain to a woman that you need some time to think, and that you'll get back with her. She'll appreciate your honesty.

❑ **Keep up with your medical appointments.** Monitor any pre-existing conditions or others you might have in your family, such as heart disease. Be open with your doctor about problems you're having—bearing pain or discomfort in silence might just kill you.

You provide for those who love you and offer strength as well as softness. Keep yourself healthy by managing your stress, and you're well on your way to telling your grandchildren that favorite fishing story one more time.

Stress of the Midlife Crisis

Another stressor for adults occurs as the midlife crisis looms ever closer. A midlife crisis is no myth. Psychologist Carl Jung first noticed the trend in middle-aged adults to explore their life's meaning. If you or a loved one is struggling with who he is and what he wants, take heart. It's perfectly normal.

Unfortunately, midlife crisis has a bad reputation. Everyone knows of someone who lost a spouse or experienced a radical shift, such as a divorce, as a result of the soul-searching from a midlife crisis. These events are tragic and create even more stress about the possibility of a midlife crisis. No one really wants that much change, right?

Embrace Midlife Crisis for Healthier, Happier Life

A little change, however, is good. If you're experiencing discontent, emotional outbursts, a heightened sex drive, or a childlike drive for adventure, you may just be beginning an exciting part of your life. A midlife crisis, when handled well, can inspire you to make positive changes in your life to increase your personal health and happiness.

ESSENTIAL

Hollywood goddess Sophia Loren offers the following advice for embracing the second half of life: "There is a fountain of youth; it is your mind, your talents, the creativity you bring to your life, and the lives of the people you love. When you learn to tap this source, you will truly have defeated age."

To embrace your midlife crisis and all the fun and excitement of change, consider the following:

- What have you always wanted to do, but never gotten around to?
- What do you hate about your current life and most want to change?
- When you are dying, what do you need to do to be fully content with your life?

Figure out what you need to do to ease the crisis bug, and do it. If your spouse, children, and other friends think you're crazy, invite them to be a part of this exciting new time in your life. A little sky-diving is good for everyone, right?

Vacations: Dream or Nightmare?

Dread vacation because it's more stress than it's worth? You're not alone. Vacations stress out many people. Though you may desperately need it, sometimes it's more stressful to be at home than it is to be at work. All those home-improvement projects that need to be addressed, the pet wanting attention, a salesman banging on the door—is there ever a break? Even planning a vacation away from home is fraught with stressors, such as the cost, the travel, the planning, and the fear of Montezuma's revenge, to name a few.

Take Vacation Time to Bust Stress

Whatever your reason for hoarding your vacation days, get over it. Vacations are good for your health. The Framingham Heart Study of 12,000 men found that those who took frequent vacations lived longer than those who didn't. Not only is a vacation good for your heart, but it also boosts your resilience to stress. Remember the image of investing in relaxation to bust stress? If you're not regularly filling your relaxation tank with days off, you're not building up the relaxation you need to bust really stressful life events when they happen.

Whether your vacation is a series of get-away-weekends with the family or a week in the Bahamas with your beloved, make sure you're getting away. There's no better way to take a break from the stresses of your adult life than by putting it all on hold, however that works best for you, your schedule, and your budget.

Seize the Day: Transform Adult Stress

Much of an adult's stress is rooted in perspective. Work is only all-consuming if you let it be. There may be friends or family willing to give you a break from the kids if you ask. Most employers offer vacation days, so use them! Use all the tools at your disposal to bust the stress in your life. Be creative, flexible, and persistent, and stress cannot win.

Too many adults cave in to the demands of modern life and sacrifice themselves in attempts to get it all done. Gambling your Big Five Tools for Stress Resilience: healthy diet, adequate sleep, water, exercise, and fun, for extra hours at work is a recipe for disaster. Instead, invest in the best asset you have: your health and happiness.

Open up your stress journal, grab a proven stress-management tool, or go out there and experiment with a new one. Nothing's more stressful than a stressed-out provider. Your children, your family, your coworkers, the grocery store clerk, and everyone else you love and care for will be grateful.

CHAPTER 18

Stress and Senior Adults

Senior adults enlighten others with their wisdom and experience. As the age group who traditionally enjoys retirement, what could possibly stress out retirees? Plenty. No one, no matter her age, is stress-free. Explore stressors unique to senior adults and discover tools to bust them as the journey to mastermind stress continues.

What Stresses Out Senior Adults?

Many world cultures revere their elders. Elders guide, teach, and nurture the future generation. In the modern world, however, society nurtures a culture of youth. People dress younger than they actually are, and procedures for defying age, such as plastic surgery, are wildly popular. What does this mean for those mature in age?

Youth Culture

Many senior adults struggle with accepting their age and limitations in a culture that encourages youth and independence. No one wants to admit she has limits and can't do whatever she wants. As the body ages, physical and mental limitations increase. Seniors must rely on loved ones for support more and more, a humbling and painful process.

FACT

The American Association of Retired Persons (AARP) began in 1958 to increase awareness of social issues facing senior citizens. Today, the AARP champions living the best life possible after fifty with their monthly publication, discounts on food and travel, and insurance and financial services.

Loss of Independence

Many senior adults struggle with a loss of independence. The body begins to shut down, and health problems are common. Sleeping becomes difficult, and it's not possible to move as fast or do as much. Entering assisted living or another group-care facility is a heart-breaking transition for seniors, and many struggle with depression and loneliness.

The golden years aren't all gloom and doom, though. Many seniors enjoy the real world post-career with a full and active life of social and community activities. Suddenly, there's time to expand the garden, redecorate the empty nest, vacation in Tahiti, and spoil the grandkids without the responsibilities of parenting. For these active seniors, they are as young as they feel, and nothing can stop them.

Self-Evaluation: Is a Senior Adult Stressed Out?

Even though you may be a senior adult—age sixty-five and above—your stressors are unique to you. Take the following quiz to ascertain the stressors most affecting you now. Ponder each question carefully, and answer on a scale of 1 (minimal stress) to 5 (maximum stress).

1. Your work and family obligations are more than you can manage sometimes. _____
2. You miss your spouse or another person close to you nearly every day. _____
3. Your body prevents you from doing what you love. _____
4. You struggle with loneliness and helplessness. _____
5. Your living arrangements aren't what you'd like. _____

QUESTION 1, your work and family obligations, gauges how much your obligations stress you out. Some seniors hate retirement, and others desperately need it but can't afford it. If you answered 1 or 2, you have a healthy balance of activities—family, friends, and maybe a sprinkling of work—to keep you occupied.

If you answered 3, 4, or 5, you are doing more than you have energy to do. Maybe you're raising the second generation of your family. Maybe you're nursing a beloved spouse or cannot afford to leave the work force. Whatever your reason for a full plate, something must change before stress begins to negatively affect you. Explore resources available to you, such as family or social services, to reduce your responsibilities. It's hard to admit you need help, but you must share your burden before you become the person needing care yourself.

QUESTION 2, you're missing someone special, explores the grief in your life. Senior adults have much to grieve as they lose their friends, spouses, health, and independence. If you answered 1 or 2, you are managing your grief by living the life you have and enjoying it to the fullest.

If you answered 3, 4, or 5, grief is stressing you out. Maybe you're pining away without your spouse. Maybe the hip replacement has got you down. Whatever you've lost, only you can lose your will to enjoy life. Stop and assess your priorities. Are you really ready to throw in the towel? Embrace something you love. Meet new people or enjoy old ones. Your life isn't over until you decide it is.

QUESTION 3, your body prevents you from doing what you want, explores your stress from losing your personal freedom. If you answered 1 or 2, you are either a senior adult blessed with a sound body and mind, or you've found ways to enjoy life fully despite a body that limits you or a disease that saps your energy.

If you answered 3, 4, or 5, you struggle to create a new life for yourself in the face of your lost independence. Maybe a surgery has left you unable to walk. Maybe your family has moved you into a home and someone else chooses your food and activities. Maybe you have a fully functioning mind but your body has failed and you're confined to a hospital bed or wheelchair.

Whatever the reason for your stress, you have the right to be angry and upset. No adult wants to be treated like a child, yet when you lose your car and your home and your ability to care for yourself, you've lost a lot. Still, only you can let the people in your life make all your decisions. Control what you can, how you spend your time, who you talk with, and how you maintain the life you're leading. No one can take away your dignity without your permission.

QUESTION 4, you struggle with loneliness and helplessness, gauges your social and emotional support. Depression is a serious condition in seniors that remains widely untreated. Yet there's no better blues buster than someone who cares! If you answered 1 or 2, you have great support and keep yourself connected with those you love and enjoy. This is keeping you resilient to stress and happy, despite whatever other hurdles come your way.

If you answered 3, 4, or 5, isolation from people who care is getting you down. What's the reason for your loneliness? Deceased spouse, family far away, friends lost over time, hobbies you can no longer do? There's no better time to meet new people than now. Most communities and group-living centers are filled with senior-friendly activities and volunteer opportunities. If you're homebound, there are organizations that offer visits and support. Ask, and you shall receive; but first, you have to ask.

QUESTION 5, your living arrangements are less than ideal, explores the stress from your immediate environment. Many seniors live in group homes or assisted-living facilities and struggle with the transition. If you answered 1 or 2, you are either lucky enough to still maintain your own home and independent life or you live in a community where your environment is clean, friendly, and fun.

If you answered 3, 4, or 5, where you live creates stress. Are you crammed into a room with an assigned roommate you didn't choose who drives you crazy? Do you live in a place where staff or other residents neglect or scare you? Did you move out of your home against your will? Even a palace can be a prison if you don't want to be there. Vent your frustrations to someone who cares. If a family member or staff member harms you in any way, file a complaint. Elder abuse is sadly prevalent but often goes unreported.

If you're living in your present conditions because you can no longer care for yourself, you have two choices. You can live in the past, dwelling on how wonderful your life used to be and fuming at how miserable you are now, or you can explore new opportunities around you. Is there a pretty garden outside? Does the center take field trips? Maybe you're a card shark and never knew it. A condition beyond your control may place you in community living against your will, but only you can give up your will to live.

Now that you've completed this quiz, review it again and record those questions where you received the highest scores. Select the one that is bothering you the most right now and brainstorm tools to relieve that stress in your stress journal. With time, as you manage this stressor, another one may pop up and require attention. That's okay. Effective stress management never ends because stress doesn't, either.

Maximizing Life to the Fullest

Stress is a normal response to the natural process of aging. When your body hurts and you slowly lose your independence and beloved peers, it's easy to give up on life. Many senior adults struggle with depression. According to the National Institutes of Health, 7 million people sixty-five and older have some form of depression. Causes of depression in the elderly include:

- **Death of a loved one.** The death of a spouse or sibling can cause intense grief and hopelessness that, if unmanaged, contributes to depression.
- **Feelings of uselessness.** Retired with empty nests, many seniors feel that they have no purpose in life.

- **Loneliness.** Being stuck at home or in a nursing home, unable to drive or walk, with friends dying all the time sounds like a nightmare. Welcome to the loss of a senior's social life.
- **Health problems.** Chronic disease, pain, complications from surgery, and loss of mobility all add to a senior's health worries.
- **Medications.** Some medications taken for other conditions can cause depression in seniors.
- **Fear of end-of-life issues.** Death, finances, and healthcare needs are common fears for senior adults.

Senior adults have a lot on their minds. All the more reason to bust that stress!

Depression Hits Seniors Hard

Many healthcare professionals ignore depression in seniors because they are treating other health conditions or the senior doesn't want to bother anyone. If you or a senior you love is retreating from life, unable to do what he once enjoyed, and skips meals and exercise, now's the time to act.

A root behavior of senior depression is negative thinking. "I'm old. Death's coming. What do I have left?" Plenty. Dwelling on your coming demise and limitations keeps you living in the past. Instead, live in the present and enjoy the time you have left.

Nurture hobbies, reach out to your community, pester your younger relations, give those cute nurses a hard time. Life's still interesting if you can muster the energy to plug in.

Fight the Futility of Old Age

Many seniors, especially those on the older end of the spectrum, experience a sense of uselessness that contributes to depression. They can't do what they used to do. Well, you are chock-full of wisdom and great stories from a life well lived. Share them with the younger generation, write a book, or volunteer in your community. If you're sharing what you have, rather than grumbling about what you don't have, you'll be much less stressed.

Shine Through the Golden Years

With a positive attitude, you can transform your senior years into some of the best years of your life. Consider the following suggestions to make the most of this time in your life:

- ❏ **Leave your mark on the world.** Donate to an art exhibit. Contribute your war story to the Veteran's Project of the National Archives. Mentor a child. Find something to impact the future, and shine.
- ❏ **Plug into your community.** Join a senior center, volunteer for the Red Cross, or teach classes at a youth center. You have gifts and time your community desperately needs. Just figure out how.
- ❏ **Make peace with your life.** Do you have conflicts or old wounds with family and friends? You don't have forever, so extend the olive branch. Even if they don't accept, you may just find that you have the peace you need to let go.
- ❏ **Live your life dreams.** Have a secret desire to scuba dive, rent a lighthouse, or see polar bears in the wild? It's never too late to live your dreams.
- ❏ **Let everyone know you love them.** Tell family and friends everything you want them to know. Be honest and open. Not only will it feel good, but it will free you up to enjoy life more.

Your life's still a book with many, many blank pages you can fill with adventures. Make the most of what you've got, and in the quest to enjoy life as much as possible, you may just find that you leave stress by the wayside.

When Retirement Isn't All It's Supposed to Be

Ideally, an adult will work full time for a number of years and then retire in comfort for the rest of her life. The reality, however, is much different. Some adults have inadequate income to meet their daily and healthcare needs, and must continue working past retirement age. Others never worked full time to begin with, and have no retirement to fall back on. An uncertain financial future as you age equals major stress.

The Retirement Myth

Some seniors experience the pressures of aging while working. Even worse, many seniors find themselves parenting again for adult children or abandoned grandchildren desperate for care. For these hardworking seniors, retirement and the rest and relaxation it should bring are a mere illusion.

Even those who saved adequately for retirement may find that they miss work. Work offers social connections and a sense of usefulness, in addition to an income. Some senior adults return to work after retirement just to fight boredom.

FACT

Retirement began in 1935 during the Great Depression. The Social Security Administration offered benefits to encourage older workers to leave the workforce so that younger workers could replace them, and retirement was born.

Make Your Senior Years Work for You

The dream retirement—carefree time spent lounging on a tropical beach—may not be your retirement. Figure out what you want to do with your golden years, and set goals to achieve it. If you know you'll miss your job, work part-time or stay on until your view changes. If family or finances keep you from taking some time to wind down, share your concerns with your family and brainstorm ways to lighten your load. Only you have the power to reduce your stress by changing its causes.

Stress and Health

The aging process itself creates pressure on the human body. As the body ages, it literally wears down. Joints hurt and then become arthritic. The heart and lungs weaken, and sometimes the mind, too.

Whether you're a senior watching your health deteriorate or nursing a loved one worse off than you, you know that health is a serious concern. You want to live as long as possible, and so do those you love. What's to be done, then, about the compounding stress of aging?

Plenty. Everything from enjoying your family to practicing yoga can improve your health and relaxation. Add the following tools to your stress-management toolbox to bust aging stress:

- **Nurture an open and supportive relationship with your doctor.** Be honest with your doctor about any symptoms, limitations, and pain you may have and pick his brain for ways to improve your quality of life.
- **Practice the Big Five Tools for Stress Resilience.** No matter your age, these tools will nip stress in the bud.
- **Engage your body.** Any gentle exercise routine keeps you healthy. Yoga and Tai Chi in particular can improve balance and joint functioning, decreasing your risk of a fall.
- **Engage your mind.** Learning something new not only prevents Alzheimer's, but it's fun.
- **Maintain your social networks.** Spend time with your families. Keep active with your friends in the community. Maybe even date if you're single. It's never too late in life to love.
- **Meditate.** Meditation busts stress before it even starts. Enjoy the "om" or the transcendental peace of your azaleas, whatever works for you.

The aches and pains of old age don't have to dominate your life. With stress-busting tools, you put aging in its proper place—as a stage of life—rather than as a stressor and depressor.

ALERT

Falls account for 70 percent of accidental deaths in seniors aged seventy-five and over, and more than 90 percent of hip fractures occur from a fall in the same population according to Dr. George Fuller of the White House Medical Clinic, Washington, D.C. Reduce body and fall stress by building up strong bones, and removing cords, rugs, and other items that could cause a fall, and watch where you walk.

Living When Those Around You Are Dying

The older you get, the more people around you will die. For those in the last half of life managing stress, you have two choices: let death be a stressor that masterminds you or choose to bust the stress of death. Let's be positive and chose the healthy choice. But how do you bust the stress of dying?

First, remember that death is a natural part of life. Death is the end. Death is also the unknown. Human beings like to know, and not knowing is scary. Hence, the fear of death. How do you accept that death is the unknown?

Accept Death as a Part of Life

Anyone who works in hospice or another field of end-of-life care can tell you that most people nearing death gain an acceptance of it before it happens and find peace with it. Since you're not dying, that may not make sense. Living as though death may, one day, make sense is something you can do. Yes, you are going to die. Someday. For now, do you want to worry about when that day comes or enjoy all the time you have left to the fullest?

Accepting death means making your own death a simple process with minimal suffering. A simple death . . . is that even possible? The growing hospice industry clamors, "Yes!" Hospice is a health-care service that provides you and your loved ones medical, social, and spiritual support in the home or hospital as you are dying.

Make a Plan to Manage Death

Even if you're not quite ready for a visit from a hospice nurse, you can make death easier on yourself. Make a plan. After this gloomy but necessary work is done, you can move on with enjoying life. Here are some ways you can control your dying process:

❑ **Explore hospitals and other long-term care centers in your area.** It may sound depressing to plan where you'd like to spend an illness or, heaven forbid, receive long-term care, but it's easier to make decisions when you're well. Make your power of attorney aware of your decision in case you are unable to make it yourself at the time, or better yet, include it in your living will. Do not be afraid to argue with your doctor or hospital who may want to choose services for you—you are the ultimate authority when it comes to your end-of-life care.

❏ **Decide on the medical care you would like to receive in a life-or-death situation.** Gloomy, yes, but if you know you don't want to end up a vegetable on life support, you will need to say so in writing to prevent it from happening. Many hospitals and doctors will keep you alive as long as possible unless someone—you or your family—says no. Make it easy on your family, and yourself; spell out how you'd like to spend your last days.

❏ **Plan your funeral.** If you plan your funeral, your grieving family doesn't have to. Plus, you can choose the funeral home, service, and gathering afterward. Include music, scripture, pictures, and stories that define who you are. Even write your own sermon as a goodbye to your loved ones. This surprise not only saves the pastor from slaving over what to say, but it can be a touching goodbye to those you love most.

❏ **Make and legalize your will.** No one wants the horror of hearing loved ones bickering about a legacy while they're still alive but unable to respond. Leave it in no doubt. Be honest and leave a copy with an unbiased person, such as your lawyer, to prevent family drama from misinterpreting your wishes.

❏ **Say what you want to say before it's too late.** Heal breaches, express love, and let people know what you mean to them now. They are too important to risk not having the opportunity to tell them so.

ESSENTIAL

Have grandchildren or great-grandchildren on the way you're concerned you'll never meet? Leave them a message in a bottle! Record yourself, audio or video, or write a letter telling them who you are, what you'd like them to know about you, and your advice for living a good life. What greater gift than "knowing" a loved one who died before you were even born?

There, you're done with the depressing end-of-life planning. You're not dead yet, and now that you've conquered fear of death by planning for it, there's nothing left to do but eat healthily, sleep, drink plenty of water, exercise, and have fun!

Seize the Day: Transform Senior Stress

The senior years hold many challenges. Aging is physically, mentally, and emotionally painful as seniors lose control over their bodies and, in some cases, their minds. Lost mobility often means loss of home and independence for formerly active adults. Finances and fear of the unknown can be other stressors senior adults bear in the last half of life.

With so many memories and losses, life can seem over already for many seniors dwelling in the past. Depression and despair consume many, while others worry about retirement and what it means for their lives. There are better ways to bust stress than to let it poison your remaining years. You can choose life every day in the smallest of ways.

Make the most of life, wherever you are, and share your wisdom and experience with others who need it. Be positive and look for what life's offering you now, rather than what life's taken from you. Your loved ones who've come before would want you to enjoy every ounce of life left in it. Only you can enjoy your life.

Stay active, nurture social ties, advocate for your healthcare choices, and plan the death you want in addition to the Big Five Tools for Stress Resilience. The more you embrace death and plan for it, the less time you have to dread it. Your life's never really over as long as you strive to live. Every day is a gift. Open and enjoy.

PART V

Accept Stress, Be Alive, and Thrive

CHAPTER 19

Get Out and Bust Stress

Now that you've explored stressors specific to life, family, work, finances, and relationships, as well as the stressors of each life stage, it's time to get down to the dirty work of putting what you've learned about your unique stress into practice. Explore important and popular ways of busting stress and decide which ones to add to your toolbox as the journey to mastermind your stress winds to a close.

Choosing to Master Stress

Remember the two choices for stress interaction: reacting to stress or responding to it? When you react, you let stress control you by automatically dashing into internal red-alert mode. All that mental and physical work for something as silly as a busy day or a crying child. Surely there are better ways to handle the stressors of life?

There are. You can respond to stress and consciously choose how to act. First, be aware of the stressor. Then, decide how to manage the stressor. Here's an example:

Dave runs a small auto parts store. It's Friday, and he's had a long day. He reaches for the door to flip the closed sign, and he notices his least favorite customer, a grumpy old lady with a habit of shaking her cane at him, approaching the door. Dave clenches his teeth. It's ten past five. The last thing he wants is to waste another hour of his time when he's supposed to take his son out to the movies tonight.

Dave has several choices. He can go on autopilot, serve this difficult customer, and risk ruining the rest of his evening, or he can stop and be aware of the situation. Dave considers his options: he could gently but firmly let this woman know they are closed, he could ignore her completely, he could pay another employee overtime to wait on her, or he could call his son and reschedule. Dave realizes he has a choice in managing this stressor. Rather than letting the stress of a difficult customer mastermind him, Dave remains in control.

Like Dave, you make choices every day about how you handle stressful situations. Sometimes, you make the choices on autopilot and cause yourself much unnecessary pain and misery. With practice you, like Dave, can plan for stressors and form options that work in your best interest.

Exploring the Inner Landscape

Choosing to master stress is a lifelong challenge for everyone. Some stressors get you every time, while others you can manage with practice and patience. Maintain that stress journal to increase awareness of your stressors as they crop up, and constantly seek new tools to bust the stress that you already have.

Self-Awareness Is Key to Busting Stress

The more you understand yourself, the better you'll be at busting your stress. Why? Well, stress is the reaction to internal and external pressure, right? Internal pressure results when you're not meeting your own inner needs. Ignore your emotions, dreams, physical or mental health, and you will experience stress. Unless you know what you need to be happy and healthy, you won't be effective at masterminding your stress.

ESSENTIAL

Curious about how to connect with your inner self? Pose the question to yourself daily in the mirror, "What do I really want today?" The answer just may surprise you. Living the answer, well, that's happiness.

Journaling, therapy, and other activities that promote personal growth develop your ability to understand your inner landscape. The more you journey inside yourself, the more you'll understand why stress pressures you from within your mind.

Pressure is also external. External pressure comes when forces outside you violate your boundaries. If you know what your boundaries are, you can protect them. Wonder why having to stay late at work without any notice leaves you with a headache? Your body is trying to tell you, yet again, that your boss violated your boundary.

Put Awareness Into Practice

Anytime someone or something upsets you, reflect upon why that bothered you. Many people aren't in the habit of saying no to intrusions on their time and energy simply because they don't even notice that the violation occurred. Assertiveness, prioritizing your time, and practicing honesty with yourself and others are important in minimizing external stressors in your life.

The more you learn about yourself, the greater your understanding of what you need to be happy and healthy. Your inner landscape is rich with gems of awareness just dying to surface and help mastermind the stress that keeps you bound in exhaustion, unhappiness, and fear. Begin a crusade against stress; practice awareness so that you can identify the enemy trying to destroy you.

Connecting Mind, Body, and Spirit

As a human being, you aren't just a body with physical needs or a mind with disembodied thoughts. You're a combination of mind, body, and spirit. Caring for your mind and body together is essential in a successful stress-management plan.

Why? Your mind and body, as separate but connected parts, both experience stress and need relief. You can't expect to have a healthy diet by eating healthy foods if you drink a lot of soda. It's also absurd to nurture one stress buster for the mind, such as meditation, while skimping on another that nurtures your body, such as exercise.

The Head- or Body-Centered Self

Most people gravitate to one extreme or the other. They are either very physical and body centered, or they are more intellectual and mind centered. Figure out which one you are by analyzing the tools you automatically use to bust stress. If they are heavy on one or the other, take note.

FACT

According to the Myers Briggs Personality type, there are two ways of engaging the world. Sensing people see life through the five senses, while intuitive people connect through their thoughts and insights. Roughly 60 percent of the U.S. population are sensing, while 40 percent are intuitive.

Common body-centered stress-busting tools include:

- Exercise
- Healthy eating
- Massage

- Gardening
- Salsa dancing
- Karate or other forms of martial arts

Common mind-centered stress-busting tools include:

- Meditation
- Nature escapes
- Traveling
- Art or other creative pursuits
- Therapy
- Addictive substances such as alcohol or nicotine

Next, work to develop stress-busting tools for your weaker area. Experiment with the ones above or mentioned throughout the book. Explore on your own, too. Diversifying your stress toolbox will make you more resilient to stress in your life, so it's well worth your time and effort. Read on to explore some popular tools that others use to manage stress in their lives.

Biofeedback

Biofeedback is a technique some people use to gain awareness of how their body functions. A practitioner will connect a client to a machine to explore involuntary bodily functions such as blood pressure and heart rate. The machine may beep or flash when the client tenses, encouraging her to do something different.

A client learns how certain actions, such as laughing, talking softly, and even positive thoughts, positively impact these bodily functions. Over time, the client learns behaviors that calm down her body, inspired by literally seeing proof of how these behaviors decrease her blood pressure.

Many people find biofeedback to be a helpful stress-reduction tool, as they have proof of how certain behaviors affect their brains. Enthusiasts insist, over time, that biofeedback retrains the automatic nervous system to be healthier. Whatever the case, biofeedback may be a tool you'd like to explore as you fill in your stress-management toolbox.

Creativity Therapy and Dream Journaling

Creative therapy and dream journaling are two popular ways to manage stress. Creative therapy employs any of the fine arts like music, dancing, painting, or writing for self-expression and healing. It can be done with a professional or on your own. Buy a painting set. Write a story. Take a mamba class. You are only limited by your own creativity.

Expressionism is an early twentieth century art movement in which artists expressed their emotions in vibrant colors and lines. Only later did art therapists encourage the stress-busting properties of this art technique.

Creativity, the Stress Reducer

Creativity is a powerful tool for stress reduction because it takes you to another world, a world of beauty that you, yourself, have created. Studies have shown that creativity boosts the immune system and brain functioning. It teaches mainstream, fast-paced modern people to use the other side of the brain: the doodling, curious, nonlinear side. Not only will this feel good, but it will make you well-balanced. You may even have fun at the same time.

Dreams Are Key to Awareness

Dream journaling is another tool for managing stress that employs an underused part of your mind, your unconscious. For centuries, people have speculated about what dreams really mean. Recording your dreams and studying possible meanings can be a fun way to learn about yourself.

Psychologist Carl Jung even believed dreams express urges hidden deep within your unconscious. Jungian dream work views every character in a dream as a part of you, interacting with another part of yourself. Each dream, according to Jung, is a cry from your unconscious mind for change of some kind.

Whether you explore your dreams for fun or to communicate with your unconscious mind, dream therapy is another way to focus on your inner life and bust stress by boosting self-awareness.

Friend Therapy

Another easy tool for stress management is friend therapy. It sounds professional, but really friend therapy is as simple as a weekly coffee date. Too many adults neglect their social needs in the frenzy of modern life. There's nothing like a true friend, someone who understands you and cares for you just as you are.

With more people substituting work for social time, maintaining good friendships is often a casualty. Remember that human beings are social creatures who need others to survive. Like eating and drinking, everyone needs a laugh, a shoulder to cry on, or someone who cares enough to listen during the tough times.

A best friend doesn't have to be a childhood friend. Cultivate several best friends, people who complete you because they offer an encouraging smile, sound advice, and a nonjudgmental presence. Make time for these people in your life, and you'll have a proven tool against stress—knowing you're not alone in it!

Hypnosis

Hypnosis is a stress-busting tool growing in popularity. Hypnosis, like meditation, is an altered state of consciousness that promotes relaxation. Unlike meditation, hypnosis is induced by a practitioner. Under hypnosis, you experience a deep calm and ability to focus intently on a specific thought or feeling.

Professionals use hypnosis to treat a variety of negative behaviors, according to the Mayo Clinic, including smoking and overeating. Hypnotism also helps patients manage extreme pain, asthma, surgery, chemotherapy, and mental illness. If you have one stressor that's continually hijacking your life, hypnosis may be a tool for your toolbox.

FACT

Past-life therapists claim to use hypnosis to connect with a client's past lives. The therapist then heals current life stressors by engaging with the past-life personality. Those who find stress relief from this type of hypnosis claim that working through a past life rapidly solved whatever problem they were experiencing.

Optimism Therapy and Reward-Based Self-Training

Optimism is a type of therapy that—you guessed it—works on being positive. A therapist treats clients with extreme stress due to trauma, such as abuse or rape, and offers a positive worldview to combat the client's negativity and personal pain. After extensive exposure to positive people and thinking patterns, clients of optimism therapy in a closed setting, such as a psychiatric ward, often improve greatly in general happiness and decreased mental anguish.

Optimism therapy serves to demonstrate that if you surround yourself with positivity, inside and outside your head, you're setting yourself up for success. Choose to put optimism in your toolbox. Dwell on the positive. Give thanks for highlights of your life daily. Tape an inspiring quote on the mirror, or practice smiling. You may just find that you enjoy life despite yourself.

Reward-based self-training can also help you bust stress. If you've ever trained a dog, you've used positive reinforcement training. Don't do this (negative behavior) and you get a treat (positive reward).

Positive reinforcement can be a powerful stress buster for you, both in training a puppy and in managing your stress. Choose a bad behavior you do to manage stress, such as that high calorie latte Frappuccino with whole-fat whipped cream, and tell yourself, "If I don't drink the latte, I will make my favorite Greek salad for dinner." There. You've effectively substituted an unhealthy coping mechanism, a high calorie drink with lots of sugar and caffeine, for a healthy coping mechanism, cooking a tasty meal you love. With time and practice, you'll be trained to choose healthy stress-management tools as treats to inspire you through the day.

Tai Chi and Other Martial Arts

Many people bust stress with participation in the martial arts. Marital arts include Tai Chi, Kung Fu, Karate, Jujitsu, and several other ritualized forms of self-defense. Nothing busts stress quite like breaking a wooden board or throwing your opponent to the ground. Martial arts aren't just about power and control, though. Every martial art takes intense concentration and practice, and many include meditation in their forms.

Tai Chi is a particular martial art that promotes relaxation and healing. An ancient series of Chinese movements, Tai Chi exercises different systems of the body to achieve balance. Tai Chi is easy for any age and activity level, and a great introductory practice for someone seeking to enter the martial arts.

If you'd like to meditate but have trouble sitting still and doing nothing, a martial art such as Tai Chi could provide you the mind/body connection you're missing. Martial arts are also social activities, so you could meet more people with similar interests and even develop a hobby along the way.

Yoga

Yoga, like meditation, is a classic stress buster. A term for various Indian exercises designed to unite body, mind, and spirit, yoga includes poses that require intense concentration as well as controlled breathing. A yoga form, a series of distinct poses, done properly, induces a meditative trance that is both relaxing and refreshing.

FACT

There are six basic types of Yoga: Hatha Yoga (Yoga of Postures), Bhakti Yoga (Yoga of Devotion), Raja Yoga (Yoga of Control), Jnana Yoga (Yoga of the Mind), Karma Yoga (Yoga of Service), and Tantra Yoga (Yoga of Rituals). In the Western World, Hatha Yoga is the type most commonly practiced.

Yoga is easy to begin, but difficult to master without patience and persistence. Like meditation, yoga is a discipline that improves the more you invest in it. If you're looking for a way to relax in a group, improve your posture, and refresh your mind, yoga may be just what you're missing.

CHAPTER 20

When You Can't Manage Your Own Stress

As you've journeyed through this book, you've encountered many stressors and many stress-management tools. You have an idea of what stresses you out, and you've explored tools to manage different stressful situations. Despite the best stress-management plan, stress sometimes becomes too much to handle alone. Learn resources at your disposal in times of crisis to complete your well-balanced stress-management plan.

What Is a Crisis?

Sometimes, stress becomes so great that you simply can't manage it. Sure you can mastermind stress, and indeed should if at all possible, but some stressors are too much all at once. A crisis is just such an event.

A crisis is literally an emergency scenario where you're at a 6—the maximum stress possible. For stress-management purposes, there are external and internal crises, triggered by external and internal pressure. Examples of external crises include:

- A dangerous car accident
- Your child runs away from home
- A loved one dying suddenly and unexpectedly
- Being robbed
- Your spouse threatens you
- Terrorists bomb your city

You get the idea. The above situations, and others like them, result from stressors beyond your control. Other crises occur within your body and mind. Examples of these include:

- Depression
- Midlife crisis
- Grief
- Spiritual identity
- Fear of death
- Alzheimer's and other mind-altering conditions

Internal crises begin inside you, but eventually affect others, too. Whether a crisis begins inside or outside of you, you must make a radical shift in your stress-management approach to mastermind the crisis. You have to admit your current weakness: stress is in control and you can't stop it.

Create Stress-Management Resources

If your stress level is as high as it can possibly be, your body and mind are not functioning correctly. Your body is on red alert, primed for dangers.

Adrenaline is pumping through your body, and you can't sit still. You are not in the best condition to make important decisions.

ESSENTIAL

You also may be unable to manage the stress alone. Heck, if you could manage the stress, it wouldn't be at maximum! A smart stress-management plan includes a plan for resources that can help you bring down your stress level in a crisis.

Some crisis-busting resources are obvious—such as calling 911 if you're having a heart attack. Others, such as asking for help, counseling, spiritual direction, and medication, may not be on your radar screen. All can ease your burden in a crisis.

Ask for Help

The first step in managing crisis stress is to ask for help. No one wants to admit that she cannot handle her own problems. But the fact is, knowing you need help is a sign of strength. Congratulate yourself on the awareness that you are maxed out on stress and cannot function alone.

Support Busts Crisis Stress

Crisis stress can decrease with something as simple as another person on board. You may be so frustrated from trying to start the car so you can get to your very important job interview, that you didn't even notice the parking brake was on. After a crying fit, you finally ask your roommate for help and voila! She notices what you didn't.

FACT

Another reason to ask for help is the fact that just talking about your stress relieves it. Even though you just got fired and the company accused you of embezzling funds and has a warrant out for your arrest, at least you've gotten it off your chest!

Include a trusted person in your stress-management toolbox as an individual to call in times of crisis. Promise yourself that you will take the time to brief him on the situation before you make any decisions. Hopefully, between the two of you, you can make informed decisions about how to proceed.

Counseling: Help in a Mental-Health Crisis

If you're in crisis but have no clue how to stop it or feel mentally out of control, a counselor may be the tool for you. Awareness is the first step to managing stress. A good counselor can listen to your problems and share her assessment of what's going on, giving you the awareness you need to bust the stress. You can find the sense of direction you desperately need to start busting that crisis stress and get on with life.

Counseling for Crisis Management Support

Other people can offer counseling for general crisis management besides a traditional therapist. Social workers, ministers, chaplains, natural medicine practitioners, and institutional psychologists are other resources for talking and advice if you have no clue how to proceed in your crisis. Consider keeping a counselor's contact info in your possession, in case the day comes when you and your family need help seeing the road signs out of a crisis.

Counseling for Mental-Health Crisis

A mental-health crisis requires a counselor for different reasons. If you're struggling with wanting to commit suicide or wanting desperately to harm someone else, do not wait for an appointment with a counselor. Call 911 or take yourself to the nearest hospital. A counselor can help, however, if you know you're having trouble managing your thoughts, feelings, and behaviors but have no clue how to proceed. A counselor can recommend a course of action, such as therapy or treatment, that may ease your crisis, and he can also refer you to other mental-health professionals who may better suit your needs.

Spiritual Direction

A spiritual crisis is another source of intense stress that many people have no clue how to manage. Intense grief, anger at life, a sense of helplessness, and a yearning for answers are all signs of a spiritual crisis. While a spiritual crisis may not be as life threatening as a physical or mental crisis, a spiritual crisis is a little known but powerful source of internal stress. Examples of spiritual crises include:

- Intense fear of death
- Intense grief over a loss
- Wanting answers after a traumatic event such as abuse or rape
- Trying to make meaning out of life
- Struggling with a major life changing event such as divorce
- Seeking reconciliation with one's concept of the divine despite one's sins

Answering Life Questions with Religion

In today's world, many people are asking questions about life and death issues and want answers about life's meaning and purpose. Religion traditionally answers such questions, and if you have a religious tradition this could be a place to start. If you're asking these questions and haven't found the answers directly through your religious group, spiritual direction may be the stress-management tool you're missing.

Spiritual Direction for Spiritual Guidance

A spiritual director is a professional grounded within a religious tradition to listen to you while you explore the roots of your spiritual stress. Though a spiritual director may be a church pastor or counselor, he doesn't have to be. Spiritual directors do not force religion upon you or tell you what to believe. Rather, they encourage you as you explore the nature of your beliefs and actively support your spiritual development, through prayer or other rituals unique to a religious tradition, or by whatever means work for you.

A typical spiritual direction session lasts between thirty minutes to an hour. The spiritual director will ask you if there's a particular issue or concern that brought you to spiritual direction. The director will then encourage you to share your struggle. The more honest you are, with him and with yourself, the faster you can bust that stress.

Like a counselor, a spiritual director can offer you a direction out of your crisis. Find one through a church or retreat center in your community, and add the contact information to your stress-management toolbox.

Is Medication the Answer?

Anxiety, constant internal stress, can be a crisis in and of itself. With high anxiety, you cannot think clearly or determine which stressors are real and which are imaginary. Stress is truly masterminding your life.

If you lack the ability to figure out what's causing anxiety, prescription medication can be a useful tool to reduce your stress so that you can think clearly. Medication can literally alter the way your brain is firing, so that the stress response eases on the cellular level. Common anxiety medications include:

- Selective serotonin reuptake inhibitors (SSRIs) such as Lexapro, Zoloft, and Prozac that boost production of serotonin, a feel-good brain chemical.
- Serotonin and norepinephrine reuptake inhibitors (SNRIs) such as Effexor and Wellbutrin boost serotonin and the brain chemical norepinephrine for mood modification.
- Benzodiazepines such as Xanax and Valium calm the stress response quickly after use.
- Azapirones such as BuSpar gradually decrease anxiety symptoms.

No anxiety drug should ever be taken lightly. Many have irritating side effects such as dry mouth, shaking, constipation, and a spaced-out feeling. Anti-depressants used for anxiety (SSRIs and SNRIs) can cause depression and serious withdrawal symptoms if abruptly ended. Benzodiazepines are extremely addictive.

Not every drug works for every person, and it may be necessary to try several over a period of six months to a year to find an anxiety medication that works for you.

Medication Is Not a Magic Cure

Anti-anxiety medications aren't a cure-all for anxiety. The stress triggers are still out there, and if you're like most people, only you have the power to identify and bust your stressors to truly manage anxiety. Consider medication, along with therapy and spiritual direction, as a possible tool to manage short-term crippling anxiety, and include it with counseling for the best chance of busting crisis stress.

ALERT

SSRI anti-depressants manage depression and anxiety by changing the brain chemicals that control your moods, emotions, and thought patterns. LCD and Ecstasy are two other drugs that affect the brain in the same way. Take SSRIs only under the guidance of a mental-health professional and in the correct dosage to keep the drug working for you, and not against you.

Professionals recommend combining therapy and medication for the best chance of managing anxiety. If all you do is take medication, you'll never learn exactly why you get stressed, nor will you learn ways to cope with that stress.

The Power of Listening

Maintaining healthy and trusting relationships is an essential tool for crisis prevention in your stress-management toolbox. There's no better stress buster than sharing your burdens with someone who cares. In a crisis, a good friend keeps you sane, makes you laugh, and helps you carry the burdens of life.

Sadly, many people lack the social support they need to manage stress effectively. A study in the *American Sociological Review* found that the average American had three close friends in 1985, but only two in 2006. Sadly, 10 percent of people interviewed in 1985 had no close friends, and in 2006 the percentage had risen to 25 percent.

QUESTION

How do you make friends?
An adult makes friends the same way a second grader does: through shared life experiences. Participate in group activities, do what you love, don't be too desperate, and keep putting yourself out there no matter how tired or lonely you are. Remember, a true friend is supposed to be hard to find!

If you are one of the growing number of adults too busy for friends because you're already overworked and juggling too many things, stop and evaluate your life. Who used to be a part of your life who you really miss, but just lost track of? Who would you like to get to know better, but just haven't taken the time?

Building a friendship takes time, trust, and commitment. Why is it so much easier to work late than set a date for bowling? You fit sleep, healthy meals, plenty of water, and exercise into your schedule, right? How about making time for a friend? You are worth it.

Supporting Others in Times of Crisis

Just as you need friends and family, they need you in times of crisis. Be the best support you can be. Nothing's worse than bad advice, platitudes, or people who just won't leave; some people become a stressor when they're really trying to help. If you want to help others during times of crisis, practice the following guidelines:

❑ **Offer the person what they need.** Ask the person in crisis what you can do for her, and follow her wishes as she expresses them. No one likes others to take charge without first asking.

❏ **Jump in.** If something desperately needs to be done but isn't being done, do it. Treat the person in the way you would want to be treated, with genuine kindness.

❏ **Focus on keeping the person in crisis safe.** Keep the person safe and comfortable until other help is available.

❏ **Don't make the person talk about what's wrong if she is not comfortable doing so.** She is going through enough without the burden of others expecting her to relive it.

❏ **Watch for symptoms of shock.** Look out for denial, staring blankly into space, shivering, dizziness, clammy skin, sweating, rapid pulse, and nausea. Encourage the person to sit down and rest. Offer her water, a warm blanket, or a dark, quiet room. In extreme cases, the person may require medical attention.

❏ **Wait several days to offer your advice on the situation.** Don't volunteer your opinion right away unless the person asks you directly for it or they are in physical danger. If that is the case, call 911 immediately.

❏ **Check in with the person.** Let her know she is not alone by checking in with her daily or every couple of days to see how she is doing and offer any additional support you can.

It's easy to support others in times of crisis, becoming a tool to manage their stress, rather than an additional stressor adding to their nightmare. Plus if you're there for someone else in the worst of times, she is more likely to be with you through your crises, too.

No one has to manage severe stress alone. Indeed, your chances of braving the storm increase if you reach out around you for help. Have a life saver waiting in your stress-management toolbox for just such a day: ask a friend to be there for you in a crisis, collect the phone number for a counselor or spiritual director, and talk with your doctor if you're considering medication. The more you plan for any stress, including a crisis, the better you'll be able to mastermind it in the long run.

CHAPTER 21

Stress and Change, Hope for a Better Life

A broken-down car, chemotherapy side effects, a ranting client, a child failing math—stress never seems to end. That's because life doesn't. Life's constantly changing, and with that change comes pressure to adapt. As this journey to mastermind your stress nears its end, find hope in your power to embrace stress as a force for positive change in your life.

Stress Comes from Change

Remember stress: the reason you've stuck with this book so far. Whether stress is a headache (internal) or the screaming baby (external) you want it to end. That's normal. The problem is that stress is more than just your annoyance. Stress has a message for you: a message about how to live the best life you can possibly live.

If there's stress, something's pressuring you. What's the cause? Change. You have a headache—big deal. Something changed to cause that headache—too much work, excessive computer use—and your body screams at you because it does not like the change. So you cut back on work, watch your computer time, and take a pain pill, and figure the problem is over, right?

Not quite. Every stressor in your life is caused by change. Losing sleep over your baby girl leaving for college? Enter stress. Change, specifically the change in your family and relationship with your child, triggers pressure on you. What's happening next, what will life be like, who am I without my kids?

If change is a normal part of life, why do you stress so much? Why can't you just go with the flow? No one likes to lose control. No one likes to feel helpless. As you struggle with any change—from increased television volume to burying a spouse—you struggle with your own desire for life to be the same the way it was before the change hit.

The Benefits of Change

Even though you resist change because you like things the way they are, change benefits you in the long run. That's because, no matter how much you hate it, you're mortal. Mortals change as they grow. Children have different concerns and experiences than senior adults do, though often these two age groups share the wisdom to enjoy life fully.

If you resist the change that is a natural part of living successfully in the world, you create stress for yourself. Think of the child who refuses to learn math because he hates it. Sure he hates it, but that's because it's hard for him. If he continues to avoid math, and really never learns how to do it, then for the rest of his life any time that he has to deal with numbers, he will experience stress.

If the child sucks it up and learns math, though, then he increases his resilience to stress. Why? He knows how to do math. He still may not like it, but it no longer has power over him. Managing your stress is just like learning math as a child. You may hate it—detest even thinking about your stress when you're not actually stressed—but in the long run you're better off because you faced it.

ESSENTIAL

Buddhist leader and teacher Daisaku Ikeda encourages everyone to embrace change for personal freedom and peace. "Buddhism holds that everything is in constant flux," Ikeda writes, "thus the question is whether we are to accept change passively and be swept away by it or whether we are to take the lead and create positive changes on our own initiative." In the spirit of Ikeda, how can you accept change and release the stress surrounding it?

No one wants to deal with stress. Yet stress is a signal of change. Now, whether the change is one you want to embrace or challenge is up to you. First, you must know the difference between healthy and unhealthy change.

Embracing Change

Life is full of change. Change is neither good nor bad. It just is. Change can have healthy or unhealthy consequences on your life, though. Learn to embrace healthy change and resist unhealthy change, and add a whole new layer of prevention to your stress-management toolbox.

Resist Unhealthy Changes

Some changes can be unhealthy when they breach your boundaries: the personal security system that protects your energy, emotions, and time. If your boss, for example, makes you work overtime for weeks until a project is done and you're now skipping the gym time you need to keep your cholesterol down, that's an unhealthy change. Some boundaries, such as healthy diet, sleep, free time, relationships, and personal expression, are essential to who you are, and require your constant protection. Changes to these habits could negatively impact you: don't gamble your basic needs for less basic ones. That's unhealthy change.

Embrace Healthy Changes

Healthy change involves breaking patterns of behavior that keep you from living the healthiest and fullest life possible. What do you do now that causes you stress in the long term? Common examples include:

- Smoke or drink, which increases risk of disease and decreases life span.
- Sacrifice family time for extra work time. Someday, you may realize you don't know your kids or your spouse anymore.
- Eat whatever you want based on what tastes good at the time.
- Avoid your own inner life—your thoughts and desires. They just may hijack you during the midlife crisis or at another time when you least expect it.
- Steer clear of your deepest desire out of fear of the myth that you're "just too busy."

Anything you're avoiding that would make you healthier and happier causes stress. Again, stress is a signal that change needs to happen in your life so you can be truly healthy and happy.

Explore in your stress journal what unhealthy changes in your life violate your boundaries and what healthy changes you could make in your life to be happier and healthier. Brainstorm some ways to reverse the effects of the unhealthy change as well as ways to practice a healthy change. You may just find that some stress magically disappears as you take the pressure off yourself by knowing and considering the change in your life.

Making New Expectations of Stress

Throughout this book, you've explored various stressors—financial, family, relationships, and money to name a few—and how they affect you. The emphasis on what exactly has stressed you out offered you awareness so you could bust the stress. After all, busting stress should be your ultimate goal because stress is bad, and you don't want it, right?

Stress Can Be Good and Bad

Stress itself is neither good nor bad. Too often, stress is bad for you when it hijacks your life and ruins your day. That's why this book spends so much time encouraging you to develop a stress-management toolbox and notice your stressors, so that you have the power to see what's actually going on in your life.

Once you can manage the superficial level—what's stressing you out and how to stop it—a deeper level of stress management emerges. Stress is also a signal that something's going on in your life. Change is happening. What is the change? What are you, the harbinger of your destiny, going to do about it?

FACT

Harvard Medical School's HealthBeat online newsletter recommends having small, achieveable goals—"I will watch calories at lunch"—with practical ways to reach it—"I will substitute a salad for the French fries." Over time, more positive changes can be made in a similar slow and careful manner.

Accept the Gifts Stress Brings

Instead of moaning about stress and its power over yourself and others, consider the gift stress can bring. Something's happening in your life. Do you want it to happen? Do you want to stop it? What do you need to be healthy and happy?

Take some time in your journal and reflect on major sources of stress in your life. What changes do you see in your life at large that's fueling the stress? Examples might include:

- **Retirement stress** comes from fear of the aging process.
- **Parenting stress** comes from the fact that your kids are growing up fast, and you can't keep up.

- **Technology stress** means that you wish you were better with the computer because it would make life so much easier.
- **College stress** comes from the fear of what job you'll be doing for the rest of your life.
- **Commuter stress** comes from the fear that the back pain from driving too much is more than you can bear.

Your examples will, undoubtedly, be different. What is important is that you find answers that work for you. Did you connect your stressors with changes in your life? What changes are healthy and a natural part of life, and what changes are unhealthy and best abandoned?

Transforming Stress to Work for You

Now that you've connected major life stressors with changes in your life, you have all the information you need to transform your stress. Stress is pressure, yes, but who says that pressure can't work for you? Recall earlier when you explored a stressor and then a change in your life fueling the stressor. Whether you accept or resist that change can alter how much stress the change generates in your life.

Accept What You Can't Change

Here's an example. You connected your Level 4 severe stress over your retirement plan with your fear of aging and dying. It's not really retirement savings that stress you out; mostly it's what retirement represents: the day when you're too old to work and be independent. You have now gained some self-awareness! Aging is a natural part of life and therefore a healthy change as you continue to mature and share your wisdom with others. If you accept that you're mortal and age, you'll save yourself a lot of stress over retirement in general and aging in particular.

Resist What You Can Change

If your stress is caused by an unhealthy stressor, your plan of action would change. Let's say you connected your Level 5 stress over your irritable bowel syndrome with the change in your work schedule that caused you to you travel constantly and always eat fast food and soda. In this case, the change—a job on the go—is an unhealthy change, change that's harming your ability to enjoy life.

If you accept this change and keep working, your health is likely to deteriorate further. Be bold and say no to the change in diet that's hurting your health. Pack lunches and healthy snacks to avoid eating on the road as a short-term stress buster, and consider finding an office job as a long-term stress buster.

ALERT

In his 2009 book *The Depression Cure*, Dr. Stephen S. Ilardi credits the many changes in work, family, and technology and the stress they generate with higher levels of depression in Westernized countries.

Be Patient as You Adjust to Change

No one can fight unhealthy change, such as poor diet, or accept a healthy change, such as aging is a normal part of life, instantly. It takes time, conversations, practice, and maybe even the help of a professional counselor to figure out all the ways you are blocking your ability to be happy and healthy. One thing is for certain, when you make decisions with your health and happiness in mind, your stress will lessen considerably.

Practice with stressors and changes unique to your life. Explore in your stress journal why, exactly, this stressor bothers you. Remember that you can reduce your stress by either accepting the change or fighting it, if it's unhealthy change. Only you have the power to shape your destiny.

Mastermind Your Stress for a Balanced and Healthy Life

Masterminding stress truly takes hard work, patience, and practice. Live daily the Big Five Tools for Stress Resilience: healthy diet, adequate sleep, water, exercise, and fun. Wield other tools such as meditation and positive thinking to bust mental stress, and still others, such as exercise or massage, to bust body stress. Be sensitive to stressors particular to various aspects of modern life—technology and family—but also stressors unique to your particular stage in life. Then examine the stressors you're trying to bust to decide whether to accept or fight the change.

Stress Is Rooted in Change

All your stress is rooted in changes, large and small, that happen to you every day. A rude person can be a change that drains your energy, which equals stress. Old relationships can also dredge up painful experiences from the past that never changed and healed. The domineering mother-in-law calls with her never-ending demands, and the change of her call in your day changes the course of your afternoon. Every stressor you experience and analyze every day comes from change.

How many of these stressors you want to analyze is up to you. Small stressors, anything 1 to 2 on the stress scale, usually go away with stress-busting tools and time. Other stressors, 3 and 4, can easily flare into a 5—maximum stress—if not explored.

Stress-Management Tools Boost Stress Awareness

Your stress-management journal offers a place to explore how you're doing, what's bothering you, and what needs busting. Eventually, your stress journal may even be programmed into your head and you'll be able to make "entries" such as: "Feeling tired (stressor). Take a ten minute walk around the building (tool to bust it)." Truly, what better program could you possibly have running, all the time, in your head? You're on autopilot to nip stress in the bud, whether it's minimal or severe. Congratulations on making such a commitment to yourself. You'll never regret it.

Self-Evaluation: How Can You Mastermind Your Stress?

As this book draws to a close, your journey to mastermind your stress is just beginning. Accept the following quiz as your parting gift. Explore your power, right now, to manage your stress and discover ways to increase it in your lifelong quest to bust stress before it busts you.

For each of the following questions, rate each on a scale of 1 to 5. One means that you are very comfortable with the statement presented, and five means you are extremely uncomfortable with the statement.

1. You know consciously when you're stressed out before you experience physical or mental symptoms. _____
2. You have all the tools you need to manage your stress. _____
3. The tools you use to cope with stress are healthy, and you have no problems expressing your stress, and do not take your stress out on others. _____
4. You completely accept yourself for who you are and are proud of the life you've led. _____
5. You are aware of the changes happening in your life right now and, if you haven't already accepted or rejected them, you're in the process of actively doing so. _____

ESSENTIAL

Prepare ahead of time for a difficult person or family member intruding into your day and bringing unwanted stress. Sketch out in your stress journal what you will say or do to minimize that person's negative effects on you, and maybe role-play with a trusted friend or therapist. With practice, difficult people will lose the power to hijack your day.

QUESTION 1, your knowledge of stress as it happens, gauges your awareness in the face of stress. If you answered 1 or 2, you know yourself well enough to see when you're becoming stressed and do something about it. Maybe you're naturally talented, have had therapy for years, or this book just taught you everything you need to know. Whatever the reason for your awareness, still practice caution. Everyone has stressors that trick them every once in a while. What's important is that, most of the time, you're aware.

If you answered 3, 4, or 5, you can't always catch stress before you're riding the roller coaster. That's okay. Knowing yourself takes time, dedication, and a drive to understand who you are and what motivates you. Use your stress journal to track stressful events after they occur and notice what triggered the stress, and then practice doing something different the next time the same stressor happens. Keep trying, and your awareness will improve.

QUESTION 2, you have all the tools you need to manage stress, explores how well-organized and stocked your stress-management toolbox really is. If you answered 1 or 2, you have plenty of tools on hand to bust physical, mental, and emotional stress. The Big Five Tools for Stress Resilience are old friends for you, and you're always open to new activities and methods to bust your stress. You excel at handling the daily stressors of work and family, and you have balance and clarity in your life most of the time.

If you answered 3, 4, or 5, your stress-management toolbox could use some attention. Do you neglect sleep, healthy diet, exercise, water, or fun? Is trying something new and different for relaxation something that happens to other people? Fear not. Developing healthy tools to bust your stress is as easy as a daily walk, eight hours of sleep, and playing with the dog. Begin with the Big Five, and choose one tool a week for the next month until you've mastered them all (more than likely you already have at least one under control).

QUESTION 3, you use healthy tools to manage stress and never take it out on others, looks at how healthy your coping tools are. If you answered 1 or 2, you manage stress in healthy ways that do not harm yourself or others. You know how you cope with stress when you are cornered or tired, and you work hard not to lash out at others, be passive aggressive, or overeat—whatever your negative stress-busting tools may be. Instead, you practice the Big Five plus other tools such as friend therapy and religious guidance to keep your life balanced and fun.

If you answered 3, 4, or 5, you may cope with stress in ways harmful to yourself or others. Do you smoke or drink? Do you take out your stress on others? Do you know you're living a lifestyle that's bad for you, but don't know how to stop? It's never too late to substitute healthy stress busters for unhealthy ones. Begin with the Big Five: sleep, healthy diet, water, exercise, and fun. Seek help for copings that are especially harmful such as smoking or abusive behavior. Explore ways around you to have fun, and try something new. Select healthy tools for your toolbox, and be patient with yourself in the process. Changing habits won't happen overnight, but it will happen if you stick with it!

QUESTION 4, you accept yourself and where you are in life, measures how happy you are with your life at present. If you answered 1 or 2, you know who you are, what you want, and where you're going. You rarely, if at all, experience stress from intense fears about your identity. Congratulations! You accept yourself, and of course you want to protect yourself from stress. Your positivity about yourself is an invaluable tool for your toolbox that will guide you through many storms to come.

If you answered 3, 4, or 5, you are fighting who you are. What about yourself can you not accept: your age, sexuality, marital status, weight? You are fighting yourself at every turn, and it's stressing you out. Take some time to explore what changes in your life trigger your greatest stressors. Are these changes healthy ones you need to accept, or unhealthy ones you want to fight? You can't expect anyone else to love you until you accept who you are right now. It's never too late to get started.

QUESTION 5, what are the changes in your life, explores your current relationship with change. Is change a friend or foe? Do you fight it, embrace it, or both? If you answered 1 or 2, you're comfortable with change. You may not always like it, but you can handle it.

FACT

According to several polls, police officers have one of the most stressful jobs in America in 2010. Sergeant Neil Springer of the Parsons Kansas Police Department handles his high-stress profession by thinking first. "Plan ahead for the worst," the sergeant recommends, "and have a plan on how to deal with it."

If you answered 3, 4, or 5, you're your own worst enemy. You may fight any change, or worse, stress about all aspects of it, missing the gift of your life, now. Well, stop it. Accept that change is normal. Explore the changes in your life, and make peace with them. Knowledge about yourself and your life goals fuel any successful stress-management program. Learn who you are, where you're going, and get started protecting that very special person from the stressors of daily life.

Now that you've completed the last quiz in this book, stop and assess. Open up your stress journal one more time. Record the questions with the highest scores, and select the one that makes your life extremely uncomfortable now. This is your weakest power in masterminding stress. Take some of the included suggestions to heart, or try some of your own. Be your own friend and support the person responsible for managing your life and your stress—you.

You have two options as you journey from this book into your life. The first is that you can continue to let stress manage you. Take a moment, breathe deeply, and remember all the ways that stress ravages your body, mind, and spirit days and weeks after a stressful event or series of events. Is that really life, running ragged on the stress roller coaster against your will? Is that really the life you want for yourself and for those you love?

The other option is to accept responsibility, acknowledge that you are in charge of your life, and take control of your stress. Masterminding your stress won't be easy—work never ends, there are no vacations, you're your own worst enemy—but the reward, a healthy and balanced life, is priceless.

Your goal is to be just like a virtual Sim. Notice the bar above your head screaming red because you need food, sleep, exercise, water, or fun. Practice stress busters like a dinner party or meditation to keep that bar green and healthy, and you, too, will win at life. Good luck as you continue the rest of your journey, and remember: you are the expert on you!

APPENDIX A

Recipes for Relaxation

Whole grains, green vegetables, and lean meats are only a few foods that bust stress as part of a healthy diet. Enjoy this collection of stress-busting recipes for food, drink, and rest, and add some of your own.

Rest De-Stress Fruit Salad

Fruits high in vitamin C such as kiwi, strawberries, and oranges boost your immune system and nurture your skin, hiding any stress-induced wrinkles. Try this version of the basic fruit salad to rest and relax your senses and skin.

INGREDIENTS | SERVES 4

1 kiwi, cut into slices

1 cup strawberries, washed and diced

1 medium-sized orange, peeled, segmented, and cut into chunks

1 medium-sized crisp apple, such as Granny Smith or Braeburn, peeled and diced

½ cup washed seedless grapes of either color

½ teaspoon lemon juice

Prepare all fruit and place in a bowl. Mix in lemon juice. Chill for at least twenty minutes, and then serve with sparkling water for a refreshing and cleansing dessert or mid-meal treat.

Cinnamon Brain Boost Oatmeal

Oatmeal jump-starts your day with a heavy dose of fiber, easing digestive distress. This superfood also contains high levels of carbohydrates that stimulate serotonin, the feel-good juice, in your brain. Try oatmeal with cinnamon, nutmeg, and cloves for a warming twist on a breakfast classic.

INGREDIENTS | SERVES 1

½ cup quick oats

Dried nutmeg, cloves, and cinnamon, to taste

Sugar, to taste

Prepare quick oats according to directions on the package. When it's the desired consistency, add the spices and sugar to taste. Try using more of the spices than the sugar to enjoy their warmth and depth. Serve with a side of fresh fruit (see Rest De-Stress Fruit Salad recipe) for a balanced start to your day.

Refreshing Hydration Tea

If you get tired of drinking eight glasses of water, try this easy way to jazz up glasses four through six. Herbal teas are flavorful, scented, and have no added caffeine or calories—making your water healthy with a very little something extra.

INGREDIENTS | SERVES 4–6

Four tea bags of herbal tea, such as peppermint, chamomile, and hibiscus
A kettle full of water
Pitcher filled with ice

Boil kettle of water. Place tea bags into boiling water, and make pot of tea. Allow to steep until cool, about a half hour or longer. Pour warm tea over ice in pitcher. Serve chilled.

Sweet Dreams Hot Chocolate

Hot chocolate is a classic comfort beverage to help wind down after a long day. Try a new twist on an old classic, chili powder, for double the comfort and warmth. Digesting chili powder, even in small amounts, boosts production of endorphins, neurtransmitters that increase pain tolerance.

INGREDIENTS | SERVES 1

1 cup milk
1–2 tablespoons flavored chocolate drink mix
Ground chili powder, to taste

Warm milk in pan or microwave. Add chocolate drink mix and dash of chili powder to taste. Enjoy slowly, in fuzzy bedroom slippers, in absolute coziness and comfort.

Lavender Pillow Packs

Lavender, the flower of a spiky Mediterranean plant, induces healing and sleep. Place lavender pillow packs inside your pillowcases for a sweetly scented and restful night's sleep.

INGREDIENTS	MAKES 4–6 SACHETS

½ to 1 cup of dried lavender flowers

4–6 small transparent material sacks, normally used for rice or birdseed at a wedding

Fill each sack with lavender and pull the strings, closing the bag. Place the bags inside your pillowcase and anywhere else in the home you'd like a fresh scent, such as linen closets and clothing drawers. Note that dried lavender loses its potency in three to six months, so replenish the bags with fresh lavender as needed.

Salt of the Earth Epsom Bath

Magnesium replenishes the cells of your body and builds up muscle. It's hard to digest, but easy to absorb through the skin. Epsom salt isn't really salt, but a mixture of magnesium and sulfates. Try this relaxing bath for smooth skin and a restful end to a long day.

INGREDIENTS	FOR 1 BATH

2 cups Epsom salt

Tub full of warm water

Add Epsom salt, found at any drug store, to a tub of warm water. Soak for at least fifteen minutes to reap the full benefits of the salt. Combine a relaxing bath with a mineral soak for a truly replenishing experience. Add a drop of essential oil, such as lavender or lemon, if desired.

APPENDIX B

Professional Organizations for Crisis Assistance

Here are resources to get you and your loved ones the help you need in a major crisis in the United States.

American Association of Poison Control Centers

1-800-222-1222

Immediate assistance 24/7 in treating exposure to toxic chemicals.

American Red Cross

1-800-REDCROSS

Offers shelter, supplies, counseling, and support to those affected by natural disasters.

Cancer Care

1-800-813-HOPE

Free cancer support and referrals to counseling, financial assistance, online support groups, and other resources for people with cancer and their loved ones.

Child Help USA

1-800-422-4453

Crisis hotline staffed by mental-health professionals assists children and adult survivors of abuse on what to do next.

Spiritual Directors International

1-425-455-1565

Resource to find a professional spiritual director in your area.

Hospice Foundation of America

1-800-868-5171

Assists you in finding a grief support group or grief counseling in your community.

National Domestic Violence Hotline

1-800-799-SAFE

Support and resources for men and women in abusive relationships, available 24/7.

National Eating Disorders Association

1-800-931-2237

Trained volunteers offer compassion and resources to those struggling with eating disorders or loved ones trying to help someone with an eating disorder.

National Suicide Prevention Lifeline

1-800-273-8255

Twenty-four hour, seven-day-a-week crisis hotline that will connect you with a crisis center or mental-health professional in your area.

The Therapist Referral Network

1-800-843-7274

Connects you to mental-health professionals in your area that consider your payment and insurance needs in seeking a counselor.

APPENDIX C

Easy Meditations for Work and Home

Try these easy meditations anytime you need a break. Though they won't give you as much rest as a twenty-minute session, it could be just the break you need to make it through the day.

Catch Your Breath Meditation

Close your eyes. Breathe as deeply as you can, and focus on your breath. Continue as long as desired, or until you're relaxed and refreshed.

Nature Scene Meditation

Bring your favorite nature postcard or picture to work. For a quick break, hold the nature scene in front of you. Imagine yourself walking into the picture. Close your eyes, and engage the senses in your mind. What do you see, feel, or smell in your nature scene? Who else is there with you? What are you doing to relax? Enjoy your imaginary vacation as long as possible until you bring your mind back to the present.

Walking Meditation

Take a stroll, but instead of focusing on what you'll do when you get to your destination, concentrate on the walk itself. Notice your feet hitting the ground. Let your whole body sink into every step. Walk as slowly and carefully as desired, savoring every step. It may take you longer to get anywhere, but you'll be more refreshed when you actually get there.

Hand Lotion Meditation

Give your tired hands and mind a wake-up. Put a squeeze of your favorite lotion, particularly one that's scented such as an aromatherapy lotion, in the palm of your hand. Gently rub only the palms of your hands together slowly until the lotion is evenly distributed. Slowly and carefully rub every single finger joint on both hands in a circular motion, taking as long as you desire. Be sure to massage your wrists and the sides of your hands, too. When all the lotion is massaged into your hands, cup your hands over your nose and mouth. Breathe in the scent of the lotion deeply three times, and return to your day.

Mood Music Meditation

Everyone has a favorite song. Choose one that's relatively slow and not jarring. Lie down comfortably in a darkened room and turn on the song. Focus on your breath, and breathe slowly and deeply in time to the song's rhythm. Repeat until the song ends, and begin with the next track on the CD if desired, or repeat the same song again.

APPENDIX D

CD Contents

Track 1: The Three Assignments   1:36

Track 2: Twenty Minute Breath Control and Energy Work   18:57

Track 3: Five Minute Mid-Day Refresh   4:50

Track 4: Aum Sharavanabhava   11:00

Track 5: Great Compassion Mantra   10:08

Track 6: From Patanjali's *Yoga Sutras*   4:11

Track 7: Peace Meditation   3:11

Track 8: A Sikh Meditation   1:12

Track 9: A Prayer for Lovingkindness   2:19

Track 10: The Still, Small Voice (based on 1 Kings 19:11–13)   2:02

Track 11: Embryonic Breathing   1:50

Track 12: From the *Canticle to the Sun*   1:46

Track 13: A Meditation of Hildegard of Bingen   1:23

Track 14: A Rumi Poem: One Whisper of the Beloved   1:50

Track 15: Mahatma Gandhi: Thoughts on Self-Transformation and World Transformation   2:13

Index

Intimate Worlds, 164

Investment stress, 132–33

Jarvis, Anna, 214

Jesus, 100

Job loss, 127–29

Job stress, 137–48

Journaling, 77–79, 240–41

Jung, Carl, 217, 240

Kubler-Ross, Elisabeth, 37

Life, hope for, 255–66

Life, stress-proofing, 49–50

Listening skills, 251–52

Long distance realities, 178–80

Loren, Sophia, 217

Love and stress, 150–51. *See also* Relationships

Managing stress, 12–13, 45–54, 73–83, 207–19. *See also* Stress

Martial arts, 107, 243

Massage, 96–97, 174

Medication, 17, 250–51

Meditation
benefits of, 98–100, 105–6
easy meditations, 273–75
success with, 108–9
techniques for, 106–8

Men and stress, 215–16. *See also* Adults

Mental-health crisis, 248

Midlife crisis, 217–18

Mind and stress, 23–33, 103–16, 238–39

Mindfulness, 25, 98–101

Money and stress, 119–36

Money management, 134–35. *See also* Financial counseling

Muhammad, 100

Multitasking, 28–29

Myers Briggs Personality, 238

Nature, 115–16

Nutrition, 92–95

Obama, Michelle, 50, 90

Obesity, 89–90, 210

Ohno, Apolo Anton, 50

On Death and Dying, 37

Optimism therapy, 242

Organizations, 271–72

Orloff, Judith, 60, 158

Orman, Suze, 134

Pain, 20–21. *See also* Body and stress

Parents as stressors, 190–91, 201–2

Perception of stress, 25–27

Personal stress, 55–69

Pessimism, 104–5

Pets, 75

Phones, 47, 172–76

Physical symptoms, 16. *See also* Body and stress

Positive Energy, 60

Positive reinforcement, 242

Positive thinking, 104–5, 227

Princess Diana, 50

Professional organizations, 271–72

Ramsey, Dave, 126, 134

Recipes for relaxation, 267–70

Reiki, 96–98

Relationships. *See also* Family
boundaries in, 156–58
changing patterns in, 167–68

Wheeldon, Mark, 128–29

Women and stress, 213–15. *See also* Adults

Work

boundaries at, 141–42

breaks at, 147

eating at, 145–46

leaving work behind, 144–45

never-ending work, 181–82

relaxation at, 142–43

sanctuary at, 146–47

saying "no" to, 59, 137, 141–44, 148

stress at, 66, 137–48

Yoga, 107, 243

Young adults

boomerang generation, 203

and college, 202–4

depression in, 204–5

eating disorders in, 200

and jobs, 202–4

managing stress, 195–206

and "not knowing," 206

parents as stressors, 201–2

self-evaluation for, 197–201

stress in, 195–206

We Have

EVERYTHING®

on Anything!

The Everything® list spans a wide range of subjects, with more than 500 titles covering 25 different categories:

Business	History	Reference
Careers	Home Improvement	Religion
Children's Storybooks	Everything Kids	Self-Help
Computers	Languages	Sports & Fitness
Cooking	Music	Travel
Crafts and Hobbies	New Age	Wedding
Education/Schools	Parenting	Writing
Games and Puzzles	Personal Finance	
Health	Pets	

CD Credits

The Three Assignments [0:01:33]
Waves on Beach from Freesound by Acclivity

Twenty Minute Breath Control and Energy Work [0:18:55]
Pensive Vibes 3–5 by Daniel Cantor © 2010

Five Minute Mid-Day Refresh [0:04:48]
Magic Gong from Freesound by Gezortenplotz

Aum Sharavanabhava [0:10:58]
Misra Shivranjani Tanpura by Gretchen Ruckert © 2009 at Notable.com

Great Compassion Mantra [0:10:06]
Tibetan Chant from Freesound by DJ Griffin

Great Compassion Mantra [0:10:06]
Excerpt from "Heart Sutra" sung by Geshe Gendun from *Many Paths, One Joy* by Robert Jonas © 2005 at Notable.com. Courtesy of Emptybell.org

From Patanjali's Yoga Sutras [0:04:09]
Desh performed by George Ruckert © 2009 at Notable.com

Peace Meditation [0:00:50]
Tibetan Chant from Freesound by DJ Griffin

A Sikh Meditation [0:01:10]
Pensive Vibes 6&7 by Daniel Cantor © 2010

A Prayer for Lovingkindness [0:02:17]
Birds from Freesound by Crk365

The Still, Small Voice (based on 1 Kings 19:11–13) [0:02:00]
Flute played By Nathan Berla-Shulock © 2010

Embryonic Breathing [0:01:48]
Gongs by Daniel Cantor © 2010

From the Canticle to the Sun [0:01:54]
Excerpt from "O Virtus Sapentia" sung by June Boyce-Tillman from
Many Paths, One Joy by Robert Jonas © 2005 at Notable.com.
Courtesy of Emptybell.org

A Meditation of Hildegard of Bingen [0:01:21]
Catherine Meyer, Pipe Organist, performing *Dietrich Buxtehude:
Praeludium in G*, BuxWV 149 live at Marsh Chapel. Recorded by
Notable.com C. Meyer © 2005

A Rumi Poem: One Whisper of the Beloved [0:01:48]
Dumbek and Finger Cymbals by Daniel Cantor © 2010

**Mahatma Ghandi: Thoughts on Self-Transformation and World
Transformation [0:02:13)]**
Digital Tanpura by Daniel Cantor © 2010